"The Powers Boys"

An Historical Legend

"The Powers Boys"

An Historical Legend:

Its Formation and Function

RODERICK J. ROBERTS, JR.

CONTENTS

Acknowledgments   i

1. Introduction   1

2. Legend: A Definition   5

3. The Historicity of Legend   11

4. Principles of Distortion in Oral Transmission   25

5. The Legend Area: Graham County   39

6. The Documentary Record   55

7. The Power Legend   77

8. Conclusion   97

9. Newspaper Accounts   109

10. Legend Texts   137

11. List of Informants   223

12. Selected Bibliography   235

13. Additional Newspaper Accounts   247

ACKNOWLEDGMENTS

It is always difficult to acknowledge all of the individuals who have been helpful in any study based on field work. One must begin with his informants, whose willingness to open themselves in response to questioning makes the work of the folklorist possible. Beyond this basic level of gratitude, I would like to express my indebtedness to the New York State Historical Association for a grant that enabled me to return to Arizona and interview John Power after his brother's death, and to the following individuals: Ruth Keating and Evelyn Barron, for cheerful and efficient interlibrary loan correspondence; Wendell Tripp and Joel Schimberg, for the thankless chore of proofreading; Milo Stewart and Jerry Reese, for photographic advice and help; Robert Wildhaber, for sharing his knowledge of European legendry; and Bruce Buckley, for squeezing the reading of my work into his incredibly busy schedule and for affording me the benefit of his considerable powers of organization. I would also like to thank a series of archivists in the Cooperstown Graduate Programs: Gerry Parsons, Tom Adler, Tom Burns, Pat Foltz, and Patty McCue, each of whom occupied an office across the hall from mine for the space of a year, and each of whom lent a tolerant and perceptive ear. Finally, I would be remiss if I failed to single out my wife, Barbara, and my children, for their uncomplaining sufferance of the dislocation of their lives; Richard M. Dorson, for patience and faith; and Lou Jones, for humanity and example.

INTRODUCTION

In the early hours of February 10, 1918, a posse surrounded a small cabin in the remote Galiuro Mountains of southeastern Arizona. A gun battle ensued, and in it four men lost their lives. Their deaths precipitated not only the most intensive man hunt in the history of Arizona, but also a bitter controversy that has persisted into the present, a controversy that continues to be waged in the most frequently recounted historical legend of the area.

The popularity of the narrative is difficult to account for if one approaches it from the standpoint of the documentary evidence. The newspapers of the day recount the dastardly murders perpetrated by John and Tom Power and the family hired man, Tom Sisson, and call for their swift capture and punishment, even seeming to advocate lynching on at least two occasions. On the basis of the surviving record, the whole-hearted cooperation of residents of the area seems to have been forthcoming in the man hunt. Nowhere in any of the written accounts is there a word of sympathy for the accused men or any hint that there might have been some justification for their actions. Yet, when I began to collect in the area more than forty years after the incident, one informant after another offered texts related to the case when asked for "old stories." I had no interest in legend at that time, and I was not particularly excited by the testimonies offered until I encountered some informants who would tell the tale but not allow it to be recorded, and others who were so disturbed by the mention of it that they would abruptly conclude the interview. These extreme reactions to an "old story" seemed to reflect tensions that I had begun to feel in the community, and I speculated that the tale might provide insights into these tensions. Since some of the texts that I had collected touched each other at no point and since I had no notion of the limits of the legend, I decided to actively seek testimonies through a formula question: Do you know the story of the Powers boys? and thus allow my informants to define the legend for me.

A great many of the texts that I elicited in this fashion told a story consistent with the newspaper record, but a significant number of others recounted a narrative in almost direct opposition to that record. When it became apparent that the version told by non-Mormon Anglos was almost always favorable to the Powers, that the version told by Mormons was almost always hostile to the Powers, and that most Mexican versions had other concerns, I knew that I had stumbled upon a narrative that had a deep significance to the community in which it circulated. I also realized that in this body of tales I was presented with a splendid opportunity to observe a legend shortly after its nascence and to learn something of the ways in which an historical incident can be molded to reflect the biases of a given group and to ease the tensions to which that group is subject. The fact that the version of the story favorable to the Power boys gained sufficient currency to first bring about their parole and then their pardon without the introduction of any new evidence suggested the possibility of studying at first hand one of the functions of the historical legend.

When I began to organize what I felt I had learned, I was dismayed to discover what little progress has been made in the classification and analysis of the great body of American legendry, and I soon came to feel that this deplorable lack of progress was chiefly due to a faulty definition of the genre. Therefore, I formulated a new definition of legend, which I hope is satisfactory to others but which, at any rate, worked for me in that it allowed me to consider all the testimonies offered in response to my formula question without resorting to the bothersome criterion of subjective belief.

In the course of formulating a definition, I was forced into a considerable amount of research and thought concerning the historicity of legend and the ways in which an historian, especially a local historian, might utilize such materials in reconstructing the past. I have presented the fruits of that thought and those researches in the body of this study.

In like manner I became aware that members of my own discipline had really had very little to say over the years about the kinds of change that occur in materials that are orally transmitted, and I soon found myself in the alien world of the psychologist and the communications theorist. It remains for someone who understands the disciplines of those scholars much better than I to bridge the gap between them and the folklorist, but I hope that I have made a small, tentative step toward making some of their findings useful to the student of legend.

Finally, I must confess that I have been shamefully enthralled by the fascination of a good story, by the varied reactions of members of a community toward it, and by the opportunity to come to know, respect and like two men for whom this story is not a legend, but the central tragedy of their lives.

LEGEND: A DEFINITION

Any scholar venturing into the study of legend is soon struck by the amorphous quality of the ambience in which he finds himself. What are the common elements among the wonder-workings of a saint in the *Legenda Aurea*, an urban belief tale dealing with albino alligators in the New York City sewers, and stories about a shooting in southeastern Arizona in 1918? What characteristics do they share that move us to sort them into a common pigeonhole labeled legend?

Robert A. Georges submits a general definition: "A legend is a story or narrative, set in the recent or historical past, that is believed to be true by those by whom and to whom it is communicated."[1] This formulation should disconcert no one interested in the genre, for these traits have been singled out by scholar after scholar, and yet, as Georges points out, there are serious questions as to the applicability of these traits to the body of materials that we regard as legendary.[2] If this is so, then Georges' straw definition of the genre can be seen to be untenable or at best ambivalent, and classification of any particular item as a legend would seem to be largely an intuitive decision.

This imprecision of definition is reflected in the scholarship devoted to legend. Speaking of the difficulties experienced by the International Society of Folk-Narrative Research in discussions of the indexing of folk-legend materials, Linda Dégh states:

> The main disagreement between representatives of the many countries involved lay in their different conceptions of what is a folk-legend, and the kinds of topics, and the verbal frames belonging to this genre. Vague categories and groups

---

[1] "The General Concept of Legend," in *American Folk Legend: A Symposium*, ed. Wayland D. Hand (Berkeley, Los Angeles and London: University of California Press, 1971), p. 5.

[2] Ibid., pp. 6-19, passim.

might be attempted, based on earlier attempts, but this would not be of much help. Until we know what we want to systematize, until we have a common understanding as to what we mean by legend, it will be impossible to establish an international catalogue.[3]

This same disagreement is echoed by Wayland D. Hand in his survey of legend study:

> Why more scholars have not been attracted to legendry is easy to see, apart from the wider literary and aesthetic appeal of folk tales and related folk narrative forms. For the systematizer, folk legends seem endless in bulk and variety, and they are often so short and formless as to defy classification.[4]

It seems evident then that before any further assertions about the nature of legend or about any particular legend can judiciously be made, the objections which Professor Georges has raised to the definition of legend in general use by folklorists must be considered and some determinant or determinants must be isolated which will serve to demarcate these items from other forms of folk prose.

Georges challenges all three of the assertions of the legend definition: many of the texts collected and classified as legends are not narratives in that they lack plot, as we usually understand the term, and in that they do not begin or end with markers that clearly differentiate them from other kinds of oral expression;[5] the notion of "recent or historical past" is a largely subjective one, and individual items may be placed at various points on the time continuum, depending upon who is performing the placement;[6] and the final criterion of belief can be shown to be a relative one, subject to the collector's observation of

---

[3]"Processes of Legend Formation," in *IV International Congress for Folk-Narrative Research in Athens: Lectures and Reports*, ed. Georgios A. Megas (Athens, 1965), p. 78.

[4] "Status of European and American Legend Study," *Current Anthropology*, Vol. 6, No. 4 (1965), p. 439.

[5] Georges, "Concept," pp. 9-11.

[6] Ibid., pp. 11-15.

context and his evaluation of the informant's attitude toward the item.[7]

The first of these challenges rests on a restrictive definition of the term "narrative" which seems to be based in turn on a rather subjective esthetic judgment:

> ... if, as I suspect to be the case, most folklorists conceive of story or narrative in the literary sense as something that contains what can be called a *plot* and/or something that has a clearly marked introduction and conclusion that enable one to differentiate it readily and easily as one can presumably do with *all* story or narrative *forms* – from other *kinds* of expression within continua of communication, then the assertion that a legend is a story or narrative turns out to be a relative assertion.[8]

To speak to the second point first, it is evident that there are any number of words and expressions which do serve as legend markers; Georges himself lists thirteen of them, and this seems to be as rich an array of such items as any genre can boast. But more important than such words and expressions is the fact that the legend is marked most effectively and most distinctively by the tone and rhetorical attitude of the narrator. Since some sub-genres such as the tall tale and the shaggy dog story are distinguished solely by these attributes and any use of linguistic clues almost certainly diminishes their effect, it seems rather far-fetched to fault the legend on this count. The first point, which binds the concept of legend to some ideal notion of plot, seems to be completely arbitrary. I have before me three common desk dictionaries,[9] all of which permit the use of the term "narrative" to denote the relation of an incident or series of incidents, and even the most fragmentary and schematic texts classified as legend would seem to fit this definition of narrative. Thus it would appear that Georges' objection to the first assertion of the legend definition is not well-

---

[7] Ibid., pp. 15-18.
[8] Ibid., p. 11.
[9] *Webster's Seventh New Collegiate Dictionary* (Springfield, Mass.: G. & C. Merriam, 1963); *The American College Dictionary* (New York: Random House, 1964); *The Random House Dictionary of the English Language* (New York: Random House, 1968).

founded.

Professor Georges' challenge to the second assertion seems to be more soundly based. He states that:

> ...the assertion that a legend is set in the remote or historical past is an assertion that is too specific and yet too imprecise at the same time. For while a legend is *set* in the past, that past may be conceived to be *either* recent *or* remote and *either* historical *or* antihistorical; and while a legend is set in the *past*, it might really be conceived to be *in* and *of* the *present* (and perhaps the future as well).[10]

The validity of this statement seems obvious. Legends are set in the past, but they can and do partake of the present and the future. Evident too is the impossibility of ever reconciling what may very well be idiosyncratic senses of time achieving agreement as to the placement of a given item in the remote or recent, historical or antihistorical past. Given the relative nature of any such judgment, the cogency of this assertion to the definition of legend must be questioned.

It would seem then that we can say only that legends are traditional narratives, and that thus far we lack any means of differentiating the legend from all other forms of traditional narrative. This failure to isolate characteristics peculiar and specific to the legend lies at the root of most of the problems of legend scholarship, and upon its obviation depends the whole future of meaningful research bearing on the genre.

The essential determinant for making this discrimination may lie delitescent in the insistence of many scholars on the essential criteria of belief and objective falsity. Legends "cannot have happened, rather they have been formed by the fabulating gift of the people."[11] "The strong element of belief in the legend as told, or in the individual folk beliefs inherent in the legend, constitutes the hall mark which sets the legend apart from the folk tale."[12] "They (folklorists) recognize that

---

[10] Georges, "Concept," p. 15.

[11] Carl Wilhelm von Sydow, "Kategorien der Prosa-Volksdichtung," in *Volkskundliche Gaben John Meier dargebracht* (Berlin and Leipzig, 1934), p. 74; reprinted in *Selected Papers on Folklore* (Copenhagen: Rosenkilde and Bagger, 1948).

[12] Hand, "Status," p. 441.

legends, while frequently hard to believe, are nevertheless believed."[13]

Similar statements can be found liberally sprinkled throughout the literature of legend,[14] and it would seem safe to state that belief and objective falsity have been the key factors in the definitions of legend which most scholars have utilized.

The reliance on these two criteria has been a fool-hardy one. In most cases the transmitter of the legend is in no position to know whether what he is transmitting is true, and in some instances texts which undoubtedly belong to the demesne of legend are passed on with disavowals of belief. For example, in April, 1972, I was visiting a relative in a New Jersey hospital. In the sick room a fellow visitor, knowing of my interest in "stories," asked if I had heard the story that was going around about a marvelous event that had taken place in a Philadelphia hospital. She prefaced the story with the statement that she did not believe it and several times interrupted her account to comment on the incredible nature of the tale and the gullibility of those who accepted it as truth. The text dealt with a new-born infant in the hospital nursery who spoke to a nurse and warned her of the impending end of the world: "There will be three days of rain, three days of cold weather, three days of sunshine, and then the world will end"; this formula working out neatly to Easter Sunday. The end of the recital was punctuated by general laughter and remarks reflecting skepticism. I believe it significant and indicative of the general attitude of the group toward the item that it precipitated a joke-telling session. Yet, while waiting for the elevator, I overheard a hospital employee who had been in the room when the story was told relating it in a very earnest manner to a fellow employee. The demeanors of both were serious, almost grave; no elements of skepticism from the original telling were retained in this account, and both transmitter and receptor were moved to comment on the wonder of such an event and on the importance and urgency of the infant's message. Thus a text which was

---

[13] Richard M. Dorson, "Defining the American Folk Legend," in *American Folklore and the Historian* (Chicago: University of Chicago Press, 1971), p. 161.

[14] Will-Erich Peuckert, *Deutsches Volkstum in Märchen und Sage, Schwank und Rätsel* (Berlin: Walter de Gruyter, 1938), pp. 95-98; Carl Herman Tillhagen, "Was ist eine Sage?" in *Acta Ethnographica*, 13 (1964), p. 10; Jan Harold Brunvand, *The Study of American Folklore* (New York: Norton and Company, 1968), p. 87.

recounted without belief and so received by all the members of the audience but one, found in that single member an unexplainable credibility. Why should this be so? Why should one listener reject all the keys and signs that instructed him that this was a laughable matter?

I believe that the answer lies in the differences in individual perceptions of the nature of reality, and that the legend interacts with individual perceptions of reality in a way that no other traditional narrative does. The legend asks that the receptor measure the incidents and characters which it contains against his perception of the real world and then either accept or reject them. All of the other narrative genres free the receptor, by one device or another, from this measurement against reality: the Märchen by opening and closing formulae and marvelous characters, incidents and settings; the joke by its invitation to laughter in the punchline; the tall tale by its juxtaposition of real-world setting and preposterous events; the myth by its setting in an otherworld or a pre-world with the concomitant suspension of natural laws. Only the legend demands that the receptor make some evaluation of the objective truth of the narrative that he hears. Although the attitude of the narrator does weigh heavily in this evaluative process, the receptor is free to make his own decision, and if his notion of the real world is markedly different from the narrator's, then his assessment of the material offered may be markedly different. The narrator's joke may, in an extreme case, become the receptor's legend. In addition, the process seems to be a selective one, with the receptor rejecting some elements in the text and accepting others. When he in turn becomes a narrator, these rejected elements may be omitted or qualified in some fashion.

With this peculiarity of the legend in mind, I would like to offer a new definition of legend: the legend is a traditional narrative which makes a statement or assertion and which asks that the receiver measure its content against his perception of objective reality. We are concerned then with texts that relate an incident or series of incidents, and which are marked by words, expressions, and most importantly, by the attitude of the transmitter as material that was believed by someone at some time, and which ask that the receptor consider their content and make some judgment as to its truth or falsity.

THE HISTORICITY OF LEGEND

The question of the value of oral traditions in the study of history is a controversial one and one that seems to lead inexorably to a polarization of attitudes. In lieu of reasoned, balanced appraisals of the worth of orally collected materials, one usually encounters firmly entrenched positions at one end of the spectrum or the other, which are stoutly defended against any suggestion of attack. The most exhaustive survey of this controversy has been accomplished by Francis A. DeCaro, who in a splendid doctoral dissertation has examined an enormous body of scholarship bearing on the historicity of legendary and mythical materials and has imposed a degree of order on a chaotic area.[15] DeCaro traces the negative attitude of historians toward folklore to their desire to extirpate myths from the accounts that had served as history and to the primacy of the written word which was established by a literary culture which used literacy as a means of distinguishing itself from the vulgar mob around it.[16]

Throughout much of his study, DeCaro drew heavily on the work of Richard M. Dorson, who produced what remains the best short treatment of the subject.[17]

An examination of one or both of these aforementioned studies will lead the careful reader to the conclusion that the critical factor is the individual scholar's understanding of the term "historical fact." Some writers seem to expect of oral tradition the same preservation of specific names, dates, and chronological order of events that has

---

[15] "Folklore as an Historical Science: The Anglo-American Viewpoint," an unpublished Ph.D. dissertation, Indiana University, 1967.

[16] Ibid., p.1.

[17] "The Debate over the Trustworthiness of Oral Traditional History," in *Volksüberlieferung, Festschrift für Kurt Ranke*, eds. Fritz Harkort, Karel C. Peters and Robert Wildhaber (Göttingen: Otto Schwartz and Company, 1968), pp. 19-35.

traditionally been the aim of written history. They ask that oral tradition meet standards that it does not recognize, and therefore this level of expectation must necessarily lead to the conclusion that oral sources are not reliable ones for the reconstruction of the past. Thus it is not surprising to find strongly negative statements as to the historical value of orally transmitted materials from such students of the subject as E.S. Hartland,[18] Alfred Nutt,[19] Robert H. Lowie,[20] Lord Raglan,[21] Homer C. Hockett,[22] and Allen Johnson.[23]

It is only those scholars who perceive the term "historical fact" in some other manner who can uphold the value of oral traditions to the serious student of the past. Thus Donald Dean Parker counsels local historians: "Yet tradition should neither be despised nor accepted literally ... there is likely to be a germ of truth in every tradition. The germ may be misplaced as to time, place or person, yet it furnishes a clue which may later lead to the truth itself."[24]

In the same vein, Louis R. Gottschalk considers oral materials along with fiction, song, and poetry and concludes that the former "may tell much about the aspirations, superstitions, and customs of the peoples among whom the stories developed, provided the historian (or folklorist) is able to distinguish between the legendary embroideries and their authentic foundations."[25]

Thus it seems apparent that if one is willing to change his expectations of the kinds of data ensconced in oral testimonies, they

---

[18] "Folklore: What Is It and What Is the Good of It?" in *Popular Studies in Mythology, Romance and Folklore*, No. 2 (London: David Nutt, 1889). Reprint with minor changes of a paper read before the Gloucester Philosophical Society. Second edition, 1904. Pages 5-47. Quoted in Richard M. Dorson, *Peasant Customs and Savage Myths*, Volume I (Chicago: University of Chicago Press, 1968).

[19] "History, Tradition and Historic Myth," *Folklore*, XII (1901).

[20] "Oral Traditions and History: Discussion and Correspondence," *American Anthropologist*, XVII (1915).

[21] *The Hero: A Study in Tradition, Myth and Drama* (New York: Vintage Books, 1956).

[22] *Introduction to Research in American History* (New York: Macmillan, 1938).

[23] *The Historian and Historical Evidence* (New York: Charles Scribner's Sons, 1926).

[24] *Local History: How to Gather It, Write It, and Publish It* (New York: Social Science Research Council, 1944), p. 25.

[25] *Understanding History: A Primer of Historical Method* (New York: Alfred A. Knopf, 1965), p.114.

can provide information valuable to a reconstruction of the past. Américo Paredes speaks to the value of studying the relationship between history and folklore: "Where documents are available for comparison, one may actually trace the process--the reshaping of history to conform with the folk group's own world view, the embellishment of bare historical detail with universal folk motifs."[26] Professor Paredes goes on to comment on the acceptance by historians of traditional motifs as history and to point out their need for a knowledge of the frequency of occurrence of such motifs if they hope to successfully winnow historical fact from such material.[27] This call to historians is echoed by Merle W. Wells, who writes: "For a professional historian to avoid turning out a product that is closer to folk history than he is likely to wish, the services of a folklorist are indispensable."[28]

A very liberal and reasonable view is put forward by Austin E. Fife, who sees oral embellishment as a necessary factor in the total picture of man's past:

> If we maintain an attitude of mental reservation then both the documents and the oral materials which we collect will ultimately fit into a pattern which will form the richest possible mosaic of local history, since it will partake at the same time of authenticity and of myth, the two components which constitute the really significant consciousness of any locality.[29]

Another approach is suggested by Theodore Blegen, who feels that a true understanding of the American people is dependent upon the utilization of "folk" documents, the true indicators of history. These documents, "the literature of the unlettered," are the letters and diaries of human beings who lived out their lives at a level beneath the notice of traditional historians, and yet it is in the study of these materials that

---

[26] "Folklore and History," in *Singers and Storytellers*, ed. Mody C. Boatright (Dallas: Southern Methodist University Press, 1961), p. 58.
[27] Ibid., pp. 58-59.
[28] "History and Folklore: A Suggestion for Cooperation," *Journal of the West*, IV: 1 (January, 1965), p. 96.
[29] "Folklore and Local History," *Utah Historical Quarterly*, XXXI: 4 (Fall, 1963), p.322.

the discovery of significant cultural patterns lies. The failure to achieve such discoveries Blegen attributes to a form of cultural snobbery which he labels "inverted provincialism," the neglect of simple, readily accessible sources:

> This inverted provincialism considered itself urbane and cosmopolitan. It was little interested in the values of folk culture. It rejected the near-at-hand as local and insignificant. It cultivated the faraway, without fully understanding it because it did not understand the near-at-hand, without sensing, too, that the faraway may in its inner meaning be near-at-hand. Imitative because it lacked self-confidence, inverted provincialism in many instances established molds and patterns for our educational and institutional development that have been hard to break.[30]

Philip D. Jordan took up Blegen's idea and singled out the folklorist as the researcher best qualified to gather, interpret and animate material that could contribute substantially to our understanding of history.[31]

An appreciation of the value of oral traditions to the historian is evident in the recent enthusiasm for oral history, which had its beginning at Columbia University in 1948, and which has now spread to numerous other institutions of higher learning, presidential libraries, state and local historical societies, and museums.[32] Oral history, of course, is not new; historians since Thucydides have interviewed participants in important events. However, there is a renewed interest in the interview as a technique, and a great deal of lip service is paid to the importance of folklore to the historian.[33] The truth of the matter is

---

[30] *Grass Roots History* (Minneapolis: University of Minnesota Press, 1947), p.5.

[31] "The Folklorist as Social Historian," *Western Folklore*, XII: 3 (July, 1953), p. 195.

[32] Here is a representative listing of oral history projects together with their special interests: Brandeis University, American artists; Cornell University, American agriculture; Michigan State University, the American Negro; Tulane University, New Orleans jazz; Wayne State University, the United Auto Workers; and Western Michigan University, regional history.

[33] See Allan Nevins, *The Gateway to History* (New York: Anchor books, rev. ed., 1962) pp. 79-86.

14

that oral historians are really only documentary historians fitted out with tape recorders. They interest themselves in the recollections of important people, insiders who were privy to decision-making, members of the establishment who can provide "factual material which has otherwise gone unrecorded" and just as blithely as their unelectrified brethren turn their backs on the "most difficult part of history to obtain ... the record of how plain men and women lived, and how they were affected by the economic, social, and cultural changes of their times..."[34]

Richard M. Dorson makes what is perhaps the most telling point in this consideration of the historical value of oral traditions when he calls for the eschewal of blanket judgments: "Tradition is not cut from one cloth ... It is not a matter of fact versus fiction so much as the social acceptance of traditional history."[35] The compartmentalization of the controversy over the historicity of oral traditions and the tendency to make blanket judgments have obscured a fact of paramount importance: what the folk believe to have happened is at least as important as what actually happened.

David D. Buchan expands on this concept in his article on the ballad "The Battle of Harlow" when he says:

> The ballad, then, despite the initial impression it is likely to give, is historical in a rather extraordinary way. It reflects, although in blurred fashion, what is reckoned to be the actual pattern of events in the battle, and this pattern, it is worth remarking, is not recorded in any known document, but only in the ballad. What appears to be the ballad's largest unhistoricity actually reflects the kind of historical truth that normally never finds its way into the documents, the nature and quality of the folk's emotional attitudes over a long span of years. And the ballad's interest is more than just historical, for it also provides us with a fair insight into the ways in which the folk imagination reacted to, molded, and used for

[34] Allan Nevins, *Interpreting American History: Conversations with Historians*, ed. John A. Garraty (New York: Macmillan, 1970), pp. 85-86.

[35] "The Debate over the Trustworthiness of Oral Traditional History," in *Volksüberlieferung, Festschrift für Kurt Ranke*, eds. Fritz Harkort, Karel C. Peters Robert Wildhaber (Göttingen, 1968), p.33.

its own emotional purposes, the raw material of historical event.[36]

Buchan goes on to point out the importance of the emotional truths contained in traditional accounts of historical events and forces upon us the realization that such accounts can and do focus the emotional conceptions of a particular culture.[37]

If the historical significance of oral material is ever to be realized, evaluative procedures must be developed for the abstraction of the historical data contained in it. The difficulties and complexities of such a process are well attested by the voluminous and controversy-laden literature on the subject, but in the case of the historical legend a number of kinds of data may yield themselves to the application of such techniques: 1) Historical legends provide a ready access to the popular attitudes, prejudices, and stereotypes of any society in which they have currency;[38] 2) they contain useful information on traditional customs, practices, and mores; 3) they can serve to verify and illuminate incidents which have originally come to light through documentary or archeological evidence;[39] 4) they may sometimes be used to disentangle fact from fancy;[40] 5) they may be the first indicators of incidents that have resisted discovery by more traditional methods of historical research; 6) they can provide valuable data on minority groups in a culture when that culture has not seen fit to record such data through more formal channels; and 7) they are often the only voice of illiterate or semi-literate groups in the culture.[41]

Historical legends as received by the historian are an extremely rich source of the attitudes, prejudices, and stereotypes current in a given society at a particular time, for the popular attitudes toward institutions, professions, and ethnic groups lie exposed there. The vernacular notions of prestige, honorific behavior, wit, wisdom, and common sense are ensconced in these traditional narratives, awaiting

---

[36] "History and Harlaw," *Journal of the Folklore Institute*, V: 1 (June, 1968), p. 65.
[37] Ibid., pp. 66-67.
[38] Richard M. Dorson, "Oral Tradition and Written History: the Case for the United States," *Journal of the Folklore Institute*, I: 3 (December, 1964), p. 222.
[39] Ibid., p. 230.
[40] Ibid., p. 228.
[41] Ibid., p. 231.

only the touch of the aware and perceptive scholar for transformation into windows on cultures no longer extant. Tales from the Southwest which only peripherally involve Mexicans or Indians still accurately reflect the folk notions of the essential character of members of these ethnic groups. The conceit of the Easterner as effete, decadent and inept occurs in text after text, usually contrasted with that of the Westerner, who is presented as virile, honorable and capable, even though the point of such stories may be unrelated to this conceit. The fact that members of families that were once involved in sheep- or goat-herding often fail to mention such involvement tells us something about historical or contemporary notions of status. A veritable treasure trove of data lies ready to flesh out our perceptions of the *Weltanschauung* of historic or regional groups.

In similar fashion many of the details of everyday life (dietary habits, work practices, greeting forms, household organization) have been incorporated in traditional tales and can be recovered by the scholar willing to search for them. Thomas D. Clark points out in *The Rampaging Frontier*, which reveals frontier attitudes through folktales culled from newspapers and travel accounts of that day, that: "There is no richer source for the study of human activities on the frontier than its thousands of humorous stories."[42] More recently, Richard Dorson has written incisively of the richness of this kind of information in *The Dewar Manuscripts*.[43]

It is obvious that the historicity of the items is not of central importance to these first two uses of legendary material, for the vehicle and not its import serves as the illuminating factor here, and the most flagrant falsification may be cast in terms that can provide valid cultural insights. These uses of the vehicle of legend as a source of historical data are the most readily apparent ones and have been exploited most widely and most profitably by social and cultural historians. It is when the discussion turns to the historical uses of legend which are dependent upon the accuracy of the facts therein contained that we encounter serious difficulties. Experiments ranging in complexity from the rigidly controlled ones in the behavioral psychologist's laboratory

---

[42] *The Rampaging Frontier* (Bloomington, Indiana: Indiana University Press, 1964), p. vi.
[43] "Traditional History of the Scottish Highlands," *Journal of the Folklore Institute*, VIII: 2/3 (1971), pp. 171-172.

to the simple childhood game of "Rumor" have amply demonstrated that human beings frequently transform or pervert facts which are entrusted to them for oral transmission. The scholarship on the subject attests to the disparity of opinions advanced by anthropologists, folklorists, and historians. How can we, then, look to the end product of this kind of oral chain with any hope of discovering historically valuable information of this kind? Robert H. Lowie stated the extreme case when he said, "...I cannot attach to oral traditions any historical value whatsoever under any conditions whatsoever."[44] Lord Raglan echoed this statement when he stated categorically, "Tradition never preserves historical facts."[45] If by the terms "historical value" and "fact," we understand the accurate preservation of numbers, rigid order of events, and the correct attribution of deed to personage, measured against some absolute written record, then those statements are undeniably true. But one need only look at Napoleon's definition of history as "a pack of lies agreed upon" or at Voltaire's as "a pack of tricks we play on the dead" or to accounts of any conflict written by observers from opposing sides to realize that the truth as preserved in the documentary record is not an absolute, but necessarily represents the result of cultural and social pressures on the writer. Virtually every scrap of data with which the historian comes into contact reaches him only after filtration through some set of human biases. What is accepted as history is only what a given culture wants to be history. The fact that the distortions that take place in the oral process are more blatant and more easily demonstrable makes them no more horrific or damaging to the historic record than those which take place in the mind of the individual observer, whose distortions we have always accepted.

This is not to say that the historical legend should be accepted at face value and weighed equally with the document. Most historical legends exhibit an accretion of traveling motifs, motifs which can be found in many other localities and which may have world-wide distribution. The scholar who is equipped to identify these items is capable of evaluating a legend, for he can conclude with some certainty

---

[44] "Oral Traditions and History: Discussions and Correspondence," *American Anthropologist*, N.S., XVII (1915), p. 598.
[45] *The Hero: A Study in Tradition, Myth and Drama* (New York: Vintage Books, 1956), p. 36.

that such material is the result of a selective borrowing process on the part of the folk and is therefore not pertinent to his area of interest. The material that survives such a winnowing process, however, can be of use to the historian.

It should not be surprising, then, to learn that two archeologists, David M. Pendergast and Clement W. Meighan, concluded that "traditional histories may preserve historical information for several hundred years with a relatively high degree of accuracy."[46] This conclusion was based on the fact that Paiute informants made statements about a Puebloid people who had inhabited a site sometime previous to 1150 A. D., and that these statements dealing with migration and movements, economic patterns, physical appearance and material culture of this people, whom they term the *Mukwitch*, are to a large extent verified by archeological data or are consistent with general views on the origin and later decline of the Puebloid intrusion into Utah.[47] Pendergast and Meighan point to two other examples of the historical continuity of Indian traditional knowledge in the Southwest,[48] and in a reply to Lord Raglan's attack on this article,[49] Meighan was able to cite four additional examples.[50] These specimens are certainly indicative of the ways in which oral tradition can serve to illuminate and verify data which the scholar has first encountered through more traditional avenues of research. All too frequently the historian is intrigued by a reference in a diary or journal or letter that passes through his hands, and with infuriating regularity, all of his efforts to learn more about the incident are in vain. None of the standard sources, no newspaper account, no court record, no corroborating reference can be found. Too often the quest ends at this point, and the researcher turns his attention to a more promising matter, when all manner of verificative material might very well exist in the oral traditions of the area, awaiting only solicitation. Abundant accounts of

---

[46] "Folk Traditions as Historical Fact: A Paiute Example," *Journal of American Folklore*, LXXII (April-June, 1959), p. 132.

[47] Ibid., pp. 128-133.

[48] Ibid., pp. 131-132. Also see D.A. Gunnerson, "The Southern Athapascans: their Arrival in the Southwest," *El Palacio*, LXIII: 11-12 (1956), pp. 346-365.

[49] "Folk Traditions as Historical Facts," *Journal of American Folklore*, LXXIII (1960), p. 58-59.

[50] "More on Folk Traditions," *Journal of American Folklore*, LXXIII (1960), p. 60.

sensational crimes, lynchings, feuds, duels, fires, massacres and disasters can reward the historian who is willing and equipped to seek them. Dorothy B. Vitaliano has introduced a term, "geomythology," which she defines as the geologic application of euhemerism. In an article with that title she reviews and evaluates a body of scholarship that has sought to link geologic events and the incidents of myth and legend.[51] Thus archeology, folklore, geology and history can work hand-in-hand to illuminate past events.

The converse use of oral traditional material is the disentangling of fact from fancy. Richard M. Dorson tells us: "A knowledge of the folklore properties of oral tradition can enable the historian ... to separate fiction from fact. The history of town, country, and region abounds in legendary traditions, which often parade as real occurrences."[52] Unfortunately, sorting out traditional items from American material which purports to be historical is not an easy task. *The Motif-Index of Folk Literature* by Stith Thompson together with the *Types of the Folktale* by Antti Aarne and Stith Thompson, and the other interlocking indices, such as those of Tom Peete Cross and O'Sullivan-Christiansen for Ireland, Thompson-Balys and Thompson-Roberts for India, and Ernest W. Baughman for England and North America, are a starting point. But a great deal of the material found in American legendry is not treated in these works, and the same must be said for the one great study of the legend, Reidar Christiansen's *The Migratory Legends*.

The worlds of European and American legendry are very different ones, and very little that can be said about the one is applicable to the other, and so even the proposed international legend classification project is not likely to go very far toward easing the problem. What the study of American legendry really needs is disciplined and thorough collecting of both folk and literary legends, followed by the development of a classification system based on this body of collected material. Until such a tool is available, however, the student of local history must acquaint himself with the whole body of American

---

[51] "Geomythology," *Journal of the Folklore Institute*, V: 1 (June 1968), pp. 5-30. See also Dr. Vitaliano's book, *Legends of the Earth* (Bloomington: Indiana University Press, 1973).
[52] "Oral Tradition and Written History: the Case for the United States," *Journal of the Folklore Institute*, I: 3 (December, 1964), p. 228.

legendary material and remain constantly on guard against such items masquerading as actual local happenings.

Historical legends may sometimes be the first indicators of incidents that have resisted discovery by more traditional methods of historical research. D.K. Wilgus and Lynwood Montell write:

> This paper demonstrates the intrinsic value of a local fiddle song and a corpus of tenacious historical legends in reconstructing a century-old episode that could not have been written if the standard historiographical methods were the only means of articulation...But the events that gave rise to the song and legends about Beanie Short, a rebel guerrilla, were never placed in writing - not in newspapers, for there were none, and not in court records, for guerrilla bands during the Civil War seldom stood trial for their crimes.[53]

This deficiency of documentary evidence is frequently encountered in many regions of the United States, and the only viable alternative to leaving great gaps in the history of an area is the utilization of oral materials. In some cases resort to this latter course will bring to light incidents which can be verified by documentary or archeological evidence, but even where this is not possible, the subjection of the oral evidence to a careful evaluative procedure can produce a worthwhile record. Barbro Klein has written of such an instance in which the attempts to refute and confirm a legend have added considerably to the body of knowledge bearing on the death of Charles XII of Sweden and have also exposed some emotional truths about the attitude of the folk toward that monarch.[54]

Virtually every area of this country has had resident within it at one period of its history or another, groups whose principal orientation was not toward the dominant culture. All too frequently the documentary record of such groups, if indeed one exists, is scanty and superficial, manifesting little understanding of the group, its customs and its

---

[53] "Beanie Short: A Civil War Chronicle in Legend and Song," in *American Folk Legend: A Symposium*, ed. Wayland D. Hand (Berkeley, Los Angeles and London: University of California Press, 1971), p. 133.

[54] "The Testimony of the Button," *Journal of the Folklore Institute*, VIII: 2/3 (1971), pp. 125-146.

values, and less sympathy for them. Since such groups are usually tradition oriented, documentary evidence relating to their history is seldom available. But in the legends current among present-day members of such a group can often be found a folk history that has not only preserved information about cultural traits, ideas and institutions, but that also functions as a basis for contemporary group decisions. These oral traditions are vital links with the past for the members of these illiterate and semi-literate groups, and they exhibit a persistence not found in the oral utterances of the main-stream oriented general population. John Joseph Mathews states in his tribal biography, *The Osages*: "The history was a part of them, of the informants and the tribe, and they could not be detached from their narratives as were literate Europeans detached from their written narratives."[55]

This involvement with the legends is understandable, for they often represent the only body of inherited material that deals with the group or that interprets the past in terms meaningful to it. This material serves to balance and sometimes to correct the official record which the dominant culture has made and is therefore of the utmost importance to the minority culture. Jan Vansina tells us, "every tradition exists as such only in virtue of the fact that it serves the interests of the society in which it is preserved ... Most group testimonies are official testimonies that reflect the basic interests of the society concerned."[56] It is an appreciation of the role of legend in such groups that has allowed anthropologists to reconstruct the old life-ways of western Indian tribes, complete with significant cultural detail lost on observers of the earlier period, through interviews with the descendants of those Indians, and it is through this same appreciation that the diligent scholar can uncover valuable data on neglected sub-cultures in which he is interested.

A necessary concomitant of the heterogeneity of the American population is that throughout our history disparate groups have

---

[55] *The Osages* (Norman, Oklahoma: University of Chicago Press, 1961), p. xii, quoted in Richard M. Dorson, "Oral Tradition and Written History: the Case for the United States," *Journal of the Folklore Institute*, I: 3 (December, 1964), p. 232.

[56] *Oral Tradition: A Study in Historical Methodology*, translated by H.M. Wright (London, 1965), (Chicago: Aldine Publishing Company, 1965), p.78.

sometimes taken up residence in the same geographic area. Sometimes the result has been healthy competition resulting in mutual respect, but as often as not, the struggle has been an uneven one with one of the groups achieving an overwhelming dominance. If in the latter instance there is a subsequent conflict between the dominant group and some minority faction, the record that we inherit, although it may seem complete and voluminous, nearly always presents the view of the dominant culture since it was in control of the recording mechanisms. The sub-culture, frequently semi-literate and tradition-oriented, is deprived of its voice in such a controversy if the historian limits himself to the documentary evidence surviving from the era under consideration. The legendary accounts of the conflict preserved by descendants of the group may represent the only means of ascertaining its version of the dispute, and its version may be just as close to the "truth" as the documentary one. The *corridos* of the Texas-Mexican border that deal with Gregorio Cortez and which have been so well studied by Américo Paredes treat just such an instance.[57]

Some notion of the universality of this phenomenon of very different perceptions of a common history might be gained by comparing the versions of a particular event as offered by members of the groups in dispute.[58] A corollary to the existence of a minority view of an historical event is the fact that the circulation of tales that dispute the documentary record may give rise to oral testimonies among members of the dominant group that support the official view of the event or that question the credibility of its attackers on some other grounds. "When a public is made up of factions with conflicting interest, cleavages may be intensified through communication, as each side comes to appreciate more fully how the purposes of the opposition encroach upon its interests."[59] These new imputations

---

[57] For a full appreciation of the nuances of this particular legend phenomenon, the work of Paredes should be examined. *With His Pistol in His Hand: A Border Ballad and Its Hero* (Austin: University of Texas Press, 1958).

[58] See Richard A. Gould, "Indian and White Versions of 'The Burnt Ranch Massacre'," *Journal of the Folklore Institute*, III: 1 (June, 1966), pp.30-42, and Louis Dupree, "The Retreat of the British Army from Kabul to Jalalabad in 1842: History and Folklore," *Journal of the Folklore Institute*, IV: 1 (June, 1967), pp.50-74.

[59] Tamotsu Shibutani, *Improvised News: A Sociological Study of Rumor* (New York and Indianapolis: The Bobbs-Merrill Company, Inc., 1966) p. 137.

demand new accounts that either give the lie to establishment-oriented versions of the event or attack in turn the credibility of those who circulate them, and a cycle of particular viciousness is underway. This cycle seems destined to end in some form of violence or in a new consensus of truth in regard to the facts of the original conflict. The latter result is the one with which this study is concerned, and we will return to it in considerable detail.

It would seem then that the historical legends of a region can represent a rich depository of information available to the scholar who can develop the techniques necessary to abstract the historically valuable data. Jan Vansina, who set up a special procedure for dealing with African traditions, writes:

> What the historian can do is to arrive at some approximation to the ultimate historical truth. He does this by using calculations of probability, by interpreting the facts and by evaluating them in an attempt to recreate for himself the circumstances which existed at certain given moments of the past. And here the historian using oral traditions finds himself on exactly the same level as the historian using any other kind of historical source material. No doubt he will arrive at a lower degree of probability than would otherwise be attained, but that does not rule out the fact that what he is doing is valid, and that it is history.[60]

The challenge to American historians and folklorists is clear: we must examine our legendary inheritance and find some means of evaluating it and subsequently utilizing it to enrich our perception of the past and to increase our understanding of ourselves and those who have preceded us.

---

[60] *Oral Traditions: A Study in Historical Methodology*, trans. by H.M. Wright (Chicago: Aldine Publishing Company, 1965), p. 186.

PRINCIPLES OF DISTORTION IN
ORAL TRANSMISSION

If legends are to be used as sources for the reconstruction of the past, scholars must recognize the fact that changes occur in materials that circulate orally and develop some techniques for dealing with these changes. This recognition must be made by even the most casual student of legend, and it is very difficult to find any observer who would insist that all oral testimonies represent historical facts accurately. The development of a technique for dealing with these changes, however, is a very different matter and demands that we come to an understanding of the nature and causes of these alterations before we can pretend to be able to utilize oral traditions in reconstructing the past. We must then view carefully the changes that occur in the oral chain.

Most human beings do not possess eidetic memories, and therefore they are unable to reproduce precisely what they hear. This inability causes informants to omit information from their accounts, an omission which in and of itself is not especially harmful, for what is left is a partial account of the event. The real damage occurs when an informant, confused by his memory losses and nagged by the notion that there is more to the story, interpolates material foreign to the event in an effort to make his account more coherent. Since lapses of memory seem to be universal, one can expect to find their effects in every culture. There are those who have maintained that members of pre-literate societies possess exceptional powers of memory,[61] but the evidence would seem to indicate that these powers are developed by the circumstances of life in such societies and not by any genetic factors. Jan Vansina says:

---

[61] See Diedrich Westermann, *Geschichte Afrikas* (Cologne, 1952), pp. 16-17.

25

So far there exists no proof that there is any inborn difference in cerebral faculties between the various races of man. However, it is a well established fact that a decisive factor in the tremendous storage capacity of the human memory is the amount of attention given to the data that have to be memorized. Practice in the process of memorization is another factor that comes into play.[62]

Thus, in spite of reports of prodigious feats of memory on the part of members of pre-literate societies, one must be prepared to deal with lapses of memory and their concomitant effects in every culture.[63] Once the student of historical legend accepts this premise, and I believe that he must accept it, he is faced with the need to find some way to deal with it. If this change is truly random and indiscriminate, then the development of such a method is not feasible. But there is a great body of scholarship that argues that such lapses of memory are nearly always selective and often purposeful, and if this is the case, then these lapses can be dealt with systematically, and oral testimonies concerning historical incidents can be utilized by scholars. Unfortunately, the researchers in the field of legend study have, for the most part, chosen to ignore this question of systematic error and have instead devoted themselves to heated assertions as to the total truth or falsity of legendary accounts.[64] It is to the work of psychologists and communications theorists that we must turn for any meaningful studies of *en regle* error in oral testimonies.

There have been discussions of the unreliability of testimony by a steady stream of writers leading back to the ancient Greeks, but the

---

[62] *Oral Tradition: A Study in Historical Methodology* (Chicago: Aldine Publishing Company, 1965) p. 40.

[63] This is not to say that individuals are not encountered who exhibit phenomenal memories. In June of 1968, I interviewed a 79 year old woman in Bainbridge, New York, who was able to pace off on her front lawn an entire farmstead layout and the interior dimensions of the farm house. Her recollections checked out with the reconstructed farm house within inches. She was also able to detect every change incorporated in the reconstruction. This performance is even more remarkable in light of the fact that she lived in the house for only nine months at the age of 11 and had never visited the house again until she was taken to it on its museum site.

[64] See Chapter II.

first controlled experimental study of distortion in serial transmission was performed by William Stern.[65] It was he who laid the basic groundwork in this area of study: his conception of rumor, his formulation of the problem, and his experimental methodology have persisted to this day. His experiments were designed to isolate patterns of faulty perception and reproductive errors in serial transmission. A subject was either asked to repeat a message given him by an experimenter or to describe a picture to another subject. This subject in turn repeated the message to another subject who passed on what he had heard. At each repetition careful records were kept of additions and subtractions to the message. On the basis of an analysis of these distortions, generalizations were made about the varying length of the accounts, the content of the alterations which were incorporated during transmission, and the direction that these variations took. Stern's work caused a short-lived excitement and the development of a fairly extensive literature in "forensic psychology."[66]

It remained for Gordon W. Allport and Leo Postman to carry out the most thoroughgoing study of this kind.[67] Three concepts are central to their findings: 1) leveling, 2) sharpening, and 3) assimilation. Leveling is the omission in serial accounts of many details which are necessary for a true understanding of the event. The repeated item grows shorter and it becomes more concise, more easily grasped and told. Leveling is not random and never proceeds to the point of obliteration. Names, titles, dates and numbers are most affected by leveling. Sharpening is the reciprocal of leveling, and one cannot exist without the other. When some details are omitted, those which are selectively retained and reported necessarily gain in importance and emphasis. Odd, preservative wordings are often retained. Numbers are multiplied, movement is emphasized, and the action contemporized. Labels and familiar symbols benefit greatly from the sharpening process and often persist when the tale has lost all other significance. Closure, the subject's urge to make his experience as complete, coherent and meaningful as possible, is also a form of sharpening.

---

[65] *Zur Psychologie der Aussage* (Berlin: J. Guttentag, 1902).

[66] This literature is summarized well in Lucy Hösch-Ernst, "Die Psychologie der Aussage und ihre Beziehung zur Gegenwart," *Internationale Rundschau*, I (1915), pp.15-33.

[67] *The Psychology of Rumor* (New York: Henry Holt and Company, 1947).

Leveling and sharpening do not take place haphazardly but in conformity with the past experience and present attitudes of the informant. Assimilation is the product of the tension between the cognitive and affective:

In the initial act of perception not all of the physical "objective" characteristics of the stimulus are reproduced. From the outset perception is selective and tends to simplify the world around us. Memory continues and hastens the process. Unconstrained by the presence of the stimulus, memory accelerates the formation of "good Gestalten." The change is toward simplicity, symmetry, good configuration.[68]

These conclusions confirmed the findings of previous experimenters such as Frederick C. Bartlett,[69] and since the work of Allport and Postman, other studies have substantiated their results. We can accept as fact then that most persons cannot repeat verbatim what they hear from others, that serial transmission is usually inaccurate, and that testimonies are usually affected by the way in which the informant views the world.

Serious questions remain, however, as to the applicability of such laboratory findings to the real-world situations of rumor and legend. In the experimental situation subjects hear the message only once; they are given no opportunity to ask questions; they are instructed to be accurate and may feel some anxiety about that charge; no time is allowed to elapse between hearing and telling; and they have no assured emotional involvement with the message they are asked to transmit. This context is at a far remove from the one in which tales normally circulate, and it would be surprising indeed if the rules formulated in such a dissimilar atmosphere would prove valid to the real-life situation. We must continue to probe if we hope to discover the rules underlying the process of legend transmission.

All the researchers who have worked seriously in the field have felt some strong connection between the legend and rumor, and this perception is reinforced by the fact that the two terms are often used interchangeably.[70] La Piere and Farnsworth tell us, "a legend is a rumor

---

[68] Ibid., p. 100.

[69] *Remembering* (London: Cambridge University Press, 1932).

[70] The Chinese term *chuan* is used to denote both rumor and legend.

that has become part of the verbal heritage of a people,"[71] and Allport and Postman develop this notion:

> In order to become legendary, a rumor must treat issues that are of importance to successive generations. Topics pertaining to national origins and honor are such; so too topics of birth, marriage, death. Whatever has sweep and universal significance may become part of our folklore.[72]

If this relationship is an actual one, then we might profitably examine the work of contemporary theorists on the subject of rumor. One of the most exciting of these scholars is Tamotsu Shibutani, who speaks directly to the problem.[73] He feels that most scholars have gone astray in their work on rumor because they have based it on the erroneous assumption that normal communication is accurate, and to the degree that serial testimonies incorporate inaccuracies, they deviate from some objective standard of reality, when the truth of the matter is that any account of an event is necessarily inaccurate and incomplete. Shibutani also quarrels with the notion that rumor and the errors inherent in rumor texts are the products of individuals and offers instead a definition of rumor as:

> ... communication through which men caught together in an ambiguous situation attempt to construct a meaningful interpretation of it by pooling their intellectual resources.[74]

This collective notion of rumor is a very promising one for the student of the legend process, and Shibutani fulfills this promise when he offers an hypothesis concerning legend:

> ... whenever a situation remains ambiguous, even after

---

[71] Richard T. La Piere and Paul R. Farnsworth, *Social Psychology* (New York: McGraw-Hill, 1936), p. 65.

[72] Gordon W. Allport and Leo Postman, *The Psychology of Rumor* (New York: Henry Holt and Company, 1947), p. 163.

[73] *Improvised News: A Sociological Study of Rumor* (Indianapolis and New York: The Bobbs-Merrill Company, Inc., 1966), p.17.

[74] Ibid., p. 17.

reality testing, men are responsive to ideas that tend to support their interests. Whenever the results of reality testing are not clear-cut, where there is room for doubt, they are sensitive to ideas that are useful. The survival of given beliefs implies the continued existence of certain sensitivities. This does not necessarily involve deliberate invention, but a selective responsiveness to views that happen to justify their acts and other beliefs.[75]

In this notion of selective responsiveness lies the key to the human impulse to recount legends and to the great amount of variation evident in legendary accounts of historical events. Men approach the world with expectations that are a product of their experiences. These expectations are shaped through the successive testing of hypotheses, the rejection of unsuccessful ones and the retention of those that are successful. In cases where it is difficult to apply tests or where the results are ambiguous, men reach out for ideas or accounts of incidents that support what they want to believe. In like manner they reject ideas or accounts that run counter to their cherished preconceptions. Kimball Young tells us that legend provides a framework that makes us feel secure in the continuity of our ideologies and spares us the necessity of constantly recasting them.[76] The fact that an informant chooses to recount the text of a particular legend and the fact that his version of the legend differs from other accounts are both inextricably bound to the way in which that informant perceives and conceptualizes his world. If the careful scholar is willing to examine numbers of oral testimonies concerning historical events, weighing them carefully one against the other, he should be able to abstract from them not only data concerning the event itself, but also a fair notion of the belief systems of the informants who provide the texts.

Jan Vansina has outlined such a methodology for African materials:

The way to decide what weight should be attached to a testimony is to find out what connection there is between the initial testimony of a tradition and the facts it describes. If

---

[75] Ibid., p. 17.

[76] *Social Psychology* (New York: F. S. Crofts and Company, 1936), p. 437.

this testimony is a falsification then the facts described must have been invented, and the testimony is not based on fact at all. But the falsification to which the testimony has given rise is in itself a fact which is of relevance to the testimony. Examination of the information on which a testimony is based is therefore the first step towards evaluating its reliability.

The next step is to compare it with all other testimonies which describe the same facts. The comparative method is the one which enables the historian to arrive at an overall estimate of the relative reliability of the various testimonies.[77]

Vansina goes on to outline a specific procedure for dealing with oral testimonies in Africa,[78] a procedure that would seem to work well in a culture that produces a great number of fixed form texts and that deals heavily in genealogical records and origin myths, but one that seems of relatively little value in the study of American historical traditions.

From his work we can derive a general methodology appropriate to the American historical legend, but we must devise our own technique for evaluating systematic distortion in the testimonies with which we are concerned.

The living, breathing informant in possession of a text which is some part of the body of a legend[79] is a very different creature from the laboratory subject in a human communications experiment. First of all, he is free to sort among the many bits of information he receives and choose what he is going to pass on; secondly, he will, in most cases, be the recipient of not one but multiple inputs of information on the same subject, and he will accept some, reject others, and frequently amalgamate several inputs in a new synthesis which then becomes his account; thirdly, he is free to ask questions of his informant and to

---

[77] *Oral Tradition: A Study in Historical Methodology* (Chicago: Aldine Publishing Company, 1965), p. 114.

[78] Ibid., pp. 115-140.

[79] Richard M. Dorson speaks to the nature of the legend when he tells us, "No one individual knows the whole legend, for by definition it is a communal possession" in "Defining the Folk Legend," in *American Folklore and the Historian* (Chicago: University of Chicago Press, 1971), p. 161.

challenge statements which he finds difficult to credit; and fourthly, he usually has considerable periods of time between reception of informational inputs and the time when he is moved to pass on his synthesis of this information. These differences from the laboratory situation all point to a greater influence on the material by the informant's perception of the world. He is free of the experimenter's injunction as to accuracy and is bound only by the limits of credibility imposed by his audience. His own sense of group identity, his notions of good and evil, his ideas of meritorious behavior, his sensitivity to the beliefs of non-members of his group toward that group, and countless other factors will all play a part in his reality testing and in the final form that his testimony will take. Frederick C. Bartlett touched on this process when he said:

> When a story is passed from one person to another, each man repeating, as he imagines, what he has heard from the last narrator, it undergoes many successive changes before it at length arrives at that relatively fixed form in which it may become current throughout a whole community.[80]

This is certainly an accurate description of the process in so far as it goes, but it glosses over the fact that such a process takes place at every link in the communications chain, and that the relatively fixed form may never evolve so long as the incident being recounted retains any element of controversy. For so long as groups which had any interest in the original incident maintain their identity, members of these groups may continue to reinterpret the event. Thus the evolution of Bartlett's "relatively fixed form" may be the work of a century or even centuries.

If one keeps in mind the biases of informants and the differences between the laboratory and field situations, it is possible to borrow a set of principles from the laboratory experimenters that will be useful in the evaluation of field-collected texts. These principles as I see them are eleven:

---

[80] "Some Experiments in the Reproduction of Folk-Stories," *Folk-Lore*, XXXI (1920), p. 30.

1) Condensation

An informant's version of a legend text, if it differs from the version that he received, will generally be shorter, simpler, and less detailed than that version.[81] This is not the loss of random parts of the text. The loss will be a selective one; the overall form of the text will be retained, and the major effect of the text will survive.

2) Middle Message Loss

The beginning and the ending of a text will be better preserved in transmission than the middle. This is one of the best-documented phenomena in all of learning studies.[82]

3) Closure

This principle refers to the informant's urge to make his experiences as complete, coherent, and meaningful as possible.[83] He does this by reinterpreting information that he receives so as to

---

[81] See Gordon W. Allport and Leo Postman, *The Psychology of Rumor* (New York: Henry Holt and Company, 1947); Frederick C. Bartlett, *Remembering: A Study in Experimental and Social Psychology* (London and New York: Cambridge University Press, 1932); D.T. Campbell and W. Gruen, "Progression from Simple to Complex as a Molar Law of Learning," *Journal of General Psychology*, LXIX (1958), pp. 237-244; H.R. Crosland, "A Qualitative Analysis of the Process of Forgetting," *Psychological Monographs*, XXIX, No. 130 (1921); E.N. Henderson, "Memory for Connected Trains of Thought," *Psychological Monographs*, V, No. 23 (1903); David Krech and Allen D. Calvin, "Levels of Perceptual Organization and Cognition," *Journal of Abnormal and Social Psychology*, XLVIII, (1953), pp. 394-400; and F.H. Lewis, "Note on the Doctrine of Memory Trace," *Psychological Review*, XL (1933), pp. 90-96.

[82] See Charles E. Osgood, *Method and Theory in Experimental Psychology*, (London and New York: Oxford University Press, 1953); J. Wishner, T.E. Shipley, Jr., and M.S. Hurvick, "The Serial Position Curve as a Function of Organization," *American Journal of Psychology*, (New York: Henry Holt and Co., 1938).

[83] See Gordon W. Allport and Leo Postman, *The Psychology of Rumor* (New York: Henry Holt and Company, 1947); Jessie B. Carlson and Carl P. Duncan, "A Study of Recognition," *American Journal of Psychology*, LXVIII (1955), pp. 280-284; S.H. Lovibond, "A Further Test of the Hypothesis of Autonomous Memory Trace Change," *Journal of Experimental Psychology*, LV (1958), pp. 412-415; D.N. Michael, "A Cross-Cultural Investigation of Closure," *Journal of Abnormal and Social Psychology*, XLVIII (1953), pp. 225-230; and Charles E. Osgood, *Method and Theory in Experimental Psychology* (London and New York: Oxford University Press, 1953).

bring it in line with his past experiences and so that it will fit his perception of reality. This reinterpretation may involve the introduction of rationalizations and explanations.

4) Symmetry

An informant may distort information which he receives in the direction of greater symmetry.[84] In a culture in which a number or numbers are invested with a potency or "magic," characters and incidents may be multiplied or reduced to make them fit these cultural notions of propriety.

5) Categorization

The content of a legend text may be distorted by its division into clear-cut entities. Gradations may be reduced by ignoring some differences and exaggerating others. W. S. McCulloch states:

> For example, the eye and the ear report the continuous variable of intensity by discrete impulses ... but this process is carried to an extreme in our appreciation of the world in pairs of opposites ... our sense organs detecting regularities the same in all aspects save one, create dichotomies and decide between opposites.[85]

6) Assimilation to Prior Input

A legend text if different from the version that the informant received will generally be distorted in the direction of stories that the informant has heard previously and which are in some way similar to this text.[86] This influence of memory is extremely

---

[84] See Fred Attneave, "Some Informational Aspects of Visual Perception," *Psychological Review*, LXI (1954), pp. 183-193; Julian Hochberg and E. McAlister, "A Quantitative Approach to Figural Goodness," *Journal of Experimental Psychology*, XLVI (1953), pp. 361-364; and Robert S. Woodworth, *Experimental Psychology* (New York: Henry Holt and Company, 1938).

[85] "Why the Mind is in the Head," in *Cerebral Mechanisms*, L.A. Jeffress, ed. (New York: Wiley, 1951), p. 174. See also Charles E. Osgood, *Method and Theory in Experimental Psychology* (London and New York: Oxford University Press, 1953), and Norbert Wiener, *Cybernetics* (New York: Wiley, 1948).

[86] See Alphonse Chapanis, "The Reconstruction of Abbreviated Printed Messages," *Journal of Experimental Psychology*, XLVIII (1954), pp. 496-510; Elliot

important to an understanding of distortion in oral transmission, for it implies a pervasive bias toward typical, popular expressions and readily explains the phenomenon of legend mingling. In another area it can be seen operating quite clearly in the "proofreader's error." A special integrant of this principle is the tendency of the informant to give verbal labels to nonverbal materials, which leads to distortion in the direction of assimilation to the verbal prototype.

7) Assimilation to the Attitudes of the Informant

A legend text may be distorted in the direction of the informant's own attitudes.[87] This principle is central to an understanding of distortion in transmission, and it is so reasonable as to need little discussion; it underlies the common law of testimony in which self-interest on the part of a witness can lead to the discrediting of his testimony.

8) Distortion to Please the Receiver

The informant is usually in the position of transmitting his text to a human listener, and the relationship with that receiver will almost necessarily have reciprocal aspects. Therefore, the informant may deviate from the version of the incident which he received or which he has synthesized in an effort to please the receiver or to avoid hurting him.[88] This principle can be readily seen in the slave narratives; those collected by whites differ greatly from those gathered by black fieldworkers.

M. McGinnies, P.B. Comer and O.L. Lacey, "Visual Recognition Thresholds as a Function of Word Length and Word Frequency," *Journal of Experimental Psychology*, XLIV (1951), pp. 65-69; and Leo Postman, "The Experimental Analysis of Motivational Factors in Perception," in *Current Theory and Research in Motivation*, J.S. Brown, ed. (Lincoln, Nebraska: University of Nebraska Press, 1953), pp. 59-108.

[87] See Donald T. Campbell, "The Indirect Assessment of Social Attitudes," *Psychological Bulletin*, XLVII (1950), pp. 15-38; Herbert H. Hyman, *Interviewing in Social Research* (Chicago: University of Chicago Press, 1954); and E.L. and R.E. Horowitz, "Development of Social Attitudes in Children," *Sociometry*, I (1938), pp. 301-308.

[88] See D. Robinson and S. Rohde, "Two Experiments with an Anti-Semitism Poll," *Journal of Abnormal and Social Psychology*, XLI (1946), pp. 136-144.

9) **Distortion from Associated Cues**

If in an informant's experience, a certain kind of outcome has been associated with a certain type of individual or situation, the informant may distort a text containing that kind of individual or situation in the direction of that kind of outcome.[89] This principle, of course, is at the root of prejudice and stereotyping.

10) **Overdependence on a Single Source**

When an informant has access to multiple sources, if one of those sources is more prestigious than the others or if the source and the informant possess similar perceptions of reality, the informant's version of the legend may follow that source very closely and ignore others.[90]

11) **Conformity**

When an informant is in contact with other informants and is able to hear their versions of the legend, he may distort his version in the direction of conformity with his fellows.[91]

Thus informants who are members of the same group and who have extensive contact with each other can be expected to tell similar versions of the legend since they are constantly receiving confirmation of their version of the facts.

These eleven principles can be applied to any body of field-collected legend texts and may aid the scholar in discovering and determining the degree of distortion to be found there. The conception here should not be that of a winnowing process from which something

---

[89] See Donald T. Campbell, "The Indirect Assessment of Social Attitudes," *Psychological Bulletin*, XLVII (1950), pp. 15-38; R. Clarke and D.T. Campbell, "A Demonstration of Bias in Estimates of Negro Ability," *Journal of Abnormal and Social Psychology*, LI (1955), pp. 585-588; and T.E. Coffin, "Some Conditions of Suggestion and Suggestibility," *Psychological Monographs*, LIII, No. 241 (1941).

[90] See Edna Heidbreder, "Toward a Dynamic Theory of Cognition," *Psychological Review*, LII (1945), pp. 1-22; and J. Smedslund, *Multiple Probability Learning* (Oslo: Akademisk Forlag, 1955).

[91] See Solomon E. Asch, *Social Psychology* (New York: Prentice-Hall, 1952); J.W. Bridges, "An Experimental Study of Decision Types and Their Mental Correlates," *Psychological Monographs*, XVII, No. 1 (1914); and Muzafen Sherif, *The Psychology of Social Norms* (New York: Harper, 1936).

called "truth" will emerge. One would hope that the incredible intellectual conceit involved in the belief that the truth of any historical event is attainable no longer has a place in serious scholarship. Rather, the hope is that these principles can be utilized to detect distortion, not so that it can be discarded, but in order that it can be isolated and evaluated, for in this distortion lies the promise of extremely important insights into the world view of the individuals and groups who transmit it.

THE LEGEND AREA: GRAHAM COUNTY

Graham County was created in 1881 from the then existing counties of Pima and Apache. It was named presumably for the 10,720 feet high Mt. Graham,[92] which lies within its boundaries. The county seat was initially located at Safford, but it was moved to Solomonville in 1883, where it remained until 1915, when it was returned to the original site.

The northern fourth of the county lies within the boundaries of the San Carlos Apache Reservation and is a part of the county in name only, since the reservation has its own governmental agencies. The remainder of the county area is dominated by the upper Gila River, which runs through the county in a northwesterly direction. The valley thus created is a level one, about thirty-five miles long, opening rapidly from box canyons at both ends and bounded by the barren Gila mountains on the east and by the timbered Pinaleno Mountains[93] twenty miles distant to the south. This valley is the population center of the county, and most of the arable land is to be found here. Beyond the Pinalenos to the southwest lies the Aravaipa Valley, an area of foothills, suited to ranching and bounded on the southwest by the rugged Galiuros. To the south lies the broad Sulphur Springs Valley. The total area of the county is 6,475 square miles, just a little larger than the combined areas of Connecticut and Rhode Island.

The upper Gila Valley has a long history of habitancy:

In the upper end of the cultivated region is one of the most notable groups of ruins in the Southwest. This group, since the coming of the

---

[92] There is some mystery attached to the name of the peak itself. One might suppose, as I did, that it was named in honor of W.L. Graham, who was prominent in the boundary survey of 1850-52. However, the name "Mt. Graham" was used in a reconnaissance report of 1846.
[93] This whole range of mountains is popularly designated the Grahams, due, I suppose, to the peak which dominates it.

Spaniard, appears to have borne the name of Pueblo Viejo (Sp.: "Old Town"). Somewhere farther down the stream is assumed to have been "Chichilticalli," the "red house" mentioned in the chronicles of Marco de Niza and the Coronado expedition.[94]

In 1846 General S.W. Kearney, en route to take California from the Mexicans, traversed the valley from east to west accompanied by a dragoon escort. This command formed the advance guard for the Mormon Battalion.

There is a record of some Mexicans in the valley as early as 1871.[95] They lived around a tiny hamlet near the junction of the Gila and the San Simon, but they made very little progress in the clearing of mesquite and the development of agricultural land.[96] The town which became Solomonville was also begun at this time.[97] The first Anglo-Saxon settlement appeared in 1872 when a group of farmers from Gila Bend, who had failed in their attempts at farming on the lower river banks, settled in the vicinity of what is now Safford. The town was named for Governor A.P.K. Safford, who was then making a tour of that part of the Arizona Territory.[98] The land in the valley was rich and fertile, but it was thickly covered with mesquite, and this thorny, widely-branched, hardwood shrub made all but the most basic, subsistence agriculture impossible. Ross Calvin tells us:

> Then into their valley by a trick of fate came a wandering Israelite. Things began to prosper among the Saints from the day that Mr. Isidor Solomon came among them.[99] He set up a store by the side of the road, and then, much more important, he began to burn charcoal and sell it to the new smelter in Clifton

---

[94] James H. McClintock, *Mormon Settlement in Arizona* (Phoenix, Arizona: Manufacturers and Stationers, Inc., 1921), p. 241.

[95] Ibid., p. 242.

[96] Ross Calvin, *River of the Sun* (Albuquerque, New Mexico: University of New Mexico Press, 1946), p. 83.

[97] McClintock, *Mormon Settlement*, p. 242.

[98] Ibid., p. 242.

[99] Mr. Calvin is in error here. He believes that Mormons were already in residence when Isidor Solomon settled in the valley. The truth is that Mr. Solomon arrived in 1876 and the first Mormon settler, Apostle Erastus Snow, did not appear in the valley until 1878, and the first Mormon settlement did not take place until February, 1879.

...The immense deposits of copper ore at the Longfellow mine in Clifton had been but recently discovered, and farming began together and one helped the other. Mr. Solomon burned the mesquite in crude pits, sold the charcoal to the Lesynzsky Brothers for metallurgical processes, and the cleared acres to the Mormons for agricultural processes. Intelligence brought its own reward. And the job of clearing the land, so expensive along the Rio Grande, was here practically self-liquidating, so that economic development was greatly set forward thereby.[100]

With the exception of his error concerning the presence of Mormons in the valley in 1876, Mr. Calvin's analysis is sound.

Permanent Mormon settlement south of the Colorado began in 1876 when at a conference in Salt Lake City, a group of fifty men, many with families, was called to settle in Arizona. Several towns were built along the Little Colorado, and small villages and ranches dotted the habitable areas north of the Tonto and White Mountains.[101] The Salt River Valley had Mormon colonies at Mesa and Tempe by 1875, and settlers came to the San Pedro Valley in 1879. Many of the northern settlements proved unsatisfactory due to long, cold winters, poor soil and rampaging rivers that time and time again overflowed their banks and destroyed the work of the previous winter. There was also the problem of the people's discontent with the so-called "United Order," which held all land and produce in common. Stories of the warm, fertile valleys to the south told by members of the Mormon Battalion aroused in these settlers a desire to move into southern Arizona.

Many of these settlers left their farms and camped in small groups while scouting for favorable locations for settlement. One such group gathered on the north slope of the White Mountains. J. K. Rogers and William Teeples, leaders of the group, made a scouting trip to the Gila Valley. Teeples was impressed by the possibilities of the land, and later in the winter he made another trip accompanied by Hyrum Weech and

---

[100] *River of the Sun*, p. 84.
[101] Apache County grew from 587 Mormon people in 1878 to 6,000 in 1887. See Hubert Howe Bancroft, *History of Arizona and New Mexico, 1530-1888* (San Francisco: The History Company, 1889), p. 610.

three other men.[102] At the time when the scouting party first entered it, the valley was still covered by a dense growth of mesquite.[103]

The Teeples scouting party crossed the Gila near the western end of the valley at Fort Thomas, an adobe army post established in 1876 as an outpost against the Apaches. A freighting road, cut deep in the dust or mud depending on the season, ran from Globe eastward through the valley and on to Fort Bowie, the nearest Southern Pacific Railroad station. Fourteen miles east of Fort Thomas on this freighting road lay the little town of Safford. In 1879 Safford had two general stores, one combined with a saloon, a grist mill, and a few adobe houses clustered nearby.[104] Four miles farther east the road cut through the village of Solomonville. The farming of the valley was generally very poorly done, since most farmers in the area were cattlemen first and farmers only incidentally, employing Mexican day laborers. The soil was a fertile, sandy loam, renewed by the river floods. The richness of this soil, coupled with the warm, sunny climate which afforded a growing season of seven to eight months, made the valley seem a paradise to the scouts from the north.[105] They borrowed a horse, wagon, and tools from a local rancher and laid out sixteen quarter sections, with the corners marked by large logs.[106]

The day after the completion of this surveying project, the party set out on its return trip. On arriving at their camp in the White Mountains, the men reported their findings to Jessie N. Smith, the president of Snowflake Stake,[107] and requested permission to take their families to the Gila. President Smith organized the camp into a branch of the church with J. K. Rogers as president, and on March 20, 1879, the whole group began its trek over the mountains to the south.[108]

After a difficult journey, the group arrived at its townsite and, using

---

[102] Hyrum Weech, *Autobiography* (Hollywood, California: Lee Publishing Company, 1931), pp. 21-23.

[103] Ibid., p. 23.

[104] Ibid., p. 23.

[105] Ibid., pp. 24-25.

[106] Ibid., p. 25.

[107] The Mormon church is made up of larger territorial divisions called stakes. The stakes are each divided into wards and branches, the smallest local church units. Snowflake Stake, with its headquarters in the town of Snowflake, was composed of the settlements of northeastern Arizona.

[108] Weech, *Autobiography*, p. 25

wagon boxes as dwelling places, made camp in the mesquite. The town was soon laid out into sixteen blocks of four lots each, one and three-fourths acres in size.[109] Building locations were determined by the drawing of lots, and lot six was reserved for public buildings. On the first Sunday the land was dedicated to the gathering of the saints,[110] and the town was named Smithville.

Almost at once the settlers found themselves faced with a serious food problem. They had departed Utah with few supplies and very little money, and what little they had, had been sorely depleted in the time they had spent wandering about. The necessities of life came high in that rugged country. They arranged to buy squatter's claims to their land and to a ditch site on credit, but the land was not cleared, and they could not hope to raise a crop without some kind of irrigation. To meet the pressing need for food, they rented a farm three miles west of their townsite.[111]

On this rented land they raised a crop during the summer of 1879 that was sufficient to sustain them until their own land could be readied. Settlers continued to arrive from Utah and northern Arizona during the summer, and by fall there were thirty-six families, 148 people, living in Smithville. In December they began work on the Smithville canal. Scrapers were made of hollowed-out cottonwood logs, and a huge plow was fashioned from the forks of a tree; both implements were pointed with iron. By April, 1880, water was flowing in the canal.[112]

New land seldom produces abundantly, and the few crops raised could barely sustain life. Each family's share of food had to be continually shared with new arrivals who were destitute. Money was needed to pay for settler's claims, machinery, clothes, and other necessities. Men soon found a ready source of money in freighting. All supplies had to be hauled to the mining camps and army posts. Since every family had a team of oxen, mules, or horses, it was only natural that they should put these animals to work, and soon most of the

---

[109] Ibid., p. 26.
[110] The Mormons claim to be of the literal blood of scattered Israel, and their gathering in the West is in fulfillment of the scriptural reference to the gathering of Israel.
[111] Weech, *Autobiography*, p. 32.
[112] Ibid., p. 33.

people in the community were at least partially supported by freighting.[113]

Early in 1880 Joseph and David Matthews, brothers, and a Mr. Waddell came from Round Valley in northern Arizona and purchased 160 acres and a one-third interest in an existing canal. Two more Matthews, Solomon and Charles, arrived in 1881, and the town of Matthewsville, known in recent years as Glenbar, was founded.[114]

Another town, Graham, on the north side of the river, four miles east of Smithville, was begun in 1881 by a group of settlers from Brigham City. This settlement was operated under the United Order. The town of Curtis, now called Eden, was also begun in 1881 when Moses Curtis and William Hawkins came from Brigham City on the Little Colorado. They began the construction of a canal almost immediately and finished it early enough in 1882 to enable them to raise a small food crop.[115] Thatcher, on the south side of the river, five miles east of Smithville, was founded in 1881 by John Moody, and in 1883 Stake President Christopher Layton approved the selection of the townsite and established a school district.[116]

The Mormon population grew very rapidly in these early years, and in 1884 there were 825 church members in the valley.[117] This early influx of settlers was marked by a noteworthy spirit of cooperation. Smithville, from its foundation, had been a city of refuge for those who had failed to find satisfactory conditions in northern Arizona and southern Utah. The original settlers divided their claims with newcomers without apparent reluctance until all of the good land was dispersed. They received all immigrants of their faith with open arms and were quite willing to feed and shelter them until they could be located elsewhere.[118] This amazing cooperation was, of course, a direct result of the extremely tight-knit organization of the church, which was the focal point of the settlers' lives. From the beginnings of settlement, services were held every Sunday in addition to the social and religious gatherings held during the week. There was the Relief Society for

---

[113] Ibid., p. 33.
[114] Ibid., p. 34.
[115] McClintock, *Mormon Settlement*, p. 249.
[116] Ibid., p. 249.
[117] *Deseret News*, Vol. XXXII, p. 574.
[118] Weech, *Autobiography*, p. 43.

women, Young People's Mutual Improvement for youth, Primary for the children, and Priesthood for the men; each of which held a regular weekly meeting.[119]

Wresting a living from the land was not the only problem that these settlers faced. Indians and malaria joined with the normal hardships of the frontier to make life in the valley difficult. There were times when so many people in the communities were sick with malaria that there were scarcely enough well to care for the sick. The cause of the malady was the water supply which came from shallow wells and ditches. From 1883 the disease began to abate in direct proportion to well-digging activity.[120]

Indians were a constant source of distress and suffering. After a series of Apache raids in 1875, the government sent troops, "rounded up" the Indians, and established posts to keep them on their respective reservations. Led by Victorio, Geronimo, Juh, the Apache Kid, and others, hostile bands of Coyotero, Mescalero, and Chiricahua Apaches raided southern Arizona and New Mexico on their trips to and from old Mexico. Since the Gila Valley was along their regular path of travel, the settlers lived in mortal dread, expecting at any time, day or night, to hear that the Apaches had bolted the reservation.[121] Each community had its organized band of minutemen who kept horses and guns ready. Some settlers were killed, but the survivors soon learned that the Indians, if unopposed, usually took what stock or food they needed and went on their way.[122] The military in the area was fairly efficient and, more important, nearby. Whenever danger threatened, troops could ride out and reach any part of the valley in a few hours; thus these settlements were spared the general massacres suffered by other areas of the Southwest.[123]

The economic growth of these Mormon settlements was slow in proportion to the population increase. The earliest settlers were, in general, those who had failed to prosper in Utah. In spite of the great amount of farm land available in the valley and the ease with which this

---

[119] Ibid., pp. 44-45.

[120] Ibid., p. 48.

[121] Will H. Robinson, *Story of Arizona* (Phoenix: The Berryhill Company, 1919), p. 206.

[122] Weech, *Autobiography*, p. 47.

[123] McClintock, *Mormon Settlement*, p. 252.

land could be acquired, these early settlers gained title to only a very little, and all of their acquisitions were along the river banks because of the ease with which this land could be cultivated.[124] Some few of the later arrivals were progressive farmers, and they did come into possession of some small parcels of good land, but these forward-looking individuals were in the minority.[125]

Such conditions were only allowed to exist because church authorities in Salt Lake City had taken little interest in the Gila Valley settlements, but circumstances in Utah in 1882 caused them to cast favorable eyes on this remote colony. The Congress of the United States had passed an anti-polygamy law in 1862, but little action was taken to interfere with Mormon practices until 1879, when the United States Supreme Court affirmed the constitutionality of the measure by confirming the conviction of George Reynolds, a president of the church.[126] After 1880 many of the prominent men of Utah who were polygamists had to secrete themselves occasionally to escape prosecution.

In 1882 continued agitation resulted in Congress amending the law of 1862 under the name of the Edmunds Law. In addition to the fine and imprisonment provided for in the earlier law, this amended statute provided for disenfranchisement of polygamists, and the hunt for such offenders began in earnest.[127] Men began to seek hiding places in the mountains of southern Utah. When the strenuous hunt continued, however, it was decided that the church should locate favorable places for the settlement of polygamists in Arizona or Mexico. On December 13, 1881, a party of church leaders left Salt Lake City on a reconnaissance tour of these two areas.[128]

On March 25, 1882, this party entered the Gila Valley. They visited and held meetings at all the Mormon settlements. The party was well impressed with the valley, and Erastus Snow and Moses Thatcher, the apostles in charge, decided to establish a stake in southern Arizona. On

---

[124] Weech, *Autobiography*, pp. 49-50.

[125] Ibid., p. 50.

[126] Milton R. Hunter, *Brigham Young, the Colonizer* (Salt Lake City: The Deseret News Press, 1940), pp. 347-348.

[127] Ibid., p. 348.

[128] John Q. Cannon, *The Life of Christopher Layton* (Salt Lake City: The Deseret News Press, 1911), pp. 190-191.

the return of the party to Salt Lake City, this plan was carried out.[129] Christopher Layton decided that he should become the president of the new stake. He said:

> Finally my wives and children agreed that, although they disliked very much to be without my presence, they would rather know that I was at liberty, than have me dodging the hands of the law. Under these conditions I accepted a call to preside over and make a home for the Saints in Southern Arizona.[130]

It was decided that headquarters of the stake should be in St. David, a settlement in the San Pedro Valley, not far from the Gila and on the direct rail and wagon route into northern Mexico. In this location, it was decided, stake officials would be in the best position to aid polygamists seeking refuge from the law. On February 15, 1883, President Layton and one of his families left Ogden, Utah, by train with furniture, stock, and machinery.[131]

Prosecution for polygamy and the consequent establishment of St. Joseph Stake[132] inaugurated a new era in the growth and development of the Gila Valley. The church took active control, and, through the leadership of President Layton, a unified development of the valley as a Mormon colony began. People were no longer permitted to settle where they chose. Instead President Layton selected townsites with an eye to health conditions and protection from Indians. Towns were established on higher ground and at a greater distance from the river than had previously been the case, and the whole colony was organized as a cooperative concern.[133] In May, 1883, Layton made a trip through the Gila Valley and set up four wards of the stake. Smithville was renamed Pima and made a ward with J. K. Rogers as bishop; Graham was made a ward with J. Jorgensen as bishop; Curtis was renamed Eden with Moses Curtis as bishop; and Thatcher Ward was created with John M. Moody as bishop. Layton recognized that the Gila held

---

[129] Ibid., p. 191.

[130] Ibid., p. 191.

[131] Ibid., pp. 193-194.

[132] President Layton chose the name St. Joseph in honor of Joseph Smith. It was the first stake to extend into a foreign country.

[133] Cannon, *Christopher Layton*, p. 194.

more promise than the San Pedro, and he moved his family to Safford in 1864.[134]

Throughout Utah and the outposts of the church, the Gila was soon favorably known, and immigration increased. The Mormon population of the valley grew from 416 in 1882 to 836 by the end of 1883. By 1886 it had again increased to 1,647.[135]

With the coming of President Layton and other settlers who had energy, foresight, and money, a more rapid economic development of the valley got underway. Layton, personally, purchased the grist mill at Safford from the Tucson builders in 1884.[136] He also established a stage and freight line operating through the valley between Bowie and Globe and secured government contracts for it. These ventures proved very successful financially and provided well-paid employment for many of the Mormons of the valley.[137]

As Mormon polygamists from Utah began to take refuge in Arizona from prosecution and imprisonment in rather large numbers, the unfavorable Republican administration started to take action against them. The thirteenth legislature of 1883 passed an act disfranchising polygamists and permitting any person to challenge the vote of any member of a sect professing belief in or countenancing polygamy.[138] Republican reports and pleas against the Mormons also brought action from Washington, and in the fall of 1884 federal authorities began the prosecution of polygamists in Arizona. Awareness of this soon spread throughout the territory, and church communities organized to protect themselves. Some went to Mexico for short periods of time; others made plans to remain there permanently. Because the attitude of local Gentiles was so favorable toward Mormons, prosecutions were never so severe on the Gila as in other places. Some of those practicing polygamy remained in the valley, completely unmolested.[139] When Grover Cleveland came into office, the attitude toward Mormons changed, and the prosecutions diminished gradually until 1887, when

---

[134] Ibid., p. 195.
[135] Ibid., p. 193.
[136] Ibid., p. 200.
[137] Ibid., p. 213.
[138] James H. McClintock, *Arizona, the Youngest State*, Vol. II (Chicago: The S. J. Clarke Publishing Company, 1916), p. 457.
[139] Cannon, *Christopher Layton*, p. 208.

the disfranchisement law was repealed.[140]

Then in 1890 President of the Church Wilford Woodruff, after appealing to the Lord to determine His will, issued the "Manifesto" - a proclamation suspending the practice of plural marriage and bringing the censure of the church to bear on all those who subsequently contracted such arrangements. President Harrison followed this proclamation three years later with one of amnesty for all those who had entered into plural marriages prior to November 1, 1890, and the great breach was healed at last.[141]

From this point in time the Mormons on the upper Gila prospered. Immigrants continued to arrive and were warmly welcomed, although the older tradition of open-handed sharing became more and more infrequent. Successful farming led to cattle ranching and mining investment, and this meant that Mormons were settled at some remove from the river, in other areas of the county which were very different in character from the Gila Valley. The Sulphur Springs Valley is about twenty miles wide and fifty to sixty miles long.

In 1880 it was described as being particularly adapted to the grazing of range cattle because of its location near the railroad, climate, good forage, and the lack of chaparral.[142] The water supply was not as abundant as most ranchers would have liked, but this had not discouraged Henry Clay Hooker from establishing one of the great cattle ranches of Arizona on most of the acreage of the valley. Colonel Hooker was an extremely colorful character, a Yankee who went to California in gold rush days, and who is said to have made his fortune by driving a herd of turkeys from California to the Nevada mining camps in 1866.[143] His Sierra Bonita Ranch became one of the showplaces of the Southwest, and his policy of stocking it with new types of beef cattle - shorthorns, Durhams and Herefords - proved instrumental in changing the cattle industry in the southern part of the territory.[144] Hooker's dominance of the Sulphur Springs Valley

---

[140] Ibid., p. 209.

[141] Hunter, *Brigham Young*, p. 349.

[142] J.J. Wagoner, "Development of the Cattle Industry in Southern Arizona, 1870's and 80's," *New Mexico Historical Review*, XXVI (1951), p. 212.

[143] Rufus Kay Wyllys, *Arizona, the History of a Frontier State* (Phoenix: Hobson and Hur, 1950), p. 243.

[144] Ibid., p. 243.

forestalled any significant Mormon settlement of influence in this area, and to this day the orientation of the valley is much more toward Willcox and Cochise County than toward Safford.

The third major area of Graham County, the Aravaipa Valley, has a much more obscure history. Aside from casual mentions in newspapers, the Aravaipa seems only to figure as a background for murders and as the site of the infamous Camp Grant Massacre.[145] Oral testimony concerning early settlers centers on a very colorful figure, Epimanio Salazar, who apparently took up residence at the mouth of the Aravaipa Canyon about 1860 and remained there, in spite of the fact that his ranch lay directly on the route the Chiricahua Apaches took from their summer home to their winter camp. For some reason he was never victimized by them although on several occasions they cleared all other settlers out of the area. Epimanio retired about 1920, turning the ranch over to his son, Lupe, and returned to his birthplace in Durango, Mexico. In 1930 at the age of 110, the elder Salazar returned to the Aravaipa on muleback to check on his son's stewardship, stayed a few months, then started on his homeward trip, only to be ambushed and killed by Yaquis![146] In any event, the valley has been a mining and ranching area. At the turn of the century cattle were displaced by angora goats, which proved very lucrative for about a decade and then gave way to the increased demand for cattle during the First World War.[147] A significant number of Mormons have settled in the Aravaipa over the years, most of them since 1920, and they now represent a potent force in valley life.

In 1960 Graham County had a population of 14,045: 1,050 in the Bonita-Klondyke Division, 2,266 in the Pima Division, 9,572 in the Safford Division, and 1,157 in the San Carlos Division. The white population is listed at 12,387 and the non-white at 1,658. Of these non-

---

[145] On April 30, 1871, a citizens' organization from Tucson, led by Jesus M. Elias and William S. Oury, attacked the camp of 150 Aravaipa Apaches who were living peacefully under army protection near Camp Grant. One hundred and eight Aravaipas were killed, only eight of them men, and twenty-nine children were taken captive and brought back to Tucson.

[146] Oral interview with Guadalupe Salazar, Aravaipa Canyon, Arizona, July 29, 1961.

[147] Old ranching families are very reluctant to talk about their involvement with goats, sometimes to the point of lying. Apparently "cowboy" has acquired a cachet that "goatboy" lacks.

white persons, 360 were Negro, 1,249 Indian, 1 Japanese, 45 Chinese, and 3 of other races. Of the total of non-white persons, 1,651 were native-born, and 1,262 of these persons were born in the state of Arizona. A foreign-born population of 1,534 was listed; seventy percent of these persons were of Mexican origin. The median family income for the county was $5,277; for non-white families it was $1,943. The median level of education was 10.8 years.[148]

These statistics are misleading in several respects: they afford no means of distinguishing between Mexican and Anglo persons, although this distinction is very important in the county; they provide no clue to religious affiliation; and beyond the figures for median family income for white and non-white families, they tell us nothing about the way in which wealth is distributed in the county. A twenty year acquaintance with the area has convinced me that forty percent of the total population is identified as Mexican, a term that in popular usage has nothing to do with the birthplace of an individual but seems rather to be determined by a combination of factors including skin color, lack of identifiable Indian blood, Hispanic surname, and religious affiliation. The Anglo population is split along religious lines with about forty percent of the total belonging to the Church of Jesus Christ of Latter-Day Saints. This two-fifths of the Anglo population, however, seems to control a disproportionate share of the wealth and, consequently, the power of the county. Most of the businesses, most of the large ranches, and a very high percentage of the desirable cotton land is in the hands of members of this sect. Virtually all of the elected and appointed officials are members of the Mormon church; in 1961, for example, the total school board and school administration was Mormon with the single exception of the school superintendent, recently imported to replace a Mormon who had held the post for thirty years and apparently eager only to carry out the wishes of the board.

All things considered, Graham County in 1962-1963 presented the most repressive atmosphere that I have ever experienced. The village of Solomonville with an enrollment of 368 voters, 359 of whom were Mexican, had never in its history until 1963 elected a Mexican as its representative on the school board. An intensive campaign, organized

---

[148] All of these statistics are drawn from the *United States Census of Population, 1960, Detailed Characteristics, Arizona.* Final Report PC (1)-4D (Washington, D.C.: United States Government Printing Office, 1962).

by Father Miguel Herrara, the curate of St. Rose of Lima Roman Catholic Church in Safford, finally resulted in the election of a Mexican to that office by a margin of two votes. Most Mexican voters with whom I spoke during this campaign expressed a deep-seated fear that their jobs might be placed in jeopardy or that some other economic reprisals might be carried out against them if they voted the "wrong way." My involvement in this campaign coupled with my suspicious behavior (asking people about the Power story) resulted in my grocer refusing my custom and ordering me from his store, a discussion at the local American Legion Post as to whether or not I was a Communist agent, the hurling of invective at my children by older schoolmates, and the refusal by the editor of the local weekly newspaper to allow me to examine back issues of his paper.

Firm lines are drawn between the Mexican and Anglo worlds. Although Mexican athletes enjoy full participation on school teams and very often excel, dating between Mexicans and Anglos is still a matter for gossip and sensational comment, and Mexicans generally shun all school activities with the exception of athletic events.

The relationship between the Mormon church and the public schools in Safford is indicative of the entire situation. The constitution of the state of Arizona has always prohibited prayer in the schools, and yet every assembly at Safford High School is opened by a prayer from the industrial arts teacher, who is also a bishop in the Church of Jesus Christ of Latter-Day Saints. In addition, the Mormon seminary, a building in which children and young people are given religious instruction, is situated directly across the street from the high school, and students are issued class schedules by the high school on which "Seminary" is listed as a class on an equal footing with Algebra I or Spanish III. The seminarian, the person in charge of religious instruction, is paid by the church, but he sits in on all faculty meetings, votes on all matters concerning the faculty, and is generally accorded the perquisites of a faculty member.

The picture, then, is one of domination of the county by members of the Church of Jesus Christ of Latter-Day Saints, a domination so complete as to be unquestioned. The grumblings that one hears are nearly always directed to specific instances of injustice, and the overall situation is almost never attacked. Statements of hostility toward the Mormons are rarely heard along the Gila, but as one moves out into the Aravaipa or the Sulphur Springs Valley, they are more freely expressed.

Mormons in the county are confident and self-assured, as well they might be. They exhibit a very strong sense of group identity and take great pride in the accomplishments of their church and of individual members of the church. All of the popularly accepted millionaires of the region are members of this sect, and Mormons dominate all of the professions with the exception of medicine. With their well-attested missionary zeal the Mormons sincerely welcome converts, and many local residents eagerly accept conversion as their ticket to upward mobility. In my experience, refusal of the offer of church membership is usually greeted by astonishment at the rejection of a golden opportunity, but with respect for the decision. Apostasy, on the other hand, is not tolerated, and individuals who have chosen to leave the church are dealt with harshly in local gossip and sometimes suffer harsh social and economic reprisals. Most members of the church exhibit a high degree of parochialism and find it difficult to believe that their church does not represent as potent a force in other areas of the country as it does in their home county.

The non-Mormon Anglos in the county seem to be defined, even by themselves, by that lack of membership. Generally speaking, very little hostility is openly expressed, although there are frequent expressions of resentment at the way the Mormons "stick together," especially in the financial area, and frequent references to the failure of members of the Mormon church to live up to their own anti-tobacco, anti-stimulant regulations. These non-Mormon Anglo residents of the county seem to accept Mormon domination of most of the political and economic institutions of their region as right and proper.

The Mexicans of Graham County constitute an atypical Mexican-American society. With the exception of the adolescent males there is no expression of race pride, no awareness of the concept of *La Raza*. Even among the young most utterances are directed toward deficiencies of the Anglo world view rather than any affirmation of the correctness of the Mexican one. Their attitude is almost exclusively a defensive one. This is the only Mexican-American group in my experience in which anti-clerical stories are not popular, and I believe this situation stems from a basic doubt about the worth of Mexican-Catholic institutions. Mexicans hold only the most menial and the most undesirable jobs, and there are very few "successes" among this portion of the population. Lupe Salazar, the son of the pioneer settler of the Aravaipa Valley, is revered and to some extent idolized by the Mexican population simply because he meets and deals with Anglos as an equal. He seems to function as the living denial of the doctrine of Anglo superiority which is hammered home by their daily experience. Mexicans make the distinction between Mormons and other Anglos, but it is not a firm one, and the terms are sometimes used interchangeably.

All the evidence would indicate that the situation of the last decade has at least the same shape as the situation in the second decade of this century. One should remember that in 1918 Mormons were just beginning to exercise economic and political control of the area. In addition, the stigma of polygamy was still not completely expunged in the eyes of their Gentile neighbors, and the Mormon population was, therefore, more sensitive to criticism from outsiders and more defensive. It is significant that the only available documentary history of the area is essentially a Mormon history, affording no recognition to the contributions of non-Mormon Anglos and Mexicans, whose deeds survive only in the oral traditions of the region. The tensions produced by this minority domination of the county go a long way toward explaining a climate that could have produced the event with which we are concerned and could have made accounts of that event a matter of interest to members of the community for better than a half-century.

THE DOCUMENTARY RECORD

When working with an historical legend, one of the mandatory courses of action for the researcher is checking the documentary evidence. All of the studies that deal with the utilization of oral testimony in historical research stress comparison of the oral material with the documents available. Very little consideration is given to the possibility that the standard historical sources might contain substantial error or that such a documentary record might not exist at all. This latter condition is very nearly true in the case of John and Tom Power. There is no official record of their arrest and trial, nor even of the issuance of any warrant for their arrest. I have been told that an unsuccessful search for these records was conducted in 1921 by a writer from Willcox, Arizona, but I have no proof of the truth of that statement. These records are missing now, however, and Ryder Ridgeway, a distinguished local historian of the area, has searched assiduously for some trace of them for the last thirty years with no result except the discovery of one loose page headed "Power Trial" and covered with what appears to be someone's personal system of shorthand. I have retraced the more obvious of Mr. Ridgeway's efforts with the same discouraging lack of affirmative results, though I must point in my own case to a decided lack of cooperation on the part of officials in charge of such records. Judge G.W. Shute published an article in 1960 which he claims is based on records in the Graham County Courthouse; but since his work seems to be an effort to forestall the parole of the Power brothers, and since it consists almost entirely of accounts of the mental processes of men long dead and of conversations among them without a shred of documentation, it is safe to conclude that his claim of access to the records is a false one.[149] The only other article touching on the case is a rather tedious account of

---

[149] "Tragedy of the Grahams," *Arizona Cattlelog*, April 1960, pp. 32-37.

the experiences of an army trooper in the field while the hunt for the fugitives was on, and it comes no closer to the facts of the case than his detachment did to the men they were hunting.[150] One embarrassingly poor book on the subject exists, but it seems to be largely a product of the author's fancy, lacking documentation of any sort, filled with readily demonstrable factual errors, and written in the style of Ranch Romances.[151] The only extant contemporary account is to be found in the newspapers of the day.

The first that the Power family drew public attention was December 14, 1917. On that date the *Graham Guardian* ran a story reporting an inquest into the death of Ola May Power, aged 22 years. The girl had died suddenly at the home of her father in the Rattlesnake Mountains on December 6. Her body had been taken to the Haby ranch, where a coroner's inquest was conducted. The principal witness was the girl's father, who testified that she had been treated for throat trouble for some time, and that he had discovered her in convulsions. He tried to help her and sent the hired man for assistance, but the girl died a short time later. It was reported that after hearing all the evidence in the case, the coroner's jury brought in a verdict that Ola's death was due to some unknown cause.[152]

The language of this item is restrained and free of any hint that the Power family is anything but a respected part of the community. The facts are reported in a straightforward and dispassionate manner, and there is no indication of any dissatisfaction with the findings of the coroner's jury. The next treatment of the Power family at the hands of the press would be quite different.

The first newspaper account of the shooting which forms the core of the legend appeared in the *Arizona Daily Star* on the morning of February 12, 1918:

Headline: M'BRIDE SLAYERS SURROUNDED AT REDDINGTON; THREE POSSES CLOSING IN FOR GUN BATTLE

---

[150] McKinley Cash, "On the Track of the Power Boys," *Journal of Arizona History*, VIII (Winter, 1967), pp. 248-255.

[151] Elizabeth Lambert Wood, *The Tragedy of the Powers Mine* (Portland, Oregon: Binfords and Mort, 1957).

[152] *Graham Guardian* (Safford, Arizona), December 14, 1917, p. 1.

Subhead: Authorities of Eight Arizona Counties Lead Small Army of Officers and Cowmen After Murderers of Graham Sheriff and His Deputies; Slacker's Accomplice Ex-Convict Paroled by Governor Hunt; Outlaws Pass Reddington

Globe, Ariz., Feb. 11-- Jeff Powers, father of two of the fugitives, died this afternoon at 4 o'clock. He was shot by the officers when they attempted to take the two Powers boys at 7:30 o'clock Sunday morning.

Globe, Feb. 11-- Tom Powers, John Powers and Tom Sisson, slayers of Sheriff Frank McBride and Deputies Mart Kempton and Kain Wootan in a battle between officers and draft evaders in the Klondyke district of Graham county, are within reach of three combined posses early this morning. That a battle will be fought before the fugitives are stopped is the belief of federal and county officers. The men have been run down a mile from Reddington, 25 miles south of the scene of the murders.

Sheriff Miles and Police Chief Bailey returned about midnight, after nearly 24 hours on the trail, during which they aroused the settlers in the San Pedro valley and organized them as guards to all the passes north and west of Reddington. Shortly after they returned it was reported that the outlaws had been trailed to within three miles of Reddington at dark, indicating that the trio were driven back from the south and are headed west and north.

Sheriff Harry Wheeler at the time was reported to be heading toward Reddington with his Cochise county posse. All the country around Reddington is up in arms awaiting the approach of the outlaws.

Sheriffs' posses from eight counties and the entire military patrols of southeastern Arizona were closing in last night on the San Pedro valley, in the biggest man hunt in years, as the result of the cold-blooded killing of Sheriff R. F. McBride of Graham county, Under Sheriff M.R. Kempton and Deputy Sheriff Kane Wootan, early Sunday morning by John Powers, Jr., his brother, Tom Powers, and Tom Sessions, a notorious horse thief. The killing was the result of an attempt to arrest the Powers boys as slackers.

The posses are working under Sheriff Miles of Pima county, who, accompanied by Chief of Police Bailey and Cattle Inspector McKinney, know every foot of the ground of the San Pedro valley. A posse under Deputy Sheriff Tom Burts containing Deputy Sheriff Cummins, Jack Archer and Spears was sent out by Miles, Sunday night, but reached Reddington after the outlaws had passed through on their way south. They returned yesterday afternoon to await further orders, while Miles and his party continued down the San Pedro.

Up from Cochise, Sheriff Harry Wheeler is heading a posse. Sheriff Hall of Pima is on the trail with cowboys. Sheriff Earhart has ordered his men from Santa Cruz to close in, and Colonel Morgan, in command at Fort Huachuca, has ordered out a detachment of colored cavalry.

Story of Killing

According to the first authentic story of the killing to reach Tucson last night, McBride and his deputies were slain about 6:30 Sunday morning after a battle with the two young slackers and with Tom Sissons, a horse thief, at the home of the Powers boys, in Rattlesnake canyon, Galluro mountains.

Deputy United States Marshal Frank Haynes of Globe and Sheriff McBride and his deputies left Safford Saturday afternoon at 4 o'clock for the Galluro mountains, going by way of Klondyke to get the slackers. They reached the house, near the mine operated by John Powers, the father of the Powers boys, about daybreak Sunday morning and surrounded the house.

Slackers Open Fire

John Powers, the father, came out of the house with a gun and was ordered to throw up his hands. As he was about to do so, one of his sons opened the door and started firing at the officers. At the first volley in reply, John Powers, the father, dropped, shot through the right shoulder.

About 25 shots were fired by the officers before McBride was shot by Tom Powers and Kane Wootan was killed by John Powers, Jr. Deputy Mark Kempton rushed around the house when his comrades were killed and kicked in the door. He was killed by Tom Sissons.

Sissons is an ex-convict, convicted of stealing horses, and was paroled by Governor Hunt after he had been sentenced to five years in the penitentiary. Deputy United States Marshal Haynes escaped unhurt and returned to Klondyke for help. He arrived about 4 o'clock Sunday afternoon with the first news. A posse left immediately to bring in the bodies and pick up the trail, while the alarm was sent to the sheriffs of surrounding counties.

Allen and his partner, a man named Murdock, obeyed the order and found the father and took him into the mine tunnel and placed him on a cot.

Additional posses were dispatched from Safford, Thatcher, Fairview and Fort Thomas, Sunday night, all heavily armed. The bodies of the dead officers arrived at Safford last night.

Enter Arizona Wilds

A report from Reddington in the San Pedro valley, stated that the killers had passed through there Sunday night and gone on.

The district they have entered is one of the wildest of Arizona, without wire or telephone communication.

150 Cowmen Take Trail

Globe, Feb. 11-- From a rancher living in the Graham mountain foothills, word reached Globe early tonight that a posse of 150 cowmen and deputies from eight Arizona counties had surrounded Tom Sisson, paroled convict, and John and Tom Powers, brothers, who shot and killed Sheriff

R.F. McBride and Deputies Martin Kempton and Kane Wootan of Graham county, Sunday, when these three officers with Deputy United States Marshal Frank Haynes went to arrest them on suspicion of being draft evaders. The three fugitives who had barricaded their cabin in the foothills escaped when Haynes left the scene of the murderers [sic] to get help. They stripped the dead officers of their guns and made their getaway on the officers' horses. They appeared next at a small mountain town, Mammoth, and got grub. It was this information that led on the new posse.[153]

Thus are sketched the general outlines of the event as it is preserved in the only documentary record available to us. The writer exhibited no reluctance in the use of pejorative terms like "slayers," "slackers," and "ex-convict," but his account contains factual errors, especially in the area of proper names. The ubiquitous and gratuitous "s" added to the Power surname, the three alternate spellings of the name Sisson, the misspelling of Deputy Wootan's Christian name, and the erroneous identification of the senior Power as John, all speak to the point that proper names survive little better in newsprint than they do in oral transmission.

The edition of the *Tucson Citizen* which appeared on the afternoon of the same day blazoned a banner headline on the front page: "SLACKERS KILL SHERIFF AND TWO AIDES." The story under this headline follows the general shape of that in the morning paper with a few differences and additions. The incident is designated "the first armed resistance in Arizona to the military draft." Tom Sisson is awarded the appellation "ex-soldier" to go along with "ex-convict" and "horse thief." Sisson and Marshal Haynes are both reported wounded, Sisson seriously. The time of the incident is again established as 7:30 a.m. on the morning of February 10, after having been changed to 6:30 a.m. in the latter half of the initial Star story.[154] The Powers are described as being "engaged in the cattle business." Physical descriptions of the fugitives are offered and their mounts are described as a brown horse, a sorrel horse, and a sorrel mule.

---

[153] *Arizona Daily Star* (Tucson, Arizona), February 12, 1918, pp. 1-2.
[154] Ibid., p. 2.

The story goes on to report that the Powers had sent word to the authorities that if they wanted them, to come and get them. There is also the interesting inclusion of excerpts from a letter to the *Citizen* from a Dr. H.A. Schell, a Tucson oculist, who happened to be in Safford at that time. Dr. Schell reports that the murderers had made threats to kill any officers attempting to arrest them and that the officers were killed without warning while advancing toward the cabin.[155]

Throughout these early accounts and continuing into the present day in popular usage, the last name of two of the principals is consistently misspelled. The "s" added to the name led to considerable confusion. In this edition of the *Citizen* it is first stated and then denied that John and Tom Power are the brothers of a railroad detective, famed in the Southwest, "Maricopa Slim" Powers.

Also included in this story is a paragraph which purports to be a first-hand account of the shooting by Marshal Haynes, in which he claims that he planned to arrest the younger Power on the draft evasion charge and that the Graham County officers volunteered to accompany him in order to investigate the death of Ola Power. He further asserts that the Powers opened fire on the officers as soon as they saw them. This story closes with a report that the elder of the Power brothers was dangerously wounded in the right eye.[156]

The *Arizona Daily Star* of February 13, 1918, continued to exhibit considerable excitement in a front page story in which it was reported that $4,000 in rewards had been offered for the capture of the fugitives, dead or alive. The writer expresses considerable enthusiasm for the numbers of volunteers in the hunt and for their quality, describing them as "Southern Arizona's Best Shots," but this enthusiasm is not enough to dispel the suspicion that the hunted men may have slipped through the lines of the posses. Law enforcement contingents from Graham, Pima, Gila, and Cochise counties are reported in the field, and the fugitives are believed headed for a ranch near San Simon that the Powers had once owned. Reports from the field were quoted to the effect that the men would not be taken alive, and that they were guilty of that grievous cattle country sin, traveling by wire-cutter.[157]

---

[155] *Tucson Citizen*, February 12, 1918, p. 3.
[156] Ibid., p. 3.
[157] *Arizona Daily Star* (Tucson, Arizona), February 13, 1918, p. 1.

The afternoon *Tucson Citizen* was still excited enough to run a front page headline: "OUTLAWS HEADED FOR TUCSON."[158] Under this headline runs a story that plays down the report that the fugitives' tracks had been picked up near San Simon in favor of one that locates their trail near Reddington, seventy miles nearer Tucson, and that supposes they will cross either the Rincon or Catalina Mountains and head into Mexico. Some details are given concerning the supposed condition of the fugitives' mounts, and it is conjectured that they will soon attempt to steal fresh horses. The story includes another first-hand account of the fight, which is quite similar to that included in the edition of the previous day, and closes with a vain attempt to straighten out the surname confusion:

> The Citizen is in receipt of a letter from Ben T. Power of Winkelman, Ariz., a brother of "Maricopa Slim" Power, stating that John and Tom Powers are not members of the family. The name is spelled differently, the outlaws having an "s."[159]

The February 14, 1918, edition of the *Arizona Daily Star* reported that the fugitives had been cornered in Cochise Stronghold and then went on to report the discovery of two of the fugitives' horses very near the scene of the killings. This discovery prompted speculation about their return to the scene of the crime. One very interesting paragraph in this story recounts an interview with Wylie Morgan, an uncle of the Power boys, in which he claims that Tom Sisson was a pro-German who had influenced his nephews to the point that they had come to resist the draft. Morgan was quoted as saying that he had warned Sheriff McBride that the Power boys would kill him if he tried to arrest them and that the boys had sent word to him to keep his mouth shut or he would be killed.[160]

The afternoon *Tucson Citizen* reported the "Powers Gang" in the foothills of the Rincons, and it is stated that the tip that they had been trailed near San Simon had been checked out and proved groundless.[161]

February 15, 1918, dawned on a story on the progress of the chase

---

[158] *Tucson Citizen*, February 13, 1918, p. 1.
[159] Ibid., p. 8.
[160] *Arizona Daily Star* (Tucson, Arizona), February 14, 1918, pp. 1-2.
[161] *Tucson Citizen*, February 14, 1918, p. 1.

on page one of the *Arizona Daily Star*. The posse was located in the Chiricahuas, twelve hours behind the fugitives, who were believed to be headed toward Bowie in an effort to cross the San Simon and enter New Mexico. Full confidence was expressed in the ability of the posses to thwart this attempt. The Power trio was reported to be in bad shape, having succeeded in obtaining food only once, and they were said to be camping in rough canyons during the day, moving only at night. Their pursuers were said to number over 200 civilians, two troops of the First Cavalry, and a detachment of Mexican troops assigned to turn back the fugitives at the border. An addition by the federal government of $800 in reward money was reported, and concern was expressed for the safety of some of the volunteers drawn by the prospect of the rewards.[162]

The *Tucson Citizen* for February 15, 1918, had nothing in the way of new information but again ran a page one banner headline: "U.S. TROOPS AFTER OUTLAWS." However, this edition did include a stirring editorial, entitled "An Arizona Melodrama," that points to the Power-Sisson incident as the exception that proves the success of the draft system. The fugitives are said to have been outlaws in spirit and "half-way outlaws in fact" before the enactment of the military draft law. It is claimed that Jeff Power had been extremely litigious and extremely unsuccessful in this litigation[163] and had thus been soured toward the possibility of justice for the poor. This bitterness caused him to plot a rebellion in case the law should ever come after him or any of his sons.

The editorial writer then treats the death of Ola Power, who he says was "forced to live with these hard men in a remote mountain camp" and "to grow up illiterate and terrorized in disregard of the customs of civilization." It was the mysterious circumstances of her death that prompted Sheriff McBride to accompany Marshal Haynes on his trip to the Power camp. There is a curious passage in which it is made clear that the Powers were not nobly defiant of the law like moonshiners, but were simply intolerant of any interference in their affairs.

The conduct of the dead lawmen is defended and extolled, the value of the aeroplane in such a man hunt is discussed, and the failure

---

[162] *Arizona Daily Star* (Tucson, Arizona), February 15, 1918, pp. 1-2

[163] I could find no record of any civil suits involving Jeff Power in the Graham County Courthouse.

of the posses to locate their quarry is blamed on a lack of centralized direction.

The editorial concludes with a quaint paragraph that contrasts the murder rate in Arizona with that of New York, where a "murder story is served with breakfast every morning."[164]

The *Graham Guardian*, a weekly published in Safford, appeared for the first time since the killings on February 15, 1918. Nearly the whole issue was devoted to the case with the principal story dominating the front page. This story generally recounts the facts as they were presented in the Tucson papers, but it includes an extensive statement by Marshal Haynes in which he gives a most improbable account of events at the Power camp, claiming that after the shooting stopped, he went up to the cabin and looked in the window. He is quoted to the effect that he saw and heard nothing, so without looking inside the shack, he got his horse and rode up the trail some distance, then stopped and observed the scene. He continued this observation until 10:30 a.m. without seeing any movement and then departed for Klondyke.[165]

It is interesting that this ridiculous story is not challenged here or at any other point in the documentary record. Marshal Haynes's account of events is ludicrous when measured against the testimony of others. The Murdocks and Henry Allen arrived on the scene long before 10:30 a.m., and the Powers claim that they left the cabin to aid their wounded father as soon as shots stopped pouring into the cabin. The likelihood that a man would behave as Marshal Haynes claims that he did is slim indeed. The facts argue that his behavior did not measure up to cultural expectations for a lawman, that he panicked and ran, and that he distorted his account to make his role seem less ignominious.

This issue of the Guardian also includes a front page account of the hunt for the fugitives, which is a rehash of material that had already appeared in the Tucson newspapers except for the allegation that the Power brothers and Tom Sisson were making their way to Mexico "over an old trail they traveled when they went into Mexico to evade the selective draft last summer."[166] There is a front page account of a mass meeting called by Mayor Jacobson of Safford for the purpose of

---

[164] *Tucson Citizen*, February 15, 1918, pp. 1 and 3.
[165] *Graham Guardian* (Safford, Arizona) February 15, 1918, pp. 1-2.
[166] Ibid., p. 1.

planning the joint funeral of the slain officers. The meeting decided that all places of business should be closed from 9:30 a.m. until 5:00 p.m. on Wednesday, February 13, the day of the funeral. At this same meeting, resolutions were passed attesting to the bravery of the officers, Graham County's debt to them, and the sympathy that the residents of the county extended to the bereaved families.[167]

The same issue also includes a front page story on the rewards offered by the Governor and by the Graham County Board of Supervisors,[168] and an editorial which extols the dead lawmen, calls for the protection and guidance of God for their families, and characterizes the fugitives as "cowardly slackers, who refused to do their duty as American citizens."[169]

The February 16, 1918, edition of the *Arizona Daily Star* reported the fugitives afoot and surrounded, with capture imminent, and then resupplied them with mounts, "one bay and one sorrel horse, and a brown mare."[170] This story also reported a reward of an additional $1500 posted by the cattlemen of Graham and Cochise Counties.

The *Tucson Citizen* for the same date eschews a full front page banner headline for the first time since February 12, 1918, and contents itself with: "Battle Between Outlaws and Posses Near." The story under this headline is a rehash of what had appeared in the morning *Star*, with the exception of a report, unconfirmed and doubted, that the bandits had been captured by a lone cowboy.[171]

The Sunday, February 17, 1918, issue of the *Arizona Daily Star* had no hard news to report on the case. In its pages there appeared a summary of developments to that point, a prediction of imminent capture, and a partial explanation of the fugitives' elusiveness through their possession of "what was considered the finest pair of field glasses in the Southwest, taken from the body of Kane Wootan, the slain deputy."[172] Through these glasses and a pair taken from McBride, the fugitives are said to watch the posses from secure positions during the

---

[167] Ibid., p. 1.
[168] Ibid., p. 1.
[169] Ibid., p. 4.
[170] *Arizona Daily Star* (Tucson, Arizona), February 16, 1918, pp. 1-2.
[171] *Tucson Citizen*, February 16, 1918, pp. 1 and 3.
[172] *Arizona Daily Star* (Tucson, Arizona), February 17, 1918, p. 1.

day and to move only at night.[173]

On page four of this Sunday edition appears an editorial under a cut of an American flag. The editorial is entitled "The Outlaws." It deplores the fact that Arizona has no capital punishment law and seems to advocate the death penalty for horse theft. The parole of Tom Sisson is held responsible for the deaths of Sheriff McBride and his deputies. The Power brothers are characterized as the dupes of Tom Sisson, a dedicated pro-German. Some sympathy is expressed for the brothers in that they are depicted as ignorant, independent mountain men, incapable of appreciating their debt to their country. The editorial closes with a thinly-veiled call for lynching: ". . . the score would be evened in accordance with justice did the outlaws never come out of their hiding place alive."[174]

Neither Tucson paper had anything of consequence to report on February 18, 1918. They still looked for an early capture, but the *Citizen* was reduced to discussing the personality of one of the bloodhounds being employed in the hunt and the probability that the dogs would be shot by the fugitives if the animals were successful in their chase.[175]

On the 19th of February, the *Star* reported in a headline that Apache trailers were now being used, but for the first time the fear was voiced that the hunted men might have slipped through the cordon set for them. It was reported that the men had discarded their cowboy boots and were now wearing hobnail shoes which they had been carrying with them. This story also stated that the hunted men had acquired a fresh set of horses and that the area of the hunt was experiencing "the worst storm in the history of southeastern Arizona."[176]

The headline of the *Tucson Citizen* for the same date flatly declared that the bandits had slipped through the lines maintained by their pursuers.[177] The story goes on to report that the fugitives have escaped for the moment, but that the possemen came so close that they found freshly cooked, uneaten food.[178]

---

[173] Ibid., p. 2.
[174] Ibid., p. 4.
[175] *Tucson Citizen*, February 18, 1918, p. 3.
[176] *Arizona Daily Star* (Tucson, Arizona), February 19, 1918, p. 1.
[177] *Tucson Citizen*, February 19, 1918, p. 1.
[178] Ibid., p. 1.

On the morning of February 20, 1918, the *Star* reported that the outlaws had again been trapped, this time in Cave Creek Valley. The story is off the front page for the first time, and the writer really has very few new facts with which to work. He does provide some filler of interest to the folklorist, however:

> The Powers boys have a reputation for shooting that is second to none in that region. It is said that the eldest, John Powers, riding a horse at full speed in a revolver match, planted six bullets in a small tin can from an automatic.[179]

The afternoon *Citizen* for this same date contains a much more interesting story. The account begins tamely enough by focusing on the recent snowstorm, the hardships that it necessarily works on hunter and hunted alike, and the fact that the new-fallen snow is bound to make tracking the fugitives an easier task. To offset this advantage to the hunters, however, the *Citizen* cites the guile of the hunted in tying gunny sacks over their shoes.[180] It is reported that there are now 800 soldiers and 1,000 civilians engaged in the pursuit and that these numbers make this man hunt the largest in Arizona history. In this account there also appears for the first time an overt expression of dissatisfaction with the way in which the hunt has been conducted:

> The officers believe the law still has a chance to get the quarry but freely express the opinion that the chase has been bungled and that Wheeler has deterred the northern deputies from entering the mountains. All officers are wearing white rag bands on their hats to prevent mistaking them for outlaws.[181]

The penultimate paragraph of this story is also of considerable interest, for here, ten days after the shootings, appears the first scrap of information that even suggests that events might not have transpired in exactly the fashion which had been thus far reported:

---

[179] *Arizona Daily Star* (Tucson, Arizona), February 20, 1918, p. 2.
[180] *Tucson Citizen*, February 20, 1918, p. 1.
[181] Ibid., p. 1.

Al Kuntz prospector and trapper from Klondyke who packed out the bodies of the slain officers, says old man Powers told the murderer's nearest neighbors while dying that Kane Wootan shot him, while he had his hands up. Haynes' story is that Powers lowered his arms and Wootan, thinking he reached for his gun, fired. The story that Powers came out with a gun told by Haynes, was denied by Powers on his death bed.[182]

On February 21, 1918, the *Star* reported that the hunt had been abandoned by most of the pursuers and that only three Apache Indian trailers from San Carlos remained in the field.[183] The *Citizen* for this same date was also discouraged at the prospects for capture of the trio and devoted considerable space to descriptions of the area of the hunt and to the effect of the snowstorm on the pursuit. The story also included a paragraph on Tom Sisson in which he is again characterized as the leader of the group and in which he is credited with a thorough knowledge of the terrain over which the chase is unfolding.[184]

The February 22, 1918, edition of the *Citizen* again reflected an air of hopelessness. The story quoted Sheriff Wheeler to the effect that if the fugitives have gone over into Mexico, he will go after them. The sheriff also commented on the difficulties of the hunt and went on to hint at some sort of conspiracy to supply them with food.[185] He is also reported to have marveled at the ability of the fleeing men to move without leaving a trace: "... the outlaws had the American Indian beaten when it comes to covering his tracks."[186]

The second edition of the *Graham Guardian* to appear since the killings bore the date of February 22, 1918, and carried only one brief story on the chase, reporting its lack of success and lamenting the failure of the pursuers to follow the initial trails eagerly enough.[187]

On February 23, 1918, the *Citizen* published a short item stating that Sheriff Wheeler was looking for a new trail. This piece also commented on the physical condition of the fugitives, noting that each of the

---

[182] Ibid., p. 3.
[183] *Arizona Daily Star* (Tucson, Arizona) February 21, 1918, p. 3.
[184] *Tucson Citizen*, February 21, 1918, pp. 1-2.
[185] *Tucson Citizen*, February 22, 1918, p. 3.
[186] Ibid., p. 3.
[187] *Graham Guardian* (Safford, Arizona), February 22, 1918, p. 1.

Power boys had been wounded, and echoed the theory that they had been supplied with food and that friends of theirs in the mountains had assisted them in throwing the posses off their trail.[188]

The Sunday edition of the *Arizona Daily Star* for February 24, 1918, contained two short items pertaining to the Power case: a front page story declaring that the Apache trailers had picked up fresh tracks[189] and a piece dealing in part with another member of the Power family. This story reports that Charles Powers had come to the scene of the murders and had begun working the mine there. He had been in El Paso at the time of the shootings, but had disappeared from there, and it was believed for a time that he had gone to join his brothers and Tom Sisson in their hiding place.[190]

For the next few days the papers were barren of items relating to the case except for brief summaries of old news, but on February 28, 1918, the *Arizona Daily Star* reported that one John Kelley, an army deserter said to have given assistance to the Power brothers and Tom Sisson, had been apprehended by possemen and had then escaped from the guard house at Camp Harry Jones, fleeing into Mexico[191].

On March 1, 1918, the weekly *Graham Guardian* ran a front page story that reiterated the conspiracy theory. This account insists that the fugitives would have long since been captured if they had not been continually assisted by friends in the mountains who were strongly opposed to the draft law.[192]

The story virtually disappears from the newspapers at that point in time, and it does not reappear until March 9, 1918, when the capture of the trio by cavalrymen near Hachita, New Mexico is recounted. The capture took place without a fight eight miles south of the international boundary. A report is included of the excitement engendered in Safford by news of the capture and the fear of lynching expressed by the Graham County Sheriff's office.[193]

The *Tucson Citizen* published a more detailed account of the capture in its afternoon edition of March 9, 1918, in which the poor physical

---

[188] *Tucson Citizen*, February 23, 1918, p. 3.

[189] *Arizona Daily Star* (Tucson, Arizona), February 24, 1918, p. 1.

[190] Ibid., p. 3.

[191] *Arizona Daily Star* (Tucson, Arizona), February 28, 1918, p. 3.

[192] *Graham Guardian* (Safford, Arizona), March 1, 1918, p. 1.

[193] *Arizona Daily Star* (Tucson, Arizona), March 9, 1918, pp. 1-2.

condition of the fugitives is stressed. Lieutenant Hays, the arresting officer, is quoted to the effect that the younger of the Powers wanted to resist, but was dissuaded by his older brother and Tom Sisson. The cavalry officer was told by the men that they would never have surrendered to civil authorities.[194]

The Sunday *Star* reported that the prisoners had been moved to the Safford jail. They were said to be footsore and weary, and Tom Power was said to be suffering from a wound in the left eye, so severe that it might necessitate the removal of the eye. The story went on to describe the secret movement of the prisoners from New Mexico to the Safford jail. The prisoners are said to have expressed indifference to their fate and to regret only the killing of Martin Kempton.[195]

This same Sunday edition of the *Star* also carried an editorial entitled "Close the Gate," in which the writer laments the jurisdiction over the case of the state of Arizona. If only the case could be tried in a federal court, the death penalty could be invoked. Since Arizona law does not provide for capital punishment, the editorial suggests that the accused men might never be tried:

> Whether the three outlaws will ever be tried no one can say. It may be that once more citizens will take the case in their hands and make the punishment fit the crime. According to advices from Safford, the peaceable, law-abiding citizens of that section, where the victims of the slayers were known and where their helpless dependents live, there is a determination that justice shall be done.[196]

The editorial goes on to characterize the Powers and Tom Sisson as anarchists who have repudiated the law and are therefore undeserving of its protection. The commentary closes with a call for the restoration of capital punishment.[197]

On March 13, 1918, the *Tucson Citizen* reported that the outlaws had actually been captured by Frank Shriver, sheriff of Grant County, New Mexico, with only minor assistance from the United States cavalry, and

---

[194] *Tucson Citizen*, March 9, 1918, p. 1.
[195] *Arizona Daily Star* (Tucson, Arizona), March 10, 1918, p. 2.
[196] Ibid., p. 4.
[197] Ibid., p. 4.

that Sheriff Shriver would receive the rewards for their capture.[198] But the *Graham Guardian* of March 15, 1918, heatedly denies the accuracy of this report and reaffirms that the cavalry was responsible for the capture and states that Sheriff Shriver was nowhere in sight at the time the men were taken.

The *Guardian* also reported that James Fielder, a lawyer of Deming, New Mexico, was retained by John and Tom Power and Tom Sisson and that Mr. Fielder waived a hearing before the Superior Court.[199]

Four days later the *Arizona Daily Star* reported that the Power brothers and Tom Sisson had been granted a change of venue to the adjacent county of Greenlee due to the impossibility of their obtaining an impartial trial in Graham County.[200]

Nothing of consequence concerning the case appeared in any of the newspapers until May 17, 1918, when the *Graham Guardian* published the first report of the trial. According to this account the trial began on Monday, May 13, 1918. A jury was secured on the first day. The prosecution began its presentation of evidence on Tuesday morning, resting its case at 2:00 p.m. that afternoon. The defense presented its case on Wednesday, resting at 2:00 p.m. on that day. The case went to the jury at 2:55 p.m. on Thursday, and that panel returned at 3:20 p.m. with a verdict of guilty of murder in the first degree for all three defendants.[201]

On May 20, 1918, the three men were sentenced to life imprisonment and were transported to the state prison at Florence, Arizona, to begin serving their sentences.[202]

The next time that any of the three imprisoned men attracted the attention of the newspapers was in December, 1923, four and one-half years after they had arrived at Florence. On December 18 it was reported that Tom Power, together with another convicted murderer, Willis Woods, had escaped the state prison at Florence on December 17, and that posses were being formed to apprehend them.[203]

The escaped pair made their way to San Diego, California, where

---

[198] *Tucson Citizen*, March 13, 1918, p. 2.
[199] *Graham Guardian* (Safford, Arizona), March 15, 1918, p. 4.
[200] *Arizona Daily Star* (Tucson, Arizona), March 19, 1918, p. 2.
[201] *Graham Guardian* (Safford, Arizona), March 17, 1918, p. 1.
[202] Ibid., May 24, 1918, p. 1.
[203] *Arizona Republican* (Phoenix, Arizona), December 18, 1923, p. 6.

they were captured on January 12, 1924.[204]

The Power brothers again came to public notice in December of 1939, when they escaped from prison with another convicted murderer, William Faltin. No organized search was mounted for the men, for it was believed that they had had help from confederates outside the prison and that they had been picked up in an automobile. The warden of the Arizona State Prison was quoted as believing that the men had escaped because their sentences were not commuted.[205]

The Power brothers remained at liberty until April 15, 1940, when they were recaptured at Eagle Pass, Texas. They had been held in a Mexican military barracks on charges of illegally taking firearms into Mexico.[206]

Some few glimpses into the lives of these men while they were in prison did find their way into the record. Daniel G. Moore wrote a book of reminiscences about his career in the Arizona penal system, and the Power brothers and Tom Sisson appear there in a generally favorable light. Mr. Moore speaks of the trusty status of all three men and the fact that at one time or another each of them was responsible for the care of the dogs used in trailing escapees. He reports that Tom Sisson was permitted free access to his pet rifle for use in hunting wild burros for food for the hounds.[207] This penal officer turned author goes on to recount what he believes to have been the reason for the brothers' December, 1939, escape:

> Another meeting of the parole board was to be held soon at the prison. The brothers, John and Tom Power, after serving twenty years of their sentence, felt that they deserved a hearing. As trusties, they had been exemplary prisoners during all those years. The warden and the majority of the guards agreed that they deserved the hearing, and we circulated and signed a petition for them. The warden mailed it with a personal letter to the Reverend Walter Hoffmann, chairman of the parole

---

[204] Ibid., January 16, 1924, pp. 1-2.
[205] Ibid., December 29, 1939, pp. 1 and 7.
[206] *Arizona Republican* (Phoenix, Arizona), April 17, 1940, p. 1.
[207] *Enter Without Knocking* (Tucson: University of Arizona Press, 1969), pp. 54-55.

board, in Phoenix, but on the day the board met the list of the prisoners to appear before it did not contain the name of either brother. Notified of the request for a hearing, the interested citizens of Safford, still bitter over the massacre of their lawmen almost a generation ago, had immediately demanded that the brothers should never appear before a parole board for the rest of their natural lives.

During their time at Florence, John and Tom had seen scores of lifers released on parole; and with all the good time they had earned, plus their two for one as trusties, they had amassed almost thirty-five years by that time. It was not surprising that they were thoroughly discouraged by the board's refusal to review their cases.[208]

There is a long gap in the record, and it was not until April 28, 1960, that the name Power made the news again when the brothers were released from prison. In a by-lined story in the *Arizona Daily Star*, Bob Thomas reported the parole of John and Tom Power after forty-two years in prison. The tone of this item is significantly different from anything that had previously appeared in print concerning the brothers. There is a very real attempt here to present the paroled prisoners as human beings. They are quoted at length throughout the story, and for the first time their version of the shootings which cost them so many years appears in a newspaper. Thomas also includes a brief account of the parole hearing.[209]

Again there is a long hiatus in the public record of the Power brothers until nine years later on January 26, 1969, when a story appeared announcing that a pardon for John and Tom Power had been signed on the previous day by Governor Williams. Here again the story is told from the point of view of the Power brothers, this time in what appear to be direct quotes from them. The item speaks to the problems of prejudicial publicity and the threat of lynching, neither of which had ever been aired in the press before. John and Tom Power are also quoted here for the first time to the effect that Tom Sisson had taken

---

[208] Ibid., pp. 98-99.
[209] *Arizona Daily Star* (Tucson, Arizona), April 28, 1960, Section B, p. 1.

no part in the gunfight. There is a detailed account of the Powers' final parole hearing.[210]

What will probably stand as the penultimate entry in the public record of the lives of John and Tom Power appeared in 1970, when the death of Tom Power was reported. The youngest of the Power brothers, age 77 years, died on his brother John's seventy-ninth birthday at 1:15 a.m., Friday, September 11, 1970, in a cabin at the Joe Bull ranch, twenty miles west of Bonita. Tom was buried the next day in the Klondyke cemetery near the graves of his sister, Ola, and his grandmother. The account of his funeral is worth examining.

The composition of the party in attendance at Tom Power's funeral is interesting in that it contained representatives of all three of the groups in the county: Mormons, non-Mormon Anglos, and Mexicans. The presence of Mormons from the Gila Valley can, no doubt, be attributed to the forceful personality and considerable influence of Zola Claridge, who worked so hard for the ultimate justification of the Power brothers. The casket bearers may be the most illuminating group: two Mexicans and two non-Mormon Anglos from Klondyke, a Mormon from Klondyke, and a non-Mormon Anglo connected to the Powers through their prison experience.[211] I think it significant that no Mormon from the Gila Valley is included in this group.

And so the documentary record ends, at least temporarily. The full texts of most of these documentary reports are included in Appendix I of this work. Since they constitute the sole extant record of these events and since it is important that the reader get some sense of the "facts" as mirrored in the popular press together with the tone of those reports, I recommend a full reading of those texts. It is only with an appreciation of the tenor of this writing that the enormity of the achievement of oral tradition in overcoming this documentary record and in reversing the judicial decision based on it can be assessed. Reading through the most significant of these accounts provides not only this sought-after appreciation, but also a window on the creative world of frontier orthography, syntax and punctuation. This exercise is also illuminating for the student of legend, for in the coverage of this case some of the principles of distortion that have been put forward

---

[210] *Arizona Republic* (Phoenix, Arizona), January 26, 1969, Section C, pp. 1-2.
[211] *Eastern Arizona Courier* (Safford, Arizona), September 16, 1970, pp. 1 and 11.

for oral testimonies can be seen in these written ones. Categorization explains the quick resort to labels, the reduction of complex human beings to verbal tags like "slackers," "outlaws," "pro-German," "ex-convict," and "horse thief." Assimilation to prior input can be seen at work in the attribution of supranormal shooting and trail-covering abilities to the fugitives. The principles of condensation, closure, symmetry, distortion from associated cues, and conformity all have a hand in shaping the journalistic version of these events. Certainly, a reading of these newspaper excerpts forces a new esteem for the principle of levelling, articulated by Gordon Allport and Leo Postman, and holding that content loss in transmission is not random and that proper names are most affected.[212]

The unanimously negative press of the early years, explained presumably by the social context of hysterical wartime patriotism, is remarkable, and it may be that without it there would have been no need to circulate stories about the event, and the legend would not have evolved. Shibutani speaks of rumor as a product of ambiguity,[213] but here we have a situation in which there is no ambiguity whatsoever in the documents at our disposal, and all of the inputs that have provided that ambiguity, that have transformed the journalistic monsters of 1918 into the journalistic kindly old men of 1970, must have been oral ones. We are, therefore, presented with a situation in which the lines are firmly drawn. We have seen the written record, and it only remains for us to examine the body of oral tradition that proved so formidable a foe to this record.

[212] *The Psychology of Rumor* (New York: Henry Holt and Company, 1947), pp. 75-84.
[213] Tamotsu Shibutani, *Improvised News: A Sociological Study of Rumor* (Indianapolis and New York: The Bobbs-Merrill Company, Inc., 1966).

THE POWER LEGEND

When I first began to encounter stories about the Power boys and then came to realize that mention of them triggered some sort of reaction almost universally among the residents of Graham County, I decided, intuitively I must confess, on a course of action regarding the collection of these stories. The stories would be solicited only by the recitation of a formula question on my part: "Do you know the story of the Powers[214] boys?" The hope was that in this way the legend would be defined by the informants with a minimum of interference on the part of the fieldworker. It would be the tellers of the story who would decide what items belonged to the body of the legend and they would flesh out the shape that the total narrative would take. Richard M. Dorson has articulated the principle that formed the basis for this intuitive decision:

> The formula requires that the legend be told as if it were a straightforward, consecutive, smooth-flowing narration. And this of course is the style of writing that appeals to the reader. But it is false to the nature of oral folk legend. No one individual knows the whole legend for by definition it is a communal possession.[215]

This concept and the procedure based on it are sound. The formula question was put to very nearly 500 informants. In over seventy percent of the cases the result was a precipitous end to the interview or a too-hasty denial of knowledge of the story and a polite change of subject. This reaction is due, of course, to the controversy attached to

---

[214] Although their surname is and always has been "Power," in the area it is almost universally rendered "Powers."
[215] "Defining the American Folk Legend," in *American Folklore and the Historian* (Chicago: University of Chicago Press, 1971), p. 161.

the legend and to the very real tensions present in the county, tensions on which the legend focuses and to some degree exacerbates. The existence of these tensions also made it apparent rather quickly that collecting by tape recorder was not a practical technique, and that device was abandoned for the most part. Substituted for it was the admittedly imperfect course of jotting down key phrases and quickly retreating to reconstruct the text as completely and accurately as possible. Faulty and irresponsible as this procedure may seem, the alternative was the accurate taping of a half-dozen texts and the loss of the others. So the recorder was most often left in the car or turned off at the request of the informant when the interview moved to the Power story. The result was the accumulation of 116 texts in response to the above-stated question and one text from each of the Power boys. Many of the texts do not seem to me to belong to the legend proper, and yet the informants felt that they did and therefore they must. If an understanding of the nature of the local historical legend is to be realized, the parameters of this informant-defined legend must be explored.

The understanding of any field-collected item depends upon an understanding of the cultural biases and belief system of the informant. A number of these collected texts provide insights into this area, and they seem to divide themselves into three points of view: Mexican, pro-Mormon, and anti-Mormon.

The Mexican point of view reflects the following percepts:
1) Anglos are not rational beings (Mx6, Mx15, Mx19).[216]
2) Anglos are greedy (Mx6, Mx15, Mx19, Mx27).
3) Anglos denigrate Mexicans (Mx8).

The pro-Mormon point of view reflects these percepts:
1) Support for the Powers had its origin in envy of Mormon success (Mo4, Mo21, An18).
2) Mormons are too virtuous to be involved in crime (Mo6, Mo10, Mo14, Mo35).
3) Mormons have always been persecuted (Mo6).

---

[216] The parenthetical letter-number designations throughout this chapter are keyed to legend texts that are to be found in Appendix II.

The anti-Mormon point of view reflects the following percepts:
1) Mormons are contemptuous of non-Mormons (Mx2, Mx7).
2) Mormons are hypocritical (An10).
3) Mormons control the establishment (An10, An 11, An 19, Mx27, Mx32).

Here, apparently, are the overt expressions of the feelings of the members of one group about another group or of their beliefs about the feelings of another group toward them. In other words, what we are presented with here are manifest esoteric-exoteric expressions.[217] Yet in this appearance of candor lies a trap, for these are not really naked expressions of world view; these percepts may also contain distortions. For example, the modifications that Informants Mx6 and Mx27 incorporate in their testimonies concerning the greed of Anglos are examples of distortion to please the receiver, and these modifications would assuredly not be present if the fieldworker had not been an Anglo. Distortion of this kind is also important in assessing the nature of the informant's value system, and much more of it may lie hidden here. Only a long-term observation of individual subjects, coupled with the careful collection and analysis of their utterances, can lead to any sort of relevant conclusion as to the belief systems and cultural biases that underlie oral testimonies. Unless we are aware, however, of this very basic kind of distortion, we can never hope to evaluate those texts which it affects.

Richard M. Dorson has proposed that a great number of American folk legends might be divided into three large categories: 1) those connected with the land and communities, 2) those attached to legendary individuals, and 3) those purporting to relate experiences of a given individual, but which are in reality connected with many persons in different places.[218] Any attempt at classifying the complexus of American legendry must be applauded as a stroke at the Gordian knot, but this particular attempt may be an oversimplification. In the legend at hand can be found texts which fit all three of the above categories,

---

[217] See Hugh Jansen, "The Esoteric-Exoteric Factor in Folklore," *Fabula: Journal of Folktale Studies*, Vol. 2 (1959), pp. 205-211.
[218] "How Shall We Rewrite Charles M. Skinner Today?" in *American Folk Legend: A Symposium* (Berkeley, Los Angeles and London: University of California Press, 1971), p. 84.

and members of the groups which know and tell the story may supply any of the types as "the legend." Perhaps this complexity can best be seen in the area of character.

There are a great number of characters involved in the Power story, but only a limited number of them seem to have seized the folk imagination. Those few, however, have been fleshed out to a considerable degree, and some seem to have become the protagonists in small cycles of tales that are not at all related to the central events of the story. But they were evoked by the question: "Do you know the story of the Powers boys?", and thus fall within the legend as defined by the folk. The first of these characters to be considered is Charles Power, the older brother of John and Tom, who is not at all involved in the shooting or in any of the events leading up to it, but who, nevertheless, has a rather fat role in the legend.

Charlie was the oldest of the Power children, and the role for which he has been singled out seems clear and well-defined: he is the jester in the piece. Characterization in oral testimony is almost never subtle since it is effected through verbal stereotypes or labels (Principle 6, Assimilation to Prior Input) which do not lend themselves to fine distinctions, and depth of character comes to legendary figures only with the amassing of a great number of texts. In Charlie Power's case the labels: "silly old shit" (Mx28), "silly old fuck" (An33), "kinda touched" (Mo3), "ignorant" (Mo3, Mo33, Mx21), "no harm in him" (Mo3), "crazy" (Mo33, Mo41), and "didn't have the balls to kill a white man" (An33), paint a fairly consistent picture of a clown, belligerent and volatile, and for those reasons dangerous, but without malice. This is, of course, a stock character type, ubiquitous in local legend, and there are a great number of traveling motifs that can be centered on such a character. It is readily apparent that the legendary character, Charlie Powers, has already begun to attract such motifs. The texts offered by Informants Mo31, Mo33, An4, An13, An15, Mx4, and Mx21 all contain narrative elements that are traditional.

The development of such a comic figure and the focus upon him are significant, for they allow some portion of the legend to be recited without greatly aggravating tensions, and the absurdity of such a figure distracts from these tensions. The ludicrous figure of Charlie is also useful to tellers of versions of the legend hostile to the Powers in that the actions of his brothers seem even more monstrous when contrasted with his harmlessness and in that his anti-social behavior can be charged against the family.

The second character to have an important role thrust upon her by tellers of the legend is Granny Power. We know very little about her. A search of birth and marriage records in Kimball and Junction Counties in Texas and in Grant and Catron Counties in New Mexico unearthed no mention of her. She was the mother of Thomas Jefferson Power, Sr., the father of the Power brothers. Granny's appeal to recounters of the legend apparently stems from the incongruity of toughness in a frail old lady. Every text that I collected dealing with Granny either states that she was tough (Mo24, An11), or relates an anecdote which illustrates that fact (Mo24, An2, An11, An29, Mx28). She is also characterized as "nice" and "fair" (An11), traits that are remarkable only in the context of her toughness. The anomalistically tough character is a common one in folk legendry, and Granny has also begun to attract traveling motifs.

The third character about whom a number of opinions are expressed and stories told is the baby of the Power family, Ola May. She was born in the Mogollon Mountains of western New Mexico in 1894 and was present at the first of the known tragedies of the Power family, when she was carried as a babe in arms by her mother, Martha Morgan Power, to a neighbor's house for a visit. Granny accompanied the mother and child, and while the women were chatting in the crude house of the neighbor, the roof of the structure collapsed. One of the large limbs which had supported the roof struck Matty, and she was killed. Ola was raised by her grandmother, father and brothers.[219] She is the first of these supporting characters who may have played a central role in the events leading up to the shooting on February 10, 1918.

The legend texts present antithetical views of Ola's character: a negative one which portrays the girl as brawling (Mo36, Mo37, An24), thieving (Mo17, Mo18, Mo36, Mo37), profane (Mo37), and promiscuous (Mo18, Mo36); and a favorable one which depicts her as virtuous, almost saintly. Each of these views is, of course, supported by verbal labels. The negative texts utilize terms such as "awful" (Mo26), "a real hell-raiser" (Mo36), and "really no good" (Mo18); while the

---

[219] Casual conversation with John and Tom Power and Ryder Ridgeway, Informant An29.

positive side employs adjectives like "pretty" (An16), "beautiful" (Mo7), "sweet" (Mo7, An16), "nice" (Mx28), "fine" (An32), and "proper" (Mo7). This stereotypical terminology is a function of testimonies concerned with subjects of controversy, and it falls under Principle 5, Categorization, the reduction of gradations by ignoring some differences and exaggerating others. Thus, some degree of polarization is to be expected in testimonies about characters who are central figures in controversial events. It is also important to note that of seven negative testimonies, six were offered by Mormon informants, and of six favorable testimonies, only one was collected from a Mormon. Thus the factions begin to define themselves, and the disparate versions of the legend begin to appear.

The other characters who are developed to any extent in the oral versions of the story were all present at that crude cabin, high in the Galiuros on that chill Sunday morning. Three of these characters were members of the Power family: Jeff, the father; John, the middle son; and Tom, the youngest son. One was the Powers' hired hand, Tom Sisson, and another was a member of the posse, Kane Wootan. The Powers are treated not only individually, but also as a unit.

The attitudes toward the Power family and the allegations made about it range over a wide area. Each informant strives to make a statement or relate an incident that he believes exemplifies honorific or opprobrious behavior. It is enlightening to examine these testimonies by group. The Mormon view alleges that the Powers were: belligerent (Mo4, Mo5, Mo6, Mo11, Mo14, Mo15, Mo46, Mo47), bloodthirsty (Mo42), cowardly (Mo1, Mo22, Mo23, Mo28, Mo40, Mo41, Mo42), crude (Mo24), universally disliked (Mo14, Mo46), godless (Mo4), gun-toting (Mo11, Mo41, Mo46), ignorant (Mo24, Mo33), illiterate (Mo24, Mo38, Mo47, An 15, Mx31), immoral (Mo4, Mo14, Mo28, Mo46), dirty (Mx4), low-class (Mo27, Mo38), mean (Mo5, Mo15), no good (Mo3, Mo36, Mo40, Mo47), property-less (Mo11, Mo14, Mo38), a sorry lot (Mo46), white trash (Mo47), and without respect for the property of others (Mo6, Mo11). Non-Mormons characterize them as: church-going (An23), expert shots (An32, An34), fine people (An17, An23), formidable (An14, An15, Mx9, Mx25, Mx30), good cowboys (An15, An29), good neighbors (An15), good people (An21, Mx12), hard-working (An15, An17, An29, Mx12), honest (An15), self-reliant (An29), truthful (An15), unbluffable (An15), unsociable (An15), tough

(Mx9, Mx28), sad (Mx11), kind (Mx20), and nice (An22, Mx2).

The terms in which these statements are couched can go a long way toward defining the *Weltanschauung* of the informant, as can be seen in the use of terms like "white trash," "hillbillies," and "lower than Mexicans." Sometimes these statements and incidents are ambiguous. For example, is it a good thing to be illiterate? Ordinarily the answer is a negative one, but if that illiteracy explains and justifies antisocial behavior, then it may very well be stressed by an informant who is very sympathetic toward the Powers (Mx31). This ambiguity seems to be lacking when the focus is on an individual.

Thomas Jefferson Power, Sr., the father of Charlie, John, Tom, and Ola, is usually referred to as Jeff Power or "Old Man" Power. He receives relatively little attention outside the narration of the events of February 10, 1918, but he is characterized as a "little funny" (An32), patriotic (An17), and quiet and unsociable (Mx28).

John Grant Power, on the other hand, is limned in considerable detail. Mormon informants generally avoid discussion of the male members of the Power family as individuals, preferring to characterize them as a group. Texts gathered from non-Mormons, however, dwell on John more than on any other figure involved in the shootings, and these texts afford a depth and complexity of character lacking in these other figures. The picture that emerges is one of an impressively redoubtable individual (An33, Mx25), utterly fearless (An27, Mx28), not given to facile social interaction (An27, An32, Mx28), and well-versed in the skills necessary for survival in the frontier milieu (An7, An25, An27, Mx28), who would kill if crossed and had killed many times before the incident in Kielberg Canyon (An14, An27, Mx28). Although he is characterized as "a cantankerous old bastard" (Mo45), it is also pointed out that "he never started no trouble, never bothered nobody". (An28). Another and very different side of John's character is apparent in those texts which treat his love for and skillful handling of animals (An20, An27, An29, Mx28).

The picture that we are given of the youngest brother, Tom Power, is a less detailed, but more consistent one in which he is portrayed as light-hearted, gregarious and fun-loving (An14, An32, Mx28), with a basic dignity that would tolerate no violation (An14).

The Powers' hired hand and friend, Tom Sisson, also receives some little attention in the oral accounts. Non-Mormon testimonies very seldom touch upon him except to stress his solid citizenship up until his arrest for stealing horses (An29) and the field skills that he acquired during his army experience (An25). Mormon texts stress the fact that he was arrested for horse theft (Mo3, Mo5, Mo11) and that he had served time in prison (Mo5, Mo14).

The posse is also treated as a group in the oral testimonies, but only in those obtained from Mormon informants, and for that reason the treatment is a consistently favorable one that stresses the respectability of all its members (Mo1, Mo10), their church-going propensities (Mo2, Mo14, Mo27, Mo35, Mo38, Mo47), and their essential goodness (Mo2, Mo10, Mo14, Mo16, Mo27, Mo38, Mo45, Mo47). No negative assessments of the character of the members of the posse before the central event are to be found. Of the four members of that posse, only one receives any degree of individual attention, and that one is the lowest ranking member, Deputy Sheriff Kane Wootan, who is painted in a generally unfavorable light. Non-Mormon texts assert that Wootan was a "hot shit" (An30, Mx28), a loudmouth (An30, Mx30), a womanizer (Mx28), and a bully (An30, Mx12, Mx25, Mx28, Mx30), who was especially hard on Mexicans (Mx12, Mx30). He is characterized as mean (Mx12), "screwy (An32), always on the prod (An32), and ambitious (An32, Mx28, Mx30).

The careful reading and consideration of the orally-collected texts of the Power legend will serve to delineate several points relevant to characters in historical legend. It becomes evident after such a perusal that a character in a local historical legend will sometimes attract traveling tales and motifs that are appropriate to his role in the story. Charlie, Granny, and John can all be seen to be functioning as the central figures in small, personal, anecdotal cycles of tales. It may be that we can see here the beginning of a true hero cycle centered on John Power. At least the stories of his shooting prowess and his power over animals would seem to represent the foreshadowing of the mythical gun and horse to which all proper heroes are entitled.[220] There is little doubt that in the pro-Power testimonies Kane Wootan has been cast in the role of villain. There are no favorable testimonies about Wootan aside from those in which he is treated as a member of the

---

[220] See Richard M. Dorson, *American Folklore* (Chicago and London: University of Chicago Press, 1959), pp. 209-211.

pose. In addition, it is quite easy to see the principles of categorization, the tendency to see the world in pairs of opposites, and Assimilation to Prior Input, the tendency to give verbal labels to non-verbal materials, at work here. One can only speculate at the subliminal significance or the consistent use of the demonstrative adjective "that" with the name of Tom Sisson in the unfavorable testimonies which deal with him (Mo3, Mo9, Mo11, Mo32, Mo46).

It now seems appropriate to move toward the event itself by examining those texts which treat the preliminaries to the actual shooting. On a Sunday early in November of 1917, Granny and Ola Power left their house in Klondyke and drove up the canyon to have dinner with their male relatives, who were engaged in a road-building project on Rattlesnake Mesa, southwest of the Haby ranch. The women made the trip in a buggy behind a borrowed horse. The family spent a pleasant afternoon, and toward evening the women started home. As they approached their house, the horse ran away; the buggy hit a woodpile in the yard and overturned, killing the old woman and injuring the girl (An15, An29, Mx11).[221]

Here we have a fairly straightforward account of another sad chapter in the tragic history of the Power family, the death of Sarah Elizabeth Power.[222] But there is a text bearing on this event which casts Granny's death in a different light and opens a window on a whole set of sordid allegations that have come to be an essential and sensational feature of the total legend:

> I heard that all four of them, the two brothers, the old man, and that hired man was all fuckin' that sister up there. And the old grandmother found out about it and raised hell, so they killed her (Mo32).

---

[221] I could find no documentary record of this event.

[222] Added in 2014: It is not clear where Roderick Roberts received this information. According to her gravestone, which did not exist when this was written, the grandmother's name is Martha Jane Power and her death was in 1915. An article in the *Eastern Arizona Courier* (September 16, 1970; pp. 1 and 11) also refers to the grandmother as Sarah Elizabeth Power. In *Shoot-Out at Dawn: An Arizona Tragedy* (Phoenix, Arizona: Phoenix Books, 1981), the book Tom Power wrote with John Whitlatch, the grandmother is called "Jane Power" (p. 7) and her death is said to have occurred in 1916 (p. 18). No documentary evidence of the year of death could be found.

This is the only text that links Granny's death to alleged incestuous activity in the Power household, but there is no shortage of averments to such activity. Veiled allegations of incestuous activity may lie behind statements concerning Jeff Power's possessive attitude toward his daughter (An29, An30, Mx10) as evidenced by its characterization as "quite a psychological thing" (An29). However, not all informants feel a need to mask their beliefs in this area. Some versions of the legend link Ola and her two younger brothers in such a relationship (Mo40, An37, Mx4); another adds her father to the group (Mo36); and a third cluster maintains that Tom Sisson was also an active participant (Mo13, Mo23, Mo32, Mo43, Mo46).

There are also a number of claims that Ola was sexually involved with a more conventional lover. Some of these texts identify the lover as a cowboy in the region (An8, An29, An30); others claim that he was a young man from Safford (Mo34, Mx10); and a third group insists that Ola's lover was the brother of Kane Wootan, the slain deputy (Mo34, Mx29). A pair of texts claims that the Powers were so affronted by Ola's involvement in a love affair that they killed her lover (Mo34, Mx10), while a single text maintains that her involvement moved her father and brothers to murder her (Mo8).

There are also a great many assertions that Ola was pregnant at the time of her death. Some texts make only this naked statement (Mo6, Mo17, Mo36), but others insist that this pregnancy was the result of an incestuous relationship (Mo23, Mo36, Mo43, Mo46, Mo47, An37) or of her involvement with the conventional lover mentioned above (An30). Many texts go on to declare that Ola was killed by her father and brothers because of her gravidity (Mo23, Mo36, Mo43, Mo46, An37).

Considerable disagreement exists among various versions of the legend as to the cause of Ola's death. Most informants who offer a cause of death as a part of their testimonies agree that she died of a broken neck (Mo2, Mo11, Mo19, Mo36). Others agree as to the cause of death but state further that this injury was incurred when her brothers frustrated her elopement (Mo32, An19, An29) or roped her in play (An29). Another body of opinion holds that Ola died as a result of poisoning, either accidentally (An29, An32) or willfully at the hands of Mormons (An27). There are at least two statements that imply a dark significance to the allegation that Ola had been dead longer than her family claimed (Mo19, An29), and two other testimonies insist that Ola suffered from convulsions before she died (An27, An32). There is one very interesting testimony that traces the cause of the girl's death to the buggy accident that claimed her grandmother's life (An32). A number of texts stress Ola's high moral character and her family's regard for her in an attempt at refuting testimonies that allege salacious behavior (An15, An29, An32, An41).

Thus run the oral accounts of the first truly controversial event in the Power saga. We are free to choose between the promiscuous strumpet, pregnant and mired in depravity, and the innocent young lady. We can select either the tragic mysterious death or the callous, expedient murder. The fact is that Ola did die, suddenly and inexplicably. The allegations that her neck was broken apparently stem from the fact that there was considerable discoloration in the throat area. Since the coroner's inquest did not seize upon a neck fracture as the cause of death, that possibility would seem to be precluded, for even a frontier practitioner should have been able to diagnose such an injury, especially if it were the result of so violent an occurrence as being roped from a horse. We are left with an unexplained discoloration in the throat area, convulsions prior to death, and a nagging suspicion in some segments of the folk mind that Ola's death was somehow linked to the accident in November, 1917, which had claimed Granny's life. Armed with these symptoms and goaded by that suspicion, I ventured into the murky world of medicine in an effort to discover some disease consistent with these conditions, and I believe I have found one in pulmonary embolism, a widespread disease which still accounts for 47,000 deaths per year in the United States.[223]

The basic concept of embolism was delineated by Rudolf Virchow, a German pathologist, in clinical, pathological, and experimental observations between 1846 and 1856. He was the first to show that when thrombi are present in the pulmonary vasculature, they are rarely due to *in situ* thrombosis, but rather they form in peripheral veins, dislodge, and then pass to the pulmonary circulation as emboli.[224] A trauma in any area of the body can cause the formation of thrombi; those thrombi tend to propagate toward the heart where they are

---

[223] James E. Dalen and Lewis Dexter, "Diagnosis and Management of Massive Pulmonary Embolism," *Disease-a-Month* (August, 1967), p. 3.
[224] Ibid., p. 3.

fragmented and then lodge at the bifurcation of the main pulmonary artery or in the proximal right and/or left pulmonary arteries. When embolism is sufficiently massive to occlude pulmonary blood flow, the brain is deprived of oxygen, and convulsions, collapse, and death can occur within minutes. Violent convulsions often cause cyanosis in the face and neck area.[225] Since this occlusion of pulmonary blood flow can occur after a traumatic event, Ola's sudden death may very well have resulted from some apparently minor injury received in the accident that took her grandmother's life.

Such theorizing matters not a whit, for it will in no way affect the whole-hearted belief in one or another of these versions of the event by those who possess these tales; nor will it change the fact that their beliefs will affect their views of events subsequent to this one and of the participants in those events.

On February 10, 1918, a posse surrounded the Power cabin. There is general agreement in the documentary record as to what brought them there. However, no such consensus is available in the oral testimonies. Many informants assert that the motivation for the formation of the posse and its movement into the Galiuros was a federal warrant for draft evasion (Mo2, Mo4, Mo6, Mo9, Mo10, Mo19, Mo38, Mo39, An15, An29, An32, Mx8, Mx22). Other texts admit the Powers' refusal to comply with draft regulations, but supply circumstances that are more or less mitigating. There is a statement to the effect that the boys would have gone in to register as soon as they had put their mine on a paying basis (An17). John Power asserts that he was not liable to the draft (An27). The failure of the brothers to register is also explained by statements to the effect that they were never notified of their obligation (Mx9) and that their refusal to comply was in retaliation for the denial of franchise as a result of their inability to read the constitution of the state of Arizona (Mx22, Mx31).

Another body of opinion holds that the posse came after the Powers for questioning in their sister's mysterious death (Mo2, Mo4, Mo6, Mo9, Mo10, Mo38, An8, An16). In one of these texts the Powers' resistance to the posse is explained by the fact that there was "bad blood" between the family and Kane Wootan and thus they

---

[225] R.T. Breckenridge and O.D. Ratnoff, "Pulmonary Embolism and Unexpected Death in Supposedly Normal Persons," *New England Journal of Medicine*, 270 (1964), p. 298.

feared that they would not receive a fair trial (An8).

Several other explanations are offered for the presence of the posse at the Power cabin. Some informants allege that the posse came with the express purpose of killing the Powers and in this fashion obtaining their valuable mine (An27, Mx9, Mx27), but many more see Kane Wootan as the Machiavellian force behind the posse's attempt to murder the Powers. A number of texts comment on the poor relationship between the Powers and Wootan, which is alleged to have resulted from the failure of the Powers to knuckle under to Wootan's bullying or from John Power's public humbling of the deputy sheriff (An27, An33, Mx7, Mx29). Other informants see the root cause of the tragedy in Wootan's lust for the Power mine (An14, An17, Mx14) or in his unbridled ambition (An32, Mx14, Mx28, Mx30). A number of informants agree that Wootan had been warned of the inadvisability of approaching the Powers in force (Mo45, An33, Mx22, Mx28, Mx30), and most of these attest that Wootan expressed a naked contempt for the fighting proclivities of the Power family (Mo45, An32, Mx22, Mx28). One informant puts forth the unlikely view that one of the posse's members had been Ola's lover and that the purpose of the posse's appearance in Kielberg Canyon was revenge for her murder at the hands of her father and brothers (Mo8).

The stage is now set for the main event; the characters that possessors of the legend have chosen as the principals have been brought to some semblance of life, and explanations have been supplied for the presence of this party of lawmen in the Galiuros on this cold, grey morning. The choice of explanations for the presence of the posse is wide indeed:

1) Ola's lover's revenge for her murder
2) An official investigation of Ola's death
3) An attempt to arrest the boys for draft evasion
4) A combination of 2 and 3
5) Wootan's desire for the Powers' mine
6) The posse's desire for the Powers' mine
7) Wootan's ambition
8) Wootan's desire for revenge for humiliation suffered at the hands of the Powers

These and other choices are available as well as almost any combination of them. These testimonies are also replete with rationalizations of and explanations for the behavior of one or another of the principal characters. This rationalization is a manifestation of Principle 3, Closure, the urge to make experiences as complete, coherent, and meaningful as possible. To satisfy this urge, informants reinterpret information they receive to bring it in line with their perceptions of reality and their past experiences. This phenomenon very often accounts for the introduction of new material as the informant strives after meaning. Since, for all practical purposes, there is no other record of the event in question, the only sensible course is to reserve judgment and allow the event to play itself out.

Some of the testimonies trace the progress of the posse from Safford to the Power cabin (Mo2, An29). There are two texts which deny that the posse members were drunk (Mo2, Mo45), although I collected no texts that allege that they were. The testimonies present antithetical views of the posse's approach to the cabin, some asserting that its members approached in plain view of the occupants of the cabin (Mo10, Mo11) and were shot down without warning (Mo1, Mo4, Mo9, Mo10, Mo11, Mo19, Mo32, Mo38, Mo39, An26, An37), and others insisting that the posse surreptitiously surrounded the cabin (An15, An34). The latter view is sometimes accompanied by the statement that the posse or at least one of its members intended to kill the Powers and Tom Sisson (Mo2, An27). The notion is also put forth that this was not the ideal manner of approaching the Powers; that if they had been approached openly with a rational appeal, they would have given themselves up (An34, An36). At any rate, those texts which do not support an ambush of the lawmen offer a picture of the unwary Powers going about the business of rising. While rousing themselves, dressing and building a fire (An27, An28), they were alarmed by some loose horses galloping through the yard (An27, An28, An29), and Jeff Power stepped out onto the front porch with either a rifle or a shotgun (Mo2, An27, An28, An34, Mx31). He was commanded to raise his hands (Mo2, An28, Mx31) and then shot (An5, An27, An28, Mx31), some insist with his hands raised (Mo2, An27, Mx31).

It is at this juncture that these oral testimonies focus on a point that is central to events as they transpired and which appears nowhere in the documentary record. Jeff Power was killed in the fight, and most of the informants who deal with his shooting insist that he was shot while outside the house and that the shot that killed him was the first shot fired in the battle. But others maintain that the shooting was accidental (Mo2, An1, An12, An29, An33, Mx25), that the posse was not bent on murder (Mo2), and that the blame can be placed on a borrowed rifle (Mo2, An12, An29, An33, Mx25) that had a hair trigger (An1, An12, An29, An33, Mx25). The shooting is variously attributed to Marshal Haynes (Mo2), to Sheriff McBride (An1), or to Deputy Wootan (An12, An29, An33, Mx25).

The motif of the hair trigger rifle is extremely important to tellers of the legend because it humanizes the behavior of the posse. It is difficult for informants who come into daily contact with descendants of posse members to believe that the ancestors of their acquaintances and friends could have been guilty of such a calculated murder. The accidental nature of the shooting makes the event understandable and plausible.

Many informants ignore the shooting of the boys' father entirely and gloss over the pivotal question of who fired the first shot in the battle, but others strive to unravel the puzzle. Was a cowardly ambush prepared by the Powers, or did the posse, wittingly or unwittingly, shoot Jeff Power with his hands raised? A number of informants insist that after Jeff Power died, the wound in his chest could only be probed to its full depth if his arms were raised high over his head (Mo2, An6, An21, An31, An34, An35, Mx7: Mx26, Mx31), thus proving to their satisfaction that the old man was shot after he had complied with the lawmen's order. The importance of this motif to the pro-Power version of the event cannot be overestimated, for if it can be established that the father was killed in this fashion, then the ensuing actions of the Power boys is adjudged to be understandable, appropriate, and laudable (Mo2, Mo45, An10, An21, Mx30). Therefore this bit of folk forensic medicine serves as a charter for the subsequent behavior of John and Tom Power.

The fight itself is not sketched in detail by most informants. We are told that one or both of the Power boys was wounded in the battle (An27, An28, An34), that John killed McBride and Kempton and Tom was responsible for Wootan's death (An27, An28), and that Tom Sisson took no part in the fighting (An27, An28).

Considerably more attention is paid to events subsequent to the shootings. A number of informants state that a party from the Murdock ranch arrived on the scene shortly after the firing stopped and that the dying Jeff Power was entrusted to the care of its members (Mo2, An28, An29, Mx22, Mx26, Mx31). We are also told that the Powers had no notion whom they had been fighting until they examined the dead after the battle (An28). Realizing they were in serious trouble and fearing a lynching, they fled on the posse's mounts (An28). Some informants fault the Powers for leaving their dying father to flee the scene (Mo9, An18), but most do not comment on it, apparently regarding this as a sensible course of action, given the circumstances. One informant relates that Jeff Power's remains were never buried; the pursuing posse simply threw the body in a nearby sandwash (Mx23).[226]

One of the more amazing aspects of this case was the ability of the Powers and Tom Sisson to remain at liberty with the greatest man hunt in Southwestern history mounted against them. Some explanation is needed to make this fact coincide with past experience, and the informants provide these explanations in a variety of ways, one of which is the borrowing of motifs from other tales. This borrowing is a manifestation of Principle 6, Assimilation to Prior Input. It is interesting to note that the Mormon informants who deal with this question attribute assistance to the Powers to non-Mormon Anglos (Mo19, Mo21), Apaches (Mo20, Mo41), and Mexicans (Mo20). Mexican informants eagerly volunteer that Mexicans did aid the Powers and focus their testimonies on the Powers' payment for the kindnesses they received (Mx2, Mx3, Mx15, Mx16, Mx18, Mx20). Two comments by Mexican informants are particularly enlightening: "She always said that it wasn't any of our business" (Mx16), and "it was usually Mexican people they stayed with because they knew they wouldn't turn them in" (Mx18). In addition to the "Robin Hood" motifs, there are other traditional elements present in these texts. Some informants allege that the Powers deceived the posses by shoeing their horses backwards (Mo20, Mo26, Mo29). Others state that the fugitives availed themselves of an underground connection between Colossal Cave and Carlsbad Caverns (Mo12, Mo25, An39). Motifs present in the legendary

---

[226] I could find no record of an interment for Jeff Power's body. Ryder Ridgeway and the Power brothers believe that the posse disposed of it in the above-mentioned manner.

accounts of other outlaws are also to be found here, such as overhearing the plans of their pursuers while hiding in a hollow log (Mo26, An27, Mx1), and conversing with members of the hunting party who are unaware of their identity (An28). Some texts claim that the Powers remained in the general vicinity of the Galiuros because they wanted to retrieve the gold that they had cached in the area (Mo16, An3).

After eluding their pursuers for twenty-nine days, the Powers and Tom Sisson were captured. The oral testimonies reflect some disagreement as to whether or not the capture took place in Mexico (Mo10, Mo39, An15, An27, An28, An29, An34, An36, An37), but this seems to be a matter of concern only to Mexican informants who resent this violation by United States troops of the territorial integrity of Mexico (Mx3, Mx30). Several texts state that the Powers and Tom Sisson had an opportunity to kill the soldiers who captured them but forbore to do so (An26, An27, An28, An29).

Oral testimonies state that the prisoners were taken to Safford (An28, An29, An34) or to Duncan and then to Clifton because of the fear that they would be lynched in Safford (An26). The fear of lynching is a recurring theme (An26, An34), and it is further asserted in some texts that only the presence of federal troops prevented such an occurrence (Mo16, An27, An28, Mx13, Mx31). These texts concerned with a lynching attempt are interesting in view of the fact that there is no documentary evidence to support the belief in such an attempt. Yet a change of venue was requested, and that request was quickly granted, and there were two thinly veiled calls for lynching published in editorials in the *Arizona Daily Star* on February 17, 1918, and March 10, 1918. John Power is insistent on the truth of his account of events after the arrest, especially in regard to the lynching attempt and his intentional and malicious blinding (An27).

The point has been made that records of the trial are for all practical purposes non-existent. The oral accounts focus on the fairness of the trial (Mo6, Mo7, Mo14, Mo28, Mo39, An17, An28), the absence of capital punishment as a possible penalty (Mo10, Mo28, Mo39, An29), and on the introduction of the last character in the drama, the Powers' lawyer. James Fiedler was an attorney from Silver City, New Mexico, with whom they had become familiar during their residence in that state. Tom Power states that Fiedler made no efforts in their defense (An28); John Power claims that he was "bought off" by a $300,000 payment from the Mormon Church (An27); and other informants borrow floating motifs to paint a picture of a drunken, unethical attorney (An9, An15, Mx31).

Some texts give an account of the life of the Powers and Tom Sisson in prison (An26, An34), telling of Sisson's death (An34), the Powers' escapes (An26, An29), their parole hearings (An34), and their eventual release from prison (An26, An29, An34). One of the interesting facets of these oral testimonies is that statements for or against freeing the Powers are most often cast in the future tense in spite of the fact that none were collected before the Powers' parole. This fact would seem to speak for the traditional nature of this cycle of tales and for its independence of the popular media. The statements advocating the release of the Powers are comparatively mild (An22, Mx8, Mx20) beside the passionate, even virulent, calls for their retention in prison (Mo5, Mo6, Mo14, Mo22, Mo39, An18), their bizarre executions (Mo9, Mo30), or lynching (Mo44). This passion serves as an indicator of the relevance and significance of the Power story to residents of the area.

Another cycle of tales, traditional in the Southwest, has attached itself to the Power story, especially with Mexican participants in the legendary process. There are a number of accounts concerned with the Powers' hidden gold, with treasure lights that indicate its presence (Mx5, Mx9, Mx18, Mx23, Mx24), perils that threaten those who would unearth it (Mx5, Mx8, Mx24), ghosts that guard it (Mx17, Mx23), and means by which it can be safely obtained (Mx5). The significance of this cycle of tales may lie in the fact that it allows Mexicans in the county to participate in the legend without choosing sides in the conflict between Mormon and non-Mormon Anglos.

This then is the thrust of the statements, allegations, and stories that comprise the Power legend. It is by no means a complete record of that legend; far too many of those who are privy to some portion of the legend were unwilling to entrust it to a bearded outlander whom they thought unsympathetic. The texts presented in Appendix II, however, do define the boundaries of the cycle as it had developed through 1962, and a careful reading of these texts will provide some sense of the tone and flavor of the oral testimonies. As it stands, thus defined, it affords a number of possibilities for belief, but inevitably the choice must come between those texts which present the Powers as immoral, cowardly murderers and those which portray them as the innocent victims of a gross miscarriage of justice, brought to their misfortune by circumstance or the malevolence of their neighbors. Obviously, individuals who transmit the legend have made their choices based on the inputs they have received, their personal belief systems, and their special interests. But just as obviously, the version favorable to the Power boys worked quietly, inexorably, and successfully to overcome not only the oral testimonies that told a different story, but also the total weight of the surviving documentary evidence. The true measure of that success was the full pardon, issued to the boys in January, 1969, by Governor Jack Williams, returning to them their civil rights and the full privileges of citizenship.

CONCLUSION

The motivation for this study was fourfold: 1) the primal, human urge that keeps all folklorists in business, the desire to tell a good story; 2) a nagging discontent with the way in which legend has been defined and the inapplicability of that definition to much of the material that the American folklorist encounters; 3) a desire to apply some of the principles formulated by communications theorists to field-collected materials; and 4) the belief that legendary accounts of historical events can be useful and sometimes essential in constructing a balanced chronicle of those events.

The story can stand on its own merits; any narrative containing ambush, murder, an extensive man hunt, buried treasure, incest and comic relief can hardly lose its appeal no matter how stilted and pedantic its relation, and such a tale is its own justification. The treatment of the other points, however, demands discussion.

The standard definition of legend has been found operationally deficient. Scholars utilizing it have found themselves unable to plot the boundaries of the genre with any degree of certitude. Hinging as it does on the criterion of belief, this standard definition has proved of very little value in the study of field-collected materials, for it is very nearly impossible to make intelligent decisions about the credence that any informant places in a given item without an extensive period of behavioral observation. The unease of scholars with regard to the generally accepted definition of legend has long been evident and is reflected in the writings of most of the workers in the field, and this unease has, in turn, been largely responsible for the fact that relatively little progress has been made toward the classification and analysis of the large body of legendary material that has been collected. Before such progress can be effected, some determinant or determinants must be isolated that will serve to demarcate the legend from other forms of folk prose.

The key determinant does lie in the sphere of belief, but at a stage preliminary to that whole-hearted acceptance of an item as "truth." The legend asks not that the receptor believe, but rather that he measure the incidents and characters which it contains against his own perception of the real world and then either accept or reject them. Thus the legend interacts with individual perceptions of reality in a way that no other traditional narrative does. All the other narrative genres free the receptor by one device or another from performing this reality evaluation of their contents. The texts with which we are concerned then are those which relate an incident or series of incidents, and which are marked by words, expressions, and most importantly, by the attitude of the transmitter as material that was believed by someone at some time, and which ask the receptor to consider their content and make some judgment as to its truth or falsity. Let it be submitted then that a legend is a traditional narrative which makes a statement or assertion and which asks that the receiver measure its content against his perception of objective reality.

Moving from the general area of legend study to the more specific concerns of the historical legend and its ability to preserve information is marked by the transition from a world of the vague and imprecise to one in which positions are definite, clearly-marked and contradictory. This body of scholarship has been adequately summarized elsewhere,[227] but the positions espoused by various writers on the subject seem to have been determined by their differing understandings of the term "historical fact." Negative estimates of the historicity of legend seem to have been occasioned by the application of the standards of written history to oral materials and dismay at the failure of such materials to preserve specific names, dates, and chronological order of events in the same way that written history ideally does. Those scholars who have approached historical legends with a different and more flexible set of expectations have been able to discover a number of avenues through which legendary material can be profitably utilized by the historian.

---

[227] See Francis A. DeCaro, "Folklore as an 'Historical Science': The Anglo-American Viewpoint," an unpublished Ph.D. dissertation, Indiana University, 1967, and Richard M. Dorson, "The Debate over the Trustworthiness of Oral Traditional History," in *Volksüberlieferung, Festschrift für Kurt Ranke*, eds. Fritz Harkort, Karel C. Peters and Robert Wildhaber (Göttingen: Otto Schwartz and Company, 1968), pp. 19-35.

Historians can employ legendary material in the reconstruction of the past in at least these ways: 1) they provide a ready access to the popular attitudes, prejudices, and stereotypes of any society in which they have currency;[228] 2) they contain useful information on traditional customs, practices, and mores; 3) they can serve to verify and illuminate incidents which have originally come to light through documentary or archeological evidence;[229] 4) they can sometimes be used to disentangle fact from fancy;[230] 5) they may be the first indicators of incidents that have resisted discovery by more traditional methods of historical research; 6) they can provide valuable data on minority groups in a culture when that culture has not seen fit to record such data through more formal channels; and 7) they are often the only voice of illiterate or semi-literate groups in the culture.[231] Legends can and do represent a valid source for the historian.

If some portion of the past is to be reconstructed through the use of legend, the fact that changes occur in materials that circulate orally must be recognized, and techniques for dealing with these changes must be developed. If such change is truly random, then it is impossible to deal with, but there is a great body of scholarship that insists that transmission error is nearly always selective and purposeful. Unfortunately, students of legend have generally ignored such systematic error; the only significant work in the field has been accomplished by psychologists and communications theorists. A careful scrutiny of this literature will yield a number of principles that are applicable to field-collected legend texts.

The first of these principles of systematic error in materials in oral transmission is **Condensation**, which states that the general tendency of oral accounts is to become shorter, simpler and less detailed. There is some evidence that this principle may not be universally valid, since in India and China there is a demonstrated tendency toward the consistent elaboration of oral accounts,[232] and even though the

---

[228] Richard M. Dorson, "Oral Tradition and Written History: the Case for the United States," *The Journal of the Folklore Institute*, Vol. I, no. 3 (December, 1964), p. 222.

[229] Ibid., p. 230.

[230] Ibid., p. 228.

[231] Ibid., p. 231.

[232] See Gordon W. Allport and Leo Postman, *The Psychology of Rumor* (New York: Henry Holt and Company, 1947), pp. 154-155.

principle is valid within the American cultural context, it is of relatively little importance to the folklorist since there seldom exists a means of establishing the primacy of legend texts, and because the principle makes no allowance for the creative, individual storyteller, who will often embellish texts which fall into his hands. A good example of condensation in operation can be seen in the comparison of the testimonies of Informants Mo10 and M11. These informants are father and son, so that primacy can be established in this case. The father's text runs over 900 words and incorporates four anecdotes. The son's testimony consists of less than 200 words and contains no anecdotes, yet the judgments in each text are virtually identical. Thus it can be seen in this example that the loss is selective, consisting largely of detail and that the overall form of the text is retained with the major effect intact.

Middle Message Loss, the principle that holds that the middle portion of a text will suffer most in oral transmission, has been taken into consideration in this study not because it can be demonstrated in the testimonies that we have examined, but because it has been so well documented in laboratory studies. The folklorist may not be able to apply this principle to field situations due to the impossibility of determining the original form of a legend, but an awareness of the validity of this laboratory-established phenomenon may allow him to intelligently probe for and even recover accounts of events which are lost in most of the testimonies offered to him. In the case at hand, my commitment to a formula question precluded this kind of investigation, but another study might profitably focus on this principle and its effects.

The principle of **Closure** stems from the universal human urge to make experiences complete, coherent, and meaningful. This urge is often satisfied by reinterpreting received information and introducing new information to bring the total account in line with past experiences. This inclination explains phenomena like the "folk Bible," and can be seen at work in the Power legend in the cycles of stories that have developed around some of the characters. These cycles are the result of a desire to add dimension to figures that are essentially one-dimensional in accounts of the central event. Thus characters are isolated, and appropriate traveling motifs are gathered to them so that bearers of the legend may know the kinds of people with whom they are dealing. The emphasis on the "hair trigger rifle" and "stick in the wound" motifs are examples of this principle in operation.

The principle of **Symmetry** argues that distortion can be anticipated in the direction of regularity. In a culture which possesses a magic number or numbers, characters or incidents may be added or subtracted to fit cultural notions of propriety. The happy accident in the Power story that allowed the number of slain lawmen and the number of fugitives to coincide with the most potent number in European tradition meant that no such changes were necessary in these texts, but such alterations can readily be seen in other bodies of legend.

The principle of **Categorization** states that the content of a legend may be distorted by its division into clear-cut entities. Human beings experience the world and detect large areas of regularity and small but striking areas of difference. They tend to ignore the areas of regularity and focus upon the areas of difference, exaggerating them until the areas of regularity are no longer significant and the element under consideration can be fitted into an already existing category. The pejorative terms applied to members of the Power family and to Mormons are good examples of this principle in action. One facet of the complex personality of an individual is used to categorize him.

Assimilation to Prior Input is a principle which holds that distortion will often take place in the direction of similar stories to which the informant has been exposed. This principle is extremely important to an understanding of the ways in which traveling motifs attach themselves to a local historical legend. The development of sub-cycles of tales around John, Charlie, Granny, and Ola, as well as the group of tales which portrays the Powers as helpers and rewarders of those who lend them assistance in their flight, can be explained by the operation of this principle. This is a very human tendency toward error and implies a pervasive bias toward typical, ordinary, popular outputs.

Assimilation to the Attitudes of the Informant is by far the most important of the principles of distortion in oral transmission. The attitudes of the informant necessarily affect his choice of the texts that he incorporates into his version of the tale. He may refuse to listen to texts which are hostile to his attitudes. This principle is so basic and so reasonable as to need very little discussion, and it plays a role in every oral utterance.

Distortion to Please the Receiver functions whenever an

informant transmits his text to a human listener, for that informant-receptor relationship almost necessarily has reciprocal aspects. The informant is aware that the receptor will react to his output, and he may change that output in an effort to please the receiver or to avoid hurting or angering him. In the testimonies of Informants Mx6 and Mx27, the presence of an Anglo receptor caused the insertion of qualifications into these texts that certainly would not have been present if the audience had been composed entirely of Mexicans. The refusal of many informants to respond to the formula question may very well have been motivated by this desire to spare the receiver, and thus a refusal to come forward with a text may represent the ultimate distortion to please the receiver.

If in an informant's experience, personal or vicarious, a certain kind of outcome has been associated with a certain type of individual or situation, he may distort the outcome of his testimony in that direction. This is the principle of **Distortion to Associated Cues**, and it lies at the root of prejudice and stereotyping. If an informant has recourse to a label to categorize some individual, that label may very well carry with it expectations for behavior, and in accounts which feature that informant his behavior may be distorted to conform with that preconception. This principle is reflected in the labels that are employed throughout the Power legend.

When an informant has access to a number of sources, which is almost always the case in the local legend situation, the principle of **Overdependence on a Single Source** may be operative. If one source is more prestigious than the others, or if the source and the informant possess similar perceptions of the nature of reality, the informant's testimony may follow that source very closely and ignore the others. In the legend under consideration a good example can be found in a comparison of the testimonies of Informants Mo10 and Mo11. Every judgment that Informant Mo11 incorporates in his testimony can be found in the text supplied by Informant Mo10. The father-son relationship between these two informants undoubtedly explains this overdependence.

The principle of **Conformity** states that when informants are in contact, their testimonies are likely to be similar. Simple physical contact, however, does not insure that conformity of testimony will follow, for if the legend in question has any element of controversy attached to it, then "contact" may be misleading, for stories of this type may not be told freely. At any rate, this principle explains the rarity of unique legend testimonies.

This represents only the most rudimentary formulation of these principles as they apply to the local historical legend. A great deal of work remains to be done before they or something like them can prove of real value in helping us to understand the function of the local legend or in helping us to more accurately reconstruct an historical event. But these principles do offer a starting point, a base from which further and more thorough investigations of local historical legends can be undertaken with the hope that their findings will be more conclusive.

The legend under consideration in this study is an historical one. It lacks the hoary patina of antiquity that we usually associate with the legend, but its very youth may afford insights into its growth and development that are not available in older stories. Here the accretion of traveling motifs has only begun; events and characters stand sharp and clear, as yet unclouded by the mists of time, but the inevitable process that will transmute flesh and blood, multidimensional individuals into larger than life, superficial symbols of virtue and villainy is well underway. The principal characters have been singled out; the character trait or traits that distinguish them in the folk mind have been decided upon, and cycles of stories that emphasize the trait or traits have begun to develop. These figures have become folk heroes. More cogently than anyone else, Richard M. Dorson has outlined the process by which such a figure assumes his central role:

> As for the popularity of the folk hero, we must recognize that it begins with his own constituency, whose viewpoint he expresses. The outside world may know little of him, and what it knows may be inflamed by third-hand rumor and the coloring of hostile or threatened reporters. To take two outlaw heroes from the late nineteenth century, Jesse James and Billy the Kid, we perceive a sharp clash of opinion as to their merits. Midwest farmers liked Jesse because he only robbed banks and gave to the poor, and they hated Billy the Kid as a sadistic gunman and pariah. Southwest cowpunchers

admired the Kid because he fought for the open range, and they despised Jesse as a money-mad robber. Or take today's generations, among whom Abbie Hoffman and Jerry Rubin attract a cult following of hippies and Yippies and at the same time receive choice opprobrious epithets from middle America. For the folk hero to really make his mark he must broaden his support to include other than his own immediate constituency......[233]

Thus the pro-Power version of the legend has produced hero figures that have inexorably broadened their constituencies, and the completely defensive position of the Mormons has been marked by their failure to develop a single heroic figure in the legend cycle. So long as the senses of group identity in the county remain clear and distinct, controversy will continue to rage concerning the specifics of the event and the character of those who participated in it. But as the version of the story favorable to the Powers has gained the sanction of established authority, adjustments have been made in the versions hostile to them, so that many texts now have shifted their emphasis from attacks on the Powers to defenses of the lawmen and of the institutions which sanctioned their behavior.

There is no doubt in my mind that the legend as here presented accurately reflects tensions as they existed in Graham County in 1961 and 1962, and the narrative seems to provide an effective vehicle for the release of the frustrations produced by these tensions. The Mormons dominate the valley economically, politically, and socially. Non-Mormon Anglos live side-by-side with Mormons and are free to struggle alongside them for affluence, but they are effectively barred from political power and complete social success. Mexicans comprise the substructure of this society; they rank above Blacks and Indians, but the impact of these groups on life in the county is minimal. For all practical purposes, the members of the Mexican group are deprived of any chance of success in any of the significant areas of life.

This deprivation, of course, produces resentments toward the Anglo world, and since Mormons are the most successful segment of

---

[233] *America in Legend: Folklore from the Colonial Period to the Present* (New York: Pantheon Books, 1973), p. 62.

that world, most of these resentments are channeled toward them. Non-Mormon Anglos share many of these resentments, and the Power legend provides a focus for this bitterness. The events of the story seem to exemplify to members of these groups the wanton misuse of power by the Mormons, the hopelessness of any struggle against that power, and the terrible penalties that can be exacted from anyone who disregards that futility. The more firmly the innocence of the Powers can be established, the greater the crime of the Mormons becomes, and this improbity underscores the injustice of life in the county for all non-Mormons. The Mormons in turn resent these attacks on the established order and feel compelled to prove the guilt of the Powers and the innocence of the slain lawmen. If someday this situation should change and these tensions should ease or disappear completely, the legend as here constituted would lose this function, and we can speculate that a considerable change in emphasis of those portions of it which survive would take place, for it would have to find some new function if it were to continue to exist.

It is certain that the situation in which one faction gains control of the recording mechanisms in an area is not a unique one, and the local historical landscape must be liberally dotted with documentary records of conflicts that reflect only the interests and the viewpoints of such a controlling group. Since the dominant group in a region usually controls the courts, the local governmental agencies, and the newspapers, the views of a group in conflict with the dominant one will not be found in the documents produced and preserved by such institutions. In such instances the only effective argument against such a biased record, the only hope of gaining a truly balanced picture of the event in question may lie in an active search for oral traditions concerned with the event. In these legendary accounts can be found judgments, statements, and observations from that group which was denied access to the official recording mechanisms. When these folkloric items have been recovered, they must be measured against the historical accounts of the incident, but one must always remember that folklore is never really concerned with the scrupulous description of events but with their significance and with the translation of that significance into judgments which will preserve the essential truth of the event. The aim of scientific history is to perceive events as dispassionately as possible and to translate these perceptions into observations that will report as many verifiable facts as possible. Obviously, the aims of folkloric and scientific history are at cross-purposes, and any confrontation of the two is bound to work to the detriment of folklore, since the standards of evaluation will be those of scientific history. What so many observers have failed to appreciate is that even in those cases in which legendary facts are in conflict with verifiable facts, they are valuable, for they are indicative of a belief system at variance with the mainstream one, a belief system which is more concerned with preserving and transmitting the significance of events than with reporting verifiable facts, and thus may be essential to an understanding of the social and cultural history of a region. If a number of such studies were undertaken, the total body of material might well allow insights into the function and process of the local historical legend that are not available in the consideration of a single case.

The fact remains that the testimonies presented in this study have demonstrated that they possess a kind of magic. They came into being in an overwhelmingly hostile popular climate and survived in that climate, casting their insidious spell until they were able to overcome the hostility of that climate. In this case no hard documentary evidence has survived; no warrants, no official reports, no court records exist. Only the newspaper accounts remain, and they fall far short of the objective, reportorial ideal. These journalistic accounts are filled with many of the same kinds of distortion one finds and expects to find in the oral accounts. The newspapers do not accurately preserve and transmit facts, and their pages are filled with subjective judgments that interpret the facts from the point of view of the established group. Newspapers both shape and reflect popular opinion, and in this case that opinion was strong enough to actually change the laws of the state of Arizona. There is no doubt that the emotions stirred up by the Power case were responsible for the reestablishment of capital punishment in the state. It was in the face of such fervor that these tales originated, and it was against the residue of such passions that they worked to bring about, first, the release of the Powers when certain powerful elements in the society had decided they were to die in prison, and, ultimately, their popular and official vindication. An explanation for the ability of a thin localized stream of oral tradition to work this kind of change on popular opinion and to actually bring about a transformation in the popular conception of the truth of an historical event is not easy to come by, but perhaps we need look no farther than John Power's own melancholy and intuitively accurate assessment: "Folks that tells we got a raw deal tells the truth."

APPENDIX I

NEWSPAPER ACCOUNTS

Graham Guardian, December 14, 1917, p. 1:

Headline: INQUEST WAS HELD

Subhead: To Determine Cause of the Sudden Death of Klondyke Girl

---

The circumstances surrounding the sudden death of Miss Ola May Powers aged 22 years, at the home of her father in the Rattlesnake mountains, about 20 miles east of Klondyke, led to a trip for Sheriff McBride and Dr. Platt, early Friday morning, when word was received here by the sheriff of the girls' [sic] death.

They arrived at Klondyke at daylight Saturday morning and went to Haby's ranch, where the body of the girl had been brought from her home in the Rattlesnake mountains.

A coroner's inquest was held by Justice of the Peace Bleak. At the inquest the girl's father testified that his wife died when Ola was a young child and that she had lived with him all her life, at their home in the Rattlesnake mountains, where he had worked on his mining claim.

About two months ago he took her to Safford to be treated by a doctor for throat trouble, and again went with her to Safford two weeks ago to get treatment for her throat.

Late in the afternoon of last Thursday, the girl came to the house where he and a man named Tom Sisson lived, and asked him to bring her a bucket of water, which he did, and later both men went to her house for supper.

When he arrived at the house, he said he went into her room and found her lying across the bed and suffering from a convulsion. He called for Sisson and sent him to Joe Bosco's ranch, 10 miles, to get assistance, and when Sisson left, he held the girl and tried to help her, but that she died a short time after Sisson left.

Mr. and Mrs. Bosco came to the house and prepared the body for burial. The body was taken to Haby's ranch and Sisson came to Safford for a casket, leaving Safford Friday for Klondyke.

Word of the girl's sudden death was brought to Sheriff McBride, who left here with Dr. Platt to attend the coroner's inquest.

After hearing all the evidence in the case, the coroner's jury brought in a verdict that the girl had died from some unknown cause.

Arizona Daily Star, February 13, 1918, p. 1:

Headline: SOUTHERN ARIZONA'S BEST SHOTS VOLUNTEER FOR MANHUNT; ZEST GIVEN BY OFFER OF $4000 REWARD

Subhead: Report From San Simon That Slayers of Graham County Officers Were in That Section, Indicate That Outlaws May Have Slipped Through Lines of Posse; Tucsonans in Chase

The outlaws were reported shortly after 10 o'clock last night as in the vicinity of Pool, south and west of Reddington, riding the original horses taken from the murdered sheriff and his deputies. They were moving toward the Happy Valley country, where Sheriff Miles is camping with his posse.

Deputy Sheriffs Tom Burts, Cummings, Harrington and Tom Wills, with his cowboys, will start after them at daybreak from Fuller Pass. Harry Wheeler and his posse will close in from the direction of Benson.

With four thousand dollars offered for the capture of the murderers of Sheriff McBride and his deputies of Graham county, all of the country along the San Pedro valley has been effectually raised against the trio, and men were pouring into Tucson and out again all day yesterday on the man hunt.

Early yesterday Governor Hunt by proclamation authorized a reward of $1,000 for each man captured. Graham county supervisors offered a reward of $1,000 for the men, dead or alive, with one-third of the amount for one man captured or killed, two-thirds of the amount for two men and the full amount for the three men.

It was generally conceded that the men will not be taken alive, but it would be illegal for the state to advertise a reward for the bodies of the men if dead.

Reinforecemtns [sic] From Gila

Men from Gila county and Hayden arrived yesterday to reinforce Sheriff Miles and left in automobiles for the scene around Reddington.

They had hardly pulled out of the city before a report was received by Chief Deputy Marshal Willetts at Tucson declaring that the men had been detected in the vicinity of San Simon. Such a course would take them into the wildest part of the Arizona-New Mexico line, which they know well, having lived in the vicinity for some time, about a half a dozen years ago.

Relying upon the reports of Sunday and Monday, however, Sheriff Miles yesterday threw a guard of a dozen men in Fuller's Pass, between the Rincon and Catalina mountains, while he and a handful crossed the range and scouted through to head off the outlaws in case they gained Happy valley, between the two ranges.

Harry Wheeler on Trail

The last report last night was that Sheriff Harry Wheeler was trailing up by way of Benson, examining the country as he came, hoping to get the outlaws between his force and that of Miles.

If the report from San Simon proves to be true, however, the outlaws have slipped through the lines and are well on their way into the depths of the southwestern corner of New Mexico.

The report from San Simon related that the tracks of the three men had been found on an old, unfrequented trail about one mile from San Simon, going eastward. Two were the trails of horses and the third that of a mule. They were found by an old ranger, it was said. The tracks were in the trail through the San Simon and Styne's Pass and were headed for an old ranch, once owned by the Powers, who lived there about five years ago. The report was sent by A. W. Forbes.

Tucsonans Take Trail

The county court house here was virtually emptied of officials who could shoot, yesterday afternoon.

Bill Leahey of the county treasurer's office, L. E. Smith, county assessor, and Harry Batterton, deputy assessor, made up a party, headed by Louis Ezekials, for Tom Nelson's ranch. Sheriff Miles took Police Chief Bailey, Deputy Sheriff Archer and Cattle Inspector Kinney in an automobile for the Happy valley, while Deputy Spears and Tom Burts went in another machine into the Rincon mountains. H.E. Farr of the assessor's office, whose wife is a cousin of the murdered sheriff, McBride, of Graham county, left for Fort Lowell to join members of the Fort Lowell home guard, expecting to hit into the mountains on horseback.

During the day the Gila county deputies arrived and said the reports this morning were that Sheriff McBride's horse, ridden by one of the outlaws, had been traced to south of Reddington, which would seem to confirm the story of the appearance of the outlaws near San Simon. The Gila county deputies were led by Deputy Sheriff Rinehart. He left the city for Agua Calientes to reinforce the trap laid about Fuller's Pass. According to Rinehart, the outlaws had cut across country, severing barbed wire en route.

The inquest into the death of the slain officers was held yesterday at Safford, with U.S. Deputy Marshal Haynes, the only survivor of the battle, as witness.

MANY REPORTS REACH GLOBE

Globe, Feb. 12-- The three outlaws who slew three Graham county officers Sunday morning in the foothills of the Graham mountains were still at liberty late tonight. They were believed to be somewhere in the vicinity of San Simon and Former Sheriff Frank Haynes, United States deputy marshal, was heading a posse that left from Safford in their pursuit. Sheriff Harry Wheeler of Cochise county, who was at Benson, telephoned to Graham county's seat of government, Safford, that the posses under his direction were "up in the air." The capture of the fugitives at once seemed improbable.

Deputy United States Marshal Haynes said over the telephone tonight that a multitude of reports had been received as to the whereabouts of the fugitives but the one that they were near San Simon was most generally believed. He is now heading a posse that is trailing the men supposed to be the murderers of Sheriff McBride and Deputies Mart Kempton and Kane Wootan.

Sheriff's officers in this district are holding themselves in readiness for action in the event that the fugitives come within their range. Thus far their services have not been needed. There is a particular anxiety on the part of local officials to aid the Graham county officers to avenge the death of Sheriff McBride as it was he who sent a carload of deputies to Globe on July 4 when riots threatened the peace of this community.

Henry Allen, a youth living near the Powers', is now in Safford. He reports that the fugitives stopped at his ranch and told him of the killing. Apparently they did not know that Haynes was with the officers which explains the fact that he escaped with his life. The United States marshal was with Sheriff McBride when the attack was made. Haynes and McBride conferred and it was agreed that the federal officer should circle around a ridge and make a counter attack in case of trouble. Before he could reach the brow of the ridge, however, three officers had been slain and his only hope of capturing the men was by gaining reinforcements.

In the meantime the outlaws, believing they had killed the entire party of officers, mounted the slain men's horses and fled. When they reached the Allen place they told Henry that each of them had "got one officer." This bore out the belief that they did not know of the presence of Marshal Haynes.

Tucson Citizen, February 13, 1918, pp. 1 and 8:

Headline: OUTLAWS HEADED FOR TUCSON

Subhead: TRAP SET FOR POWERS GANG IN SOUTHERN MOUNTAINS

Subhead: Sheriff Miles Withdraws Forces from the North to Watch Southern Passes of Rincon and Catalina Mountains; Slayers Are Believed to Have Crossed the San Pedro River and Are Heading for Mexican Line

Convinced from the direction of tracks near Redington [sic], that the Powers-Sission [sic] outlaws are heading for the Rincon gap, the sheriff's forces are making a "squeeze play" from the north and south sides of the divide Tuesday in the hope of catching the murderers in between.

The latest information concerning the movements of the outlaws was brought to Tucson Tuesday after noon by a Gila county posse led by Deputy Sheriff Reinhart [sic]. They said that tracks of Sheriff McBride's mule ridden by one of the outlaws, had been found south of Redington [sic].

The tracks showed that the animal had cast three shoes. It is believed that the mule and horses have played out and that the outlaws will make an attempt to steal fresh mounts. Reinhart had three men with him. After dining, they left for Agua Caliente to reinforce the Pima posse in the Rincon pass.

Country Covered With Brush

The country in the Rincon pass is said to be covered with thickets of underbrush to such an extent that a rider cannot see more than 15 feet ahead of him in many places.

There are now three Pima posses in the field. Deputy Sheriff Burts is leading men on horseback from Agua Caliente. Deputy Sheriff Ezekials, L. E. Smith, H. R. Batterton, and others have gone to Tom Mills' ranch. Sheriff Miles is patrolling Happy Valley. Chief of Police Bailey, Deputy Sheriff Archer and Cattle Inspector McKinney are with the sheriff.

A sister of Mr. Wootan by the name of Mrs. Hattie Francis, who lives near Fort Lowell, and her husband, who is employed by the Midvale Farms Co., are planning to leave for Safford to attend the funeral.

The Gila posse stated, that the outlaws had cut barbed wire fences in two places.

The United States marshals office received a report late this afternoon that tracks thought to have been made by the bandits' horses and mule had been seen near San Simon, which is near the New Mexican line. If this is true, it would dispose of the theory that the men are headed south through the Rincons and Catalinas. It is known that the Powers formerly lived on a ranch east of San Simon and they may be headed in that direction.

Acting on information that the Powers gang of murderers have crossed the San Pedro river and are heading for passes in the Rincon mountains, Sheriff Miles organized civilian posses in Tucson Tuesday to assist in watching the trails in this portion of the country. The probable scene of the expected battle draws closer to Tucson.

The passes which are regarded as most strategic are the old road across the saddle of the range between the Catalina and Rincon mountains, issuing near Agua Caliente, the Rincon canyon issuing at Tom Mills' ranch and Happy Valley on the east side of the Rincon divide, reached by way of the Benson road.

The San Pedro valley being now well guarded by sheriffs' forces from the northern counties, Sheriff Miles withdrew his men from the Redington [sic] district Monday night, after 24 hours in the field, in order to watch his own territory on the southern slope of the Catalinas and the western slope of the Rincons.

Hard to Find Men

The sheriff was having some difficulty Tuesday in finding men who could spare time for picketing that might last for several days. Among the first to volunteer were J. C. Daly captain of the Fort Lowell home guards, L. E. Smith, secretary of the Tucson Rifle Club and county assessor, and Harry R. Batterton, his deputy. D. M. Penny, the attorney, offered his automobile.

The inquest into the death of the three victims of the outlaws, Sheriff McBride, and his two deputies, Mark [sic] Kempton and T. Kane Wootan, and Jeff Powers, father of the Powers boys, was in progress at Safford Tuesday. U. S. Deputy Marshal Haynes, the only one of the four officers to come out of the fight alive is there, being the chief witness.

Jeff Powers, who was shot near the heart, died at the scene of the fight, a few hours later. The bodies were taken to Safford by horseback.

Tracks in River

Tracks of the fugitives have been discovered near Redington [sic] where they crossed the river. From the direction taken it is deduced that they are heading for the southern ranges, the Catalinas or Rincons. Reports that the Powers boys and Sisson were seen at Mammoth are without foundation, so far as known. It is believed by the officers unlikely that they would go in that direction.

County Attorney Chambers of Graham county, told the Citizen over the telephone Tuesday morning of a report at Safford that the killers had been surrounded in the northwestern corner of Cochise county. The man hunt is taking place in the corners of four counties, Pima and Graham, which overlap by one township, and Pinal and Cochise which are separated by that distance. This region is in the San Pedro valley, isolated, and inhabited only by small ranchers, mostly Mexicans.

Mormons Up In Arms

Forces of Mormon settlers from Graham county, aggregating over 150 men are in pursuit of the outlaws, spurred on by the fact that two of the slain officers were of their faith.

It was learned at Tucson Tuesday that Sisson frequently came to the Bayles commissary at Redington [sic] to buy supplies, although the Powers boys were not often there. They preferred to use the Redington [sic] post office although Klondyke was nearer.

In a letter mailed from Redington [sic] on Feb. 1, T.J. Powers asked quotations from the Smith Sporting Goods company on two calibres of rifle catridges [sic]. The Powers had recently sought to get supplies of food from Redington [sic].

Wootman's [sic] Relatives Here

William Wootan, father of the slain officer and Bras Wootan, his brother called at Sheriff Miles' office Monday afternoon. They were on their way by automobile from their home on Freeman's ranch, near Florence, to Safford.

Deming Isaacson, owner of the Hot Springs ranch, mentioned in the dispatch from Safford, was in Tucson Monday, a guest at the house of Byrd Brooks and was endeavoring to get in telephonic communication with his place.

Story of the Fight

An authentic story of the encounter, telegraphed to The Citizen by the Graham county guardian [sic] of Safford, is as follows:

Sheriff R. F. McBride and deputies, Mark [sic] Kempton and T. Kane Wootan were killed Sunday morning about 6:30 o'clock in a battle with Tom Powers, John Powers, slackers, and Tom Sissons [sic], horsethief at the home of the Powers boys in Rattlesnake canyon, Galluro [sic] mountains.

Deputy United States Marshal Frank Haynes of Globe, Sheriff McBride and deputies Kempton and Wootan left Safford Saturday afternoon at 4:00 o'clock for the Galluro [sic] mountains by way of Klondyke to get Tom Powers and John Powers. They reached the house near the mine of John [sic] Powers, father of the Powers boys, about daybreak Sunday morning and surrounded the house. Old man Powers came out of the house with a gun, and was ordered to hold up his hands, as one of his boys opened the door and started firing at the officers. Old man Powers dropped, shot through the right shoulder. About 25 shots were fired by the officers.

McBride was shot by Tom Powers and Kane Wootan by John Powers. Kempton came around the house, kicked in the door and was shot by Tom Sisson, the horse thief. Sisson was sentenced to the penitentiary 5 years ago and was paroled by Governor Hunt. He lived with the Powers.

Hayes [sic] Was Unhurt.

Marshal Haynes escaped unhurt and came back to Klondyke for help. A posse from Klondyke started Sunday afternoon for the Powers camp to bring back the bodies. Haynes arrived at Safford at 4:00 o'clock Sunday with the news of the killing.

The murderers took the officers horses and ammunition and started for the border to go to Mexico. They stopped at Hot Springs, one mile from the Powers camp and told a man named Allen they had killed the officers, and that their father was shot and for him to go to the Powers home and take care of the mine.

Allen and a man named Murdock went to the house and found the old man. They took him into the tunnel of the mine and placed him on a cot. Allen then came to Safford, reaching here about 4:00 o'clock Sunday afternoon. Posses left Safford, Thatcher, Pima, Fairview, and Fort Thomas Sunday night heavily armed for the Galluro [sic] mountains to get the slackers and Sisson. A report Monday from Redington [sic] in the San Pedro valley states that the Powers and

Sisson reached there Sunday night.

The Citizen is in receipt of a letter from Ben T. Power of Winkelman, Ariz., a brother of "Maricopa Slim" Power, stating that John and Tom Powers are not members of his family. The name is spelled differently, the outlaws having an "s".

Arizona Daily Star, February 14, 1918, pp. 1-2:

Headline: SHERIFF MILES DRIVES SLAYERS OF M'BRIDE INTO STORNGHOLD [sic] OF COCHISE; HOLDS THEM AT BAY

Subhead: Tucson Sheriff, Exhausted, Had Quarry Bagged Last Night in Lair of Indian Chief, and Was Awaiting Reinforcements; Four Posses on Way From Bisbee: U.S. Cavalry Guards Border to Prevent Possible Escape

Bisbee, Ariz., Feb. 13. -- Entirely played out and awaiting reinforcements, Sheriff Rye Mile [sic] of Pima county, drove Tom and John Powers and Tom Sisson into Cochise Stronghold, a formidable natural barrier located about 10 miles west of Pearce. Four posses are being sent out of Bisbee to guard the southern edge of the stronghold and the sheriff's office is sending out men to take care of the western side of the mountains. From Johnson, Gleeson, Pearce and Willcox posses are also in action.

Sheriff Miles picked up the trail of the murderers late this afternoon and followed it across the Southern Pacific tracks between Johnson and Cochise. He was but a short time behind the men when they went into the mountains.

Chief Deputy Sheriff Guy Welch of Tombstone will go to Gleeson, near Cochise Stronghold, after midnight tonight, and take charge of the posses in that neighborhood. He will split up the organizations and station the men along the west, east, and southern side of the Dragoon mountains, in which the stronghold is located. With Sheriff Rye Miles of Pima county, and officers from Johnson, Pearce, Cochise and Willcox on the northern side of the mountains, hope is expressed that the murderers will be either apprehended or killed.

Cochise Stronghold, where the three murderers of the Graham officers are said to have taken refuge, is one of the great natural forts in the southwest.

It was made famous and named after the Apache chief, Cochise, who terrorized southeastern Arizona in the 70's. It was to this stronghold that Cochise, in July, 1871, drove a herd of cattle, stolen near Fort Bowie. Capt. Jerry Russell and his troops of the Third cavalry were ambushed by Cochise when the army officer attempted to get into the barrier.

U. S. CAVALRY IN PURSUIT

DOUGLAS, Feb. 13.--Colonel George H. Morgan, commander of the Arizona military district, tonight dispatched two troops of cavalry to patrol the international boundary east of Douglas to prevent Tom and John Powers and Tom Sisson, Graham county slayers of Sheriff R. F. McBride and two deputies last Sunday morning, from escaping into Mexico. These troops have orders to leave the border patrol if it is thought by so doing they can aid in the capture of the men. Colonel Morgan said tonight the international line would be carefully guarded to keep the fugitives from crossing.

Whether the Powers-Sisson outlaws are making their way back to the scene of the murder of Sheriff McBride and his deputies, or whether they have broken through the cordon of manhunters bent upon their capture, will become evident this afternoon when Sheriff Miles with a posse, trailing through the broken country east of the San Pedro river, northward from Benson, reaches the Powers ranch.

Discarded Horses Found

The sorrel mule and sorrel horse belonging to the murdered sheriff and his deputies were found yesterday afternoon on the Bar X ranch, about 20 miles northeast of Reddington, and at a point east of Rosfield's canyon, 25 miles from the scene of the crime.

Rosfield's canyon is the only pass into the Powers ranch through the Guluri [sic] mountains. It was down this canyon that the fugitives fled from the ranch after the murder and made their way around Reddington. Whether they released the sorrels on that trip, or when they were starting back to the ranch, will be demonstrated when Miles and his posse reach the vicinity of the ranch.

If they have not returned, it was conjectured yesterday, the release of the animals was a ruse to mislead posses while the outlaws fled eastward toward the border.

It is known and they are probably aware, that there is a veritable nest of slackers settled in the isolated corner of southeastern Arizona and southwestern New Mexico, hiding in the national forest, ready to cross the line on the approach of officers.

Among these slackers the outlaws would naturally find succor. Nothing could get them out of there excepting a company of soldiers with a field piece. All of the slackers are said to be well armed and ready to fight capture. Aliens of all breeds are among them.

Posses of deputy sheriffs or ranchers are now stationed in every pass through the mountains and on the high peaks men have been placed by Sheriff Miles. These lookouts are armed with field glasses. By day they sweep the trails and the mountain sides and by night they lie in the brush without fires alert to every sound, for it is expected that the outlaws, who have never been seen, are traveling by night

Bloodhounds on Trail

Reports from Tom Burts to the sheriff's office yesterday afternoon were that Sheriff Miles with his posse and with the county bloodhounds had swung around in an arch from Cary's ranch across the San Pedro and headed northwest along the San Pedro valley toward Reddington and Rosfield's canyon.

To the west of Reddington he has a posse posted at Agua Caliente and another at Fuller's Pass leading from the Happy valley to the Catalinas as well, as in the second pass from the Happy valley which opens into Cary's ranch. Some of Sheriff Wheeler's men are at Benson for the purpose of heading off the southward flight unless the outlaws bear far to the east out of reach.

Reports Conflicting

Reports yesterday were conflicting. It was said that a Pinal county posse was located at Pool, south west of Reddington, and had joined a posse under Sheriff Wheeler of Cochise, and that the outlaws were in the Rincon mountains, west of the San Pedro and south of Reddington.

County Ranger Burts and his party spent Tuesday night in Fuller's Pass, south of the Rincon, without detecting anything unusual.

It was also reported that Frank Wootan, a brother of Kane Wootan, one of the murdered deputies, had trailed the outlaws to within a mile of the store at Reddington. Here, it was reported, the outlaws doubled back, cutting barbed wire in four places to avoid ranch houses. They were then said to have gone upon the mesa and returned to the San Pedro river afterward.

Boys Threatened Uncle

Wylie Morgan, an uncle of the Powers boys, who was in Tucson yesterday, declared that Tom Sissons [sic] was responsible for the boys resisting the draft. Sissons, he said, was a pro-German. The older Powers boy had attempted to pass as over 31 years old. Morgan said he had warned McBride that the Powers boys would kill him if he attempted to arrest them. The boys sent word to Morgan to keep his mouth shut or he would be killed.

Arizona Daily Star, February 15, 1918, pp. 1-2:

Headline: POSSE NOW 12 HOURS BEHIND POWERS TRIO
Subhead: Slayers of Sheriff McBride in Chiricahua Mountains, Safely Hidden For Present, But With 200 Pursuers Scouring Hills

Subhead: FUGITIVES DOUBLE BACK OVER TRAIL

Subhead: Posses Headed by Sheriffs Miles and Wheeler Still in Lead of Manhunters; Mexican Troops Are Lending Aid at Border

(Special to The Star)

Bowie, Ariz., Feb. 14-- The Powers brothers and Tom Sisson, still together, were camped in Cochise stronghold Wednesday, crossed the Sulphur Springs valley going east Wednesday night, and camped in Busenback pasture, one mile from Dos Cabezas, Thursday. Sheriff Miles with over 100 men, was guarding the pasture at sundown today, with hundreds of possemen around Bowie and many machine loads are coming. The outlaws seem to be headed towards Bowie to cross the San Simon and enter New Mexico, but with little chance to break through the heavy guard line.

They are choosing the roughest canyons for day camps, moving only at night. The native trailers are doing good work and keeping them at close range. If the posses can hold them in the Dos Cabezas range tonight, there is a fair chance of their capture tomorrow, although the scene is in the roughest part of Cochise county, and it is feared some of the posse will be killed. There is only one report of the outlaws having secured food and that was near Pearce Wednesday night from a lone woman. They secured only bread, their horses being unfed and having had no water. They can't hold out long unless fresh horses are secured.

(By the Associated Press)

Douglas, Ariz. Feb. 14-- Twelve hours ahead of their pursuers, Tom and John Powers and Tom Sissons [sic], alleged slayers of Sheriff R. F. McBride and deputies Kempton and Wootan of Graham county last Sunday, tonight were swallowed up in the Chiricahua mountains of eastern Arizona, for the time being safe, while 200 civil officers, cowboys and ranchers and two troops of the First cavalry from Douglas were scouring the southeastern corner of the state.

FUGITIVES DOUBLE BACK

Doubling back over territory previously covered, the fugitives rode all last night from the Cochise stronghold in the Dragoon mountains to the Chiricahua mountains, where Sheriff Harry C. Wheeler of Cochise county and Sheriff Rye Miles of Pima county picked up the trail early today only to lose it. Most of the day was spent in recovering the trail, and early tonight the two posses, headed by Sheriffs Wheeler and Miles, were reported to be following the trio.

It was discovered that the fugitives pitched camp for breakfast near the Charles Busenback ranch in the Chiricahua foothills.

Request was made today by the sheriff's office at Tombstone for a military airplane, but it was stated that there was none nearer than Fort Sam Houston.

MEXICAN TROOPS AID

Lieut. Col. Augustine Camou, at Agua Prieta, Sonora, commander of the military forces of northeastern Sonora, has sent Mexican troops to patrol the international line on the Mexican side, with instructions to capture and turn over to the civil authorities of Arizona the three men if they cross into Mexico. Mexican troops are on patrol duty from Naco on the west to the intersection of the New Mexico state line with Mexico on the east.

Sheriffs of southwestern New Mexico counties have been requested to establish patrols and the military authorities at Hachita, N. M., have been notified.

Three Passes Guarded

Sheriff Henry Hall of Pinal and his deputy, Bob Frazier, accompanied by former Sheriff Jeff Adams of Maricopa, reached Tucson about 8:30 last night, and left in an automobile for Tombstone in an effort to head off the escape of the outlaws from the Dos Cabezas country. They planned to report on arriving at Tombstone to the sheriff's office at Tucson and unless the chase had developed important angles they would head out for Rodeo, N.M., and guard the Dos Cabezas to the west of that point as to prevent the outlaws from entering the Chiricahua national forest.

Sheriff Miles, with his posse, and Sheriff Wheeler with his men, were reported at 9 o'clock last night as working south out of Bowie with more than 100 hundred [sic] men under their command, toward Dos Cabezas and guarding the foothills which stretch to the south. Between the foothills and the Chiricahua national forest is a long valley with a pass to the south, one to the east, and one to the north. Miles is guarding the pass to the north, the pass to the south is believed to be guarded by military patrols from Nogales and the easter npass [sic] is the objective of Sheriff Hall's party. While these outlets are called passes they are really wide sweeps of level land containing many gulches and arroyas [sic].

Word that Sheriffs Wheeler and Miles had gone south to the Dos Cabezas peaks from Bowie was received at Sheriff Miles office late last night. It indicated that Sheriff Miles has grasped the value of the high land as points of observation of the level land on all sides. From the high points his men with field glasses can sweep the country for the fugitives.

Find Camp Fire

That Sheriff Miles and Wheeler are close to the trail of the outlaws was indicated by a report tonight from Willcox that when Charles Busenback discovered his fences cut this morning, he also saw traces of a camp fire where the outlaws had cooked breakfast.

With reports that the Powers outlaws had been located near Dos Cabezas yesterday morning, and that cowboys and others not in regularly organized bands had crowded into the zone of the man hunt, apprehension grew yesterday that accidental shooting is liable to occur with the result that some of the man hunters will be brought down by high power rifles in mistake for the outlaws.

Beyond the report that the outlaws had been reported from the vicinity of Dos Cabezas, no word was received during the day yesterday from the scene of the man hunt.

The report originated with Charles Busenback, who telephoned from the Adams ranch to the deputy sheriff at Benson. Busenback said he had found his barbed wire fence cut and had trailed the outlaws into the foothills of the Dos Cabezas mountains. He said the men were going east, apparently to strike the border east of Douglas.

U.S. Reward $800

The federal government has offered a reward of $800 for information leading to the arrest of the outlaws or of $200 for any information leading to the arrest of any one of them. This yesterday gave a total of $4800 in rewards to inspire the chase, which is likely to lead a large number of men to the field and may lead to the shooting of some of these volunteer workers by possemen.

The country into which the men have fled is familiar ground to Sheriff Miles, who as manager and ranger of some of the San Pedro ranches has rounded up cattle from all the mountains and canyons during a number of years.

That he has plenty of assistance was indicated by a report from Bowie yesterday that armed men were crowding into the country even youth, each armed with a rifle and a lot of ammunition.

Tucson Citizen, February 15, 1918, p. 3:

AN ARIZONA MELODRAMA

The Powers-Sisson gang's defiance of the draft is one of the infinitesimal exceptions which demonstrate upon reflection the creditable success which the United States, a self governing people, have made of the democratic method of raising an army. A solitary case of open and armed opposition proves by the furore [sic] which it has excited the state-wide peaceable acceptance in Arizona of the military obligation.

All information obtainable about the Powers-Sisson gang indicates that they were outlaws in spirit and half-way outlaws in fact outside of the consideration of military draft law. Their defiance is therefore not that of a particular law, but rather of the will of the law.

Jeff Powers, father of the boys, The Citizen has information, had been engaged in litigation for years and had been so soured by his defeats that he counseled his sons to regard the government as a government of the rich for the rich and that justice was unobtainable for such as them. It is said that for years he had planned this rebellion in case the law should come for him or any of his sons with a warrant.

The mysterious death of Olla [sic] Powers, the 20-year-old daughter, who was forced to live with these hard men in a remote mountain camp 30 miles from the nearest settlement, and the knowledge that her father had forced her to grow up illiterate and terrorized in disregard of the customs of civilization, had called Sheriff McBride to investigate the circumstances. It is not improbable that fear of disclosures in this respect, or more resentment of the law's inquisitiveness, reinforced the gang's hostility and determination not to recognize the law. Many aspects of the case show that the Powers and Sisson were not mere conscientious objectors to the draft, modeled from the same intractable spirit as those mountaineers who have from time immemorial insisted upon their right to distill liquor from their own corn and apples without paying the government its tax, but that the draft simply furnished the first occasion for a clash with the law by men who were intolerant of any interference with their affairs.

By laying down their lives in the pursuance of duty, Sheriff McBride and his deputies bore out the best traditions of peace officers in Arizona. It is reminiscent of the sacrifice of W. W. Lowther, a peace officer of Bisbee, who advanced to arrest James Daly in 1890, although warned by Daly that he would shoot. He had been warned of Daly's dangerous character, but replied that he must do his duty. Daly shot him and escaped. McBride knew of the threats that the Powers boys had made and it is unfortunate that he did not approach their cabin more warily.

Should the federal authorities succeed in locating an aeroplane which can be obtained for the man hunt, it will bring into the same chase one of the oldest and the most novel means of pursuing criminals. Sheriff Miles is using three bloodhounds of the same familiar black and reddish coloring as those which pursued Eliza to the edge of the ice. The value of an aeroplane in such a hunt is speculative, especially if the outlaws travel only at night and hide in canyons during the day, but it would certainly add romance to the story. In the case of fugitives fleeing in an automobile over open desert roads, an aeroplane would unquestionably be effective in locating them. It is even easily conceivable that it might attack the fugitives with a machine gun should they refuse to halt.

Assiduous as have been all sheriffs of southern Arizona in taking and keeping the field in pursuit of the outlaws, it looks as if swifter action, better co-operation and a more strategic direction of the campaign could be secured if there were a force of state rangers, with a commander authorized to direct such campaigns by the civilian forces of the state. If the movements of the outlaws have been correctly reported they have slipped past several posses.

There is no greater amount of serious crime in Arizona proportionately to population than in metropolitan centers such as New York and Chicago, if as much, but the picturesque and difficult terrain of mountain ranges and forests, over which the hunt must be conducted, makes of it a much more primitive and absorbing story. The state cannot avoid the news advertising which such incidents entail, but it is to be doubted that it blackens the reputation of the state with enlightened people. A New York murder story is served with breakfast every morning by the New York papers.

Graham Guardian, February 15, 1918, pp. 1-2:

Headline: OFFICERS KILLED IN BATTLE WITH SLACKERS

Subhead: Sheriff McBride and Deputies Kempton and Wootan Slain by John and Thomas Power and Tom Sisson, at the Powers' Home in the Galiuro Mountains, Sunday Morning--Deputy U.S. Marshal Frank Haynes, Member of Party, Brings in News of the Killing.

Subhead: BODIES BROUGHT HERE MONDAY NTGHT

Subhead: Posses from Graham, Gila, Pima and Cochise Counties Are On Trail of Murderers, Who Are Now Reported 25 Miles South of Busenback's Ranch in the Foothills of the Chiricahua Mountains in Cochise County

The entire community was shocked at the news received here Sunday afternoon that Sheriff McBride, Chief Deputy Martin R. Kempton and Deputy Sheriff T. Kane Wootan had been killed in a battle with the Power boys, John, aged 28 years; Thomas, aged 25 years, and a paroled horsethief, Thomas Sisson, aged 55 years, which occurred at the home of Jeff G. Power, father of the two boys, near the old Bowman gold mine, in the Galiuro mountains, 28 miles southeast of Klondyke, shortly after 7:00 o'clock Sunday morning.

The first news of the killing was brought in here by Deputy U.S. Marshal Frank Haynes, of Globe who was the fourth member of the party which left here Saturday afternoon for the Powers' home to bring back John and Tom Power, who were wanted by the government on the charge of evading the selective draft.

According to the story told by Deputy Marshal Haynes when he arrived at the court house, he had come here from Globe on orders from U.S. Marshal Dillon to get the two slackers, John and Tom Power. He secured the services of T. Kane Wootan, a deputy sheriff to accompany him, and Sheriff McBride and Chief Deputy Kempton offered their services, the government to pay the expenses of the trip. Sheriff McBride wanted old man Power and Tom Sisson for the purpose of clearing up the mystery of Ola Power's death, aged 22 years, who died early in December under suspicious circumstances.

The four officers left here Saturday afternoon, about 3:00 o'clock, in Sheriff McBride's car for Klondyke. They arrived at Upchurch's place, Klondyke, some time after 6:00 o'clock p.m., where they secured three horses and a mule.

They left Upchurch's place after 7:00 o'clock, taking the trail for the home of Jeff Power in the Galiuro mountains.

On their way they stopped at Joe Bosco's house, a cattleman, but found no one at home. Next they came to the first house and then to the second house, both of which belonged to old man Power. One of these houses had been occupied by Power's daughter Ola, who died there last December.

The party continued on until, just after 7:00 Sunday morning, they arrived in the vicinity of the Power home, a log house. This house was built about 10 feet west of a creek, up on the embankment. It fronted the east.

The officers tied up their horses in a small canyon northwest of the house and then started for the house. Sheriff McBride stationed himself at the northeast corner of the house, Deputy Marshal Haynes going to the northwest corner of the house. At the northeast corner, about two feet from the house, was the remains of a fence, built of shakes, about five feet long. Sheriff McBride was between this fence and the house.

Deputies Kempton and Wootan evidently went around the western side of the house, the house on this side being close to a high hill over which was a trail leading into the new trail which met the new road going into Klondyke. The trail on this hill was higher than the house. The two officers stationed themselves at the southeast corner of the house.

On the east front of the house are two doors. On the southeast side a fireplace has been built and east of the fireplace is a window. There is a window on the northeast side, but no door.

About the time Deputies Kempton and Wootan had reached their stations, old man Power came out of the door nearest to them. Evidently, the men in the house had heard the officers when they went around the west side of the house, for when old man Power came out of his door, he was carrying a gun.

As he stepped out in the open, the officers called to him to throw up his hands. Placing his gun between his knees, he raised his hands and as he did this, the door behind him opened wide enough for a gun to be shoved through.

Something occurred right then, either the old man Power dropped his hands to seize his gun or the man behind the door began shooting, for the battle commenced. The man in the door, with the gun just far enough out to be turned, was firing in the direction where Kempton was stationed, and then turned the gun and fired at the place where Sheriff McBride was posted.

Sheriff McBride told Deputy Marshal Haynes to watch the window, and he went in close to the house to do so, when he noticed that the sheriff had fallen and his feet protruded past the fence.

Some twenty five shots were fired, then the shooting stopped and everything was quiet.

At this time, Haynes said he went up to the window to look in, but could see nothing. There was no noise in the house, everything was perfectly quiet. He then went to the place northwest of the house, where the horses were tied, got his horse and rode up the trail on the hill west of the house, stopped for several minutes but could see no one near the house, then saw a man east of the house lying on the ground, and thought it was Wootan, but on second glance saw it was not Wootan and might be old man Power. He heard no noise and believed the men in the house were dead. He did not see Kempton or Wootan and did not know whether they had been killed or wounded.

Seeing no one moving, Deputy Haynes then started for Klondyke about 10:30 o'clock, and told of the killing of Sheriff McBride and the people started to organize a posse to go to the Power house.

Deputy Haynes then started for Safford, arriving at the court house about 4:00 o'clock p.m., and told of the battle at Power's home and the killing of Sheriff McBride.

Some time after Deputy Haynes left the scene of the battle, John and Thomas Power and Tom Sisson came out of the house and carried old man Power across the creek to within 25 yards of the tunnel to the mine. Then they came back to the house and took the guns and ammunition off the dead officers. Then they went to the place where the officers' horses and the mule were tied and got the two horses and the mule.

They then rode over to the Murdocks' house, about a mile from the Power home, where they summoned the Murdocks, father and son, and a young man named Henry Allen, who had been working for the Murdock's building a fence at Hot Springs.

They told them that they had killed the three officers and had taken their horses, the mule, their guns and ammunition. They said they got all three officers and evidently did not know there were four officers in the party that came to their home to get them. They had not seen Haynes.

They also told of the killing of Wootan, by John Power, who shot him thru the window on the south side of the house, after Wootan had fired at him thru the window, the broken glass cutting his eye. Tom Power said he shot McBride and Tom Sisson had shot Kempton.

They told the Murdocks that their father had been wounded and for them to go over and take care of him. Then they rode off.

The Murdock's [sic] and Allen went over to the Power house, reaching there about 10:30 o'clock, and found Power lying about 50 yards east of the house, across the creek. He was unconscious. They carried him into the tunnel of the mine and placed him on the cot.

Allen then went over to the house and found the body of Sheriff

McBride lying near the northeast corner of the house, and then found the bodies of Deputies Kempton and Wootan lying at the southeast corner of the house.

Allen then rode to Klondyke and told the people there that Sheriff McBride and Deputies Kempton and Wootan had been killed.

At Klondyke, a posse was organized, consisting of Drew Wilson, John F. Greenwood, John Sanford, Bert Higgins, Elmer Gardenhire, Joe Bosco, Jeff Clayton, and a young man from Pima.

This posse was to go after the bodies of the dead officers and bring them in. The posse left Klondyke at 5:00 o'clock p.m. and reached the Power home about 7:00 o'clock Monday morning.

They learned from the Murdocks and a man named Edward Knothe that Jeff Power, the father of the Power boys, had died about 4:00 o'clock Sunday afternoon.

The bodies of the dead officers were found and preparations were made to bring them into Klondyke, which were completed in several hours. The posse then started back for Klondyke, arriving there about 7:00 o'clock p.m.

At Klondyke, the posse was met by Dr. Platt, W. V. Thorpe and others from Safford, and the bodies were transferred to cars and brought here about 11:30 o'clock Monday night, and placed in the justice of the peace's room, in the basement of the court house, where the examination of the wounds was made by Drs. Platt, Schenck and Stratton.

Sheriff McBride had been shot four times through the right leg, through the lower part of the body, through the upper part of the body and through the neck.

Deputy Kempton had been shot through the neck, the bullet severing the spinal cord.

Deputy Wootan had been shot through the back, the bullet fracturing the spinal column.

The wounds were all made by a large calibre soft nose bullet.

An inquest was held at the court house Tuesday afternoon and the jury brought in a verdict that Sheriff R. F. McBride, Chief Deputy Sheriff Martin R. Kempton and Deputy Sheriff T. Kane Wootan, had died from gun shot wounds inflicted at the hands of John Power, Tom Power and Tom Sisson.

Sheriff R. F. McBride was 42 years of age. He leaves a widow and seven children.

Chief Deputy Sheriff Martin R. Kempton was 40 years of age, and leaves a widow and seven children.

Deputy Sheriff T. Kane Wootan was 36 years of age, and leaves a widow and four children.

Arizona Daily Star, February 17, 1918, p. 4:

The Outlaws

The ghost of the capital punishment law in Arizona, voted out of existence several years ago, will not down. Arizona has been reminded with increasing frequency ever since the mistaken zeal of the people led them into abolishing that necessary device for protecting society, of the powerlessness of the state to deal with cold-blooded murder in a way that would be commensurate with such murder and in a way that would adequately protect society.

Unfortunately, proof of the unsoundness of the criminological policy pursued by the state has been supplied by the application of that policy. We have no figures to show how many pardoned or paroled prisoners from the state penitentiary have been later returned to the prison as murderers, but we can recall several off-hand.

The outlaw Tom Sisson was sentenced to the penitentiary several years ago as a horsethief, a crime which the pioneers of Arizona held to be one resorted to only by the most abandoned criminals and they punished it accordingly, summarily. It was not because these pioneers were lawless. Horse-stealing involves the practice of other forms of crime, from lying to murder.

On what grounds we do not know, but Sissons [sic] was paroled from the penitentiary by Governor Hunt. As a result, three officers of the law have been murdered and as many more may be murdered before the outlaw Sisson and his associates, said to be his dupes, are captured. They are prepared to kill as many of the posse of citizens as they can, and in order to capture them the officers must take their lives in their hands. Nothing but capital punishment could be commensurate punishment in a case like this.

Yet we would not place Sissons [sic] and the Powers boys in the same criminal category. The Powers boys had lived unto themselves; they have depended upon their wits for sustenance; in the satisfaction of their selfish wants they were independent. While indebted to the common country beyond the confines of their mountain range. It must have been easy for Sisson, a pro-German, to lead the Powers boys into believing that their country had no claim upon them and induce them to evade the draft. While one may pity the Powers boys, Sisson deserves neither pity nor mercy.

The Powers brothers and Sisson are outlaws and they are outside the pale of every law, for their crime was in denying and resisting the authority of government, not merely an infraction of draft regulations; and in denying this authority they implied repudiation of all law and all government when they murdered the agents of the government. The officers in charge of the hunt for the outlaws have a high duty to perform in protecting their prisoners, but the score would be evened in accordance with justice did the outlaws never come out of their hiding place.

Graham Guardian, March 1, 1918, p. 1:

Headline: SHELTER OUTLAWS

Subhead: Friends in Mountains Help Murderers to Escape from Officers

If Tom and John Powers and Tom Sisson, fugitives, wanted for the murder of Sheriff McBride and Deputies Kempton and Wootan, had not been given help by friends in the mountains and by men who gladly shelter outlaws and are strongly opposed to the draft law, they would be in custody today, says the Douglas International.

This is the opinion of Sheriff Harry Wheeler, who has been leading a posse of men in pursuit of the fugitives since the day of the murder. The sheriff was in Douglas Tuesday morning with his posse and explained why the posses of between 300 and 400 men, for the most part unorganized and scattered, and four troops of cavalry, have been unable to capture the trio.

It looks as if providence has favored the brothers and their companion from the start. Every time the posse would get close on the trail something unpreventable would happen to throw them off. Luck, it seems, has been with the fugitives all along.

It is proved that the murderers were guided through certain parts of the country, according to the sheriff. More than one man gave them provisions and sheltered them, it was found out.

More than once when posses visited ranch houses they were told that the fugitives had not been seen. More than once posses were sent in the opposite direction from the way the fugitives went. These delays were costly.

The cavalry returned to Douglas Tuesday night. Most of the possemen have abandoned the search. But Sheriff Wheeler and a crowd of loyal followers have not been disheartened. The sheriff declares he will continue the search for the fugitives and he believes they will be caught.

After a short stay in Douglas the sheriff and his men left for Tombstone. From there they will get more provisions, a camping outfit and make plans for an indefinite search.

Arizona Daily Star, March 9, 1918, pp. 1-2:

Headline: POWERS OUTLAW TRIO CAPTURED BY TROOPS NEAR HACHITA, N.M.

Subhead: Soldiers of Cavalry Regiment Take Tom Sissons [sic] and Tom and John Powers, Draft Evaders and Slayers of Sheriff McBride and His Deputies, Without the Firing of a Shot, After Starving the Outlaws Out; Capture Is Effected Twelve Miles South of Hachita When Soldiers Chase Outlaws Across Mexican Line

(By the Associated Press)

Douglas, March 8-- Tom and John Powers and Tom Sisson, who killed Sheriff R.F. McBride, Undersheriff M.R. Kempton and Deputy Sheriff D. W. Wooten [sic] of Graham county, February 10, were captured today by soldiers of a cavalry regiment twelve miles south of Hachita, and eight miles south of the international boundary, according to word received here tonight. The outlaws were taken to Hachita and are being guarded by the soldiers.

They surrendered without a fight, it was said.

The three men were taken into custody after the soldiers had followed them into Mexico. The soldiers telephoned to Hachita late this afternoon they had just captured the fugitives and were bringing them to the camp.

Soldiers of the cavalry regiment have been on the trail of the outlaws for several days, following abandonment of the search in southeastern Arizona ten days ago, and it was believed they starved them out. Not a shot was fired b yeither [sic] side.

Safford, March 8--News of the capture of the Powers brothers and Tom Sisson so excited the people of the Gila Valley that the local officers tonight refused to give out the date of their probable arrival in Safford. The officers at the sheriff's office confessed that they feared they would be unable to prevent a lynching if the public knew when to expect the men here.

MAY JAIL MEN HERE.

When the trail of the outlaws was picked up by the posses several weeks ago, it was arranged at a conference of sheriffs in the field that the only safe place to bring the men, if taken, was to Tucson and the Pima county jail.

This was to safeguard the prisoners against any attempted capture of the men by ranchers, who had declared the men would be shot on sight. It was thought that the Pima county jail would be the only safe place for them.

Preparation was made at the sheriff's office last night to receive the me nshould [sic] they be started in this direction.

WAS GREATEST MAN-HUNT IN SOUTHWEST'S HISTORY

Douglas, March 8.--The capture of the three outlaws brings to a close what officials have said was the greatest man-hunt ever staged in the southwest. At one time 1000 men, including eight troops of United States cavalry, were searching for the three slayers of the Graham county officers. The United States troops, military headquarters here explained, sought the three men as evaders of the selective draft and not as murderers.

Tucson Citizen, March 9, 1918, p. 1:

Hachita, N.M., March 9--Their feet wrapped in gunny sacks, footsore and discouraged to the point of returning to the American side of the border and surrendering Tom and John Powers and Tom Sissons were brought here on cavalry horses today and placed in the government guard house later being taken to Safford, Ariz., to answer charges of having murdered Sheriff H. F. McBride [sic] of Graham County and his two deputies. They were captured south of the American border. The men told Lieutenant Hays [sic], in command of the cavalry detachment, that they would never have surrendered alive to the Arizona state officers, but they would rather surrender than shoot a United States soldier.

According to the cavalrymen who brought the outlaws to the border, the younger of the Powers wanted to resist arrest, but was prevailed upon by his older brother and Sissons [sic] to give up.

The three men were heavily armed each having a high-powered rifle and there were also two pistols between the three of them with 200 rounds of cartridges in each of the men's belts.

Outlaws Resting Under Mesquite

The three outlaws were found sitting beside a clump of mesquite brushes [sic] resting. Their provisions had been exhausted and they were without water, having been unable to create any waterholes in the Mexican desert. They were making their way back toward the border, having decided to surrender rather than die of thirst in a country where they had been wandering for days, without finding water.

The prisoners were placed on three cavalry horses, the soldiers riding mounts behind three of their comrades. The little detachment with the prisoners reached the international line about sunset last night and reached here at 9 p.m.

Arizona Daily Star, March 10, 1918, p. 4:

Close the Gate

Unfortunately the state of Arizona and not the United States has jurisdiction over the case of the Powers-Sisson outlaws. We say "unfortunately" because the teeth of the state law against murder have been drawn, and the worst that awaits these slayers of good men is repose and the "hard labor" of knitting socks under the tutelage of minions of the "honor" system.

The officers who were slain by these outlaws were assisting in the enforcement of the laws of the United States. Voluntarily they were rendering assistance to a deputy United States marshal, himself a representative of the United States department of justice. The outlaws were captured by United States soldiers, pursuing them into a foreign country. But they must be turned over to the state of Arizona because the crime was committed in territory over which the state courts have jurisdiction. Had it been committed on an Indian reservation, the federal courts would have had jurisdiction, and it would be possible to inflict punishment commensurate with the crime which they committed.

Whether the three outlaws will ever be tried no one can say. It may be that once more citizens will take the case in their hands and make the punishment fit the crime. According to advices from Safford, the peaceable, law-abiding citizens of that section, where the victims of the slayers were known and where their helpless dependents live, there is a determination that justice shall be done.

It would not be the first time that it has happened since Arizona substituted sentiment for justice under the leadership of the head of the theosophical cult and political posers.

There are features of the Powers-Sissons [sic] case which emphasize the inadequacy of our state law for the punishment of murder. These men were outlaws, they had repudiated the draft law--which is a statement of the theory of democracy. Are they, then, advocates of autocracy, that they defy the authority of a democracy? No, they belong to the other extreme, they are anarchists. Any law to which they object they would repudiate. So they are outlaws, outside the pale. In defying the authority of government, they took the lives of three representatives of the government.

The scene of the crime also emphasizes its outlawry. There is no more peaceable, law-abiding section of the state than the Gila valley, inhabited, developed and made prosperous largely through the thrift of the Mormon settlers. They have large families, they endow their children with a sense of responsibility to the state. They respect authority. Is it any wonder that they have been so greatly affected by this awful crime against God and country?

Society's protection of itself against crimes of this kind in Arizona is incomplete. The sentimentalists have removed a vital postern gate by abolishing capital punishment and providing, instead, that murderers shall be inducted into a city of refuge, where they may have the comforts that the children and wives of their victims are denied; and the coddling of the patrons who believe them sinned against more than sinning.

How many more times must justice be outraged and authority be brought into contempt by the unrestrained passions of strong men who substitute their collective will for the written will of the legislature?

Graham Guardian, May 17, 1918, p. 1:

Headline: GUILTY OF MURDER IN FIRST DEGREE

Subhead: Quick Verdict of Jury in the Powers-Sisson Case at Clifton

Subhead: JURY OUT ONLY 25 MINUTES

Subhead: John and Tom Power and Tom Sisson Will Get Life Imprisonment

The trial of John and Tom Power and Tom Sisson, charged with the murder of Sheriff R. F. McBride, and his deputies, Martin R. Kempton and Kane Wootan, on Sunday, February 10th, at the home of the Power boys in the Galiuro mountains, began Monday, at Clifton, in the Superior Court of Greenlee county, Judge Frank Laine, presiding.

A jury was secured by Monday night and the testimony of witnesses for the prosecution began Tuesday morning, closing at 2:00 p.m., and were followed by the witnesses for the defense.

All the testimony in the case was in at 2:00 o'clock yesterday afternoon. County Attorney Chambers gave the opening address before the jury, closing at 3:00 o'clock, and was followed by Attorney Fielder for the defense.

Attorney Fielder had not finished his address when court adjourned at 5:00 o'clock, and continued his argument to the jury when the court convened this morning, finishing at 11:00 o'clock.

Attorney Johnson, for the prosecution, made the closing address.

Court adjourned at noon for lunch and convened again at 1:30 p.m., when Judge Laine delivered his charge to the jury.

The jury was given the case at 2:55 o'clock and returned at 3:20 with a verdict of guilty of murder in the first degree for all three defendants.

The attorneys for the prosecution are County Attorney W. R. Chambers, A. R. Lynch, of Clifton, and Norman Johnson, of Globe. The attorney for the defense is James Fielder, of Silver City, N.M.

Unfortunately, we were not given permission to publish entire later articles from the *Arizona Republic*, the *Arizona Daily Star*, and the *Eastern Arizona Courier*. For those interested in reading them, we have included the pertinent information as well as a short description of the respective contents as follows.

Arizona Republic, December 29, 1939, pp. 1 and 7:

Headline: Wartime Slayers Escape

An article about how the Power brothers and another prisoner, William Faltin, escaped from the state prison, with speculation about where they might have gone and what made them do it.

Arizona Republic, April 17, 1940, p. 1:

Report about the surrender of Tom and John Power to officials after they crossed the Rio Grande as they returned from Mexico.

Arizona Daily Star, April 28, 1960, Section B, p. 1:

Superhead: Long-Awaited Day Arrives

By Bob Thomas, Star Staff Correspondent

Description of the day John and Tom Power left the Arizona State Prison after they were paroled, with quotes from the brothers, the warden, and a good friend of the Power brothers. Information about the shooting and the parole hearing.

Arizona Republic, January 26, 1969, Section C, pp. 1-2:

Headline: Pardons end brothers' 50-year wait

By Bob Thomas, Southern Arizona Bureau

Interview with John and Tom Power after they were pardoned by Governor Williams in 1969. Information about the shootout, the man hunt, the trial, the parole hearings, and the draft dodging question.

Eastern Arizona Courier, September 16, 1970, pp. 1 and 11:

Headline: Shoot-out figure Tom Power dies

Touching description of Tom Power's funeral and the people who took part.

APPENDIX II

LEGEND TEXTS

MORMON TEXTS

Informant Mo1 (Reconstructed Text)

Nobody'll ever convince me that them Powers boys did anything but murder them men. They knew they was lookin' for them, and they laid for them. They never was nothin' but trash anyway, and them men ..... them lawmen was all respectable people. They was cowards or they'da gone to fight for their country. If they hadn'ta had the drop on McBride and the rest of the posse, they'da come outa there meek as lambs.

Informant Mo2 (Reconstructed Text)

Well, I'll tell you what I know about it or rather what I've heard about it, but it may get me in trouble. The Powers boys was draft dodgers; they wouldn't come in and register. That made people mad, and then their sister's body was brought down to Pima with her neck broken, and that didn't sit any too well. So at any rate, Sheriff McBride and two of his deputies, Kane Wootan and Mark Kempton, and a federal man from Globe, name of Haynes, they went up there to bring the boys out. I've heard it told around that Kane Wootan said that he'd rather bring them out dead than alive.

Well, anyway, they drove on out there to the Upchurch ranch, and they ate dinner there and got horses to ride up the rest of the way. Now, I've heard it said that Mrs. Upchurch claimed they was drunk, but I don't believe that. They were all good members of the Church, and there wasn't a one of them that drank, so that couldn't be. But they did borrow a rifle from Mr. Upchurch because the federal man didn't bring one, and I think that's where the story lays.

Well, anyway, they rode on up into that Rattlesnake country, and they got to the Powers place early in the morning, just before day. Somehow the old man knew there was somebody out there, and he picked up a rifle and stepped out on the porch. The sheriff told him to put his hands up. Now, some say he did and some say he didn't, but I believe he did, and I'll tell you why in a minute. Well, anyway, right after he was told to put up his hands, the old man was shot and fell on the porch. Well, the boys and Tom Sisson took to firing from the cabin, and it wasn't long before McBride and Wootan and Kempton was dead. The government man sneaked on down the wash and got a horse and rode on outa there. When he got down to the Aravaipa, he was so scared he was out of his mind, couldn't tell them what had happened up there.

Well, the Powers got the Murdocks to come over and take care of their father, and they and Sisson rode on out of there. But I'll tell you what I think happened, and I'll tell you why. Jay Murdock says that when the old man died, they examined the wound on his chest, and the boys had told him that he'd been shot while he had his hands up. And Jay, knowin' that the old man wasn't one to be caught with his pants down like that, wondered about it. So he took a little stick, and he tried to push it in the wound, and it wouldn't go. So he fooled around and tried different things, and the only way it would go in was to raise the arms way above the head. So he must a been shot with his hands up. Now them men was good men, and they didn't go out there to murder anybody. So all I can figure is that that government man, Haynes, was scared shitless by all the stories he'd heard about how tough the Powers was, and he had a gun he'd borrowed, and he just shot the old man by accident. Now, that's what I figure happened, and I don't figure it was really anybody's fault. And once the old man was shot, it just had to happen. The Powers and Sisson had the cover, and they just shot until all the return fire stopped. You might say it was all an accident.

The only fault I can find is with the Powers for not coming in to register, and we don't know all the reasons that went into that. I've heard people say that they never got the word to come in, but I don't know the truth of it. I think maybe they was like all people ... not as black as they're painted. And I think no matter what they done, they've been punished enough for it.

But don't you go tellin' nobody I said that or I'll be run right out of the Stake. You hear?

Informant Mo3 (Reconstructed Text)

They wasn't no good, I know that. That Tom Sisson was a horse thief. Mr. Ellsworth told me that he used to own a little paint pony that Sisson got arrested for stealin' off the reservation. And they sent him to prison on that deal.

I could tell you stories about that girl, too, if we wasn't in polite company. She was about on the par with the rest of that bunch.

The only one I could say a good word for was old Charlie, and I believe he was kinda touched. He was always a-sayin' somethin' stupid. He was awful ignorant. And then he'd wanta fight anybody that laughed at him, and he was pretty good in a tussle, too. But there wasn't no harm in him. He wasn't like the rest of them.

Informant Mo4 (Reconstructed Text)

I don't come from around here, you know; I come from Mesa. But even before I come down here to school, I heard about the Powers. A bishop come one time, and he talked about the whole case and give the true story. He told how it all come about. He said that the Powers was the worst kinda people, sinnin' and never went to church or nothin'. Then when they said they wouldn't go in the army to fight for their country, people got kinda upset, and then when they killed their sister, well, there wasn't nothin' the law could do but go after them. And when he talked about how the Powers laid for them and killed them without a chance, the tears begun to roll down his cheeks, and you could hear a pin drop. Man, nobody made a sound! Then he went on to say that all the support for the Powers really came from the people that was envious of the Church and how prosperous it was, and they figured it was a good chance to sling some mud at it. Now that's the truth of it.

Informant Mo5 (Reconstructed Text)

I don't see why everybody feels so sorry for those Powers. I think they got just what they deserved. I heard that they kept real mean dogs and sicked them on people, and then laughed when the people ran. That Powers girl wasn't any good, and that old man Sisson was a convicted horse thief. And yet people choose to believe their story instead of the word of a marshal and all the evidence.

Informant Mo6 (Tape Transcript)

This whole controversy stems from hatred of the Mormons. We've been persecuted every place we've ever been. They've burned us out and killed us and lied about us ever since the Church has existed. They killed Joseph Smith, and then they persecuted thousands of Mormons just for practicing their religion, and that's in violation of the Constitution. And wherever the Church has been too strong to persecute, then the most terrible lies are told about it.

That's the case with the Powers, I think. From all that I've heard and read, the facts are clear. They were a bunch of no-goods who were always fighting with their neighbors. My dad told me how they insisted on watering some diseased horses at a tank where a man kept his horses, and all of his horses caught the disease and died. And some of them were very valuable animals. But they didn't care. They always carried guns and were always ready to fight if anyone made them mad. And then they wouldn't register for the draft to fight for their country, and that was a crime. But nothing was done about that. And then they brought their sister down dead, claiming they just ..... she just died, but her neck was broken and she was pregnant.

Then when the officers went up there to bring them back to stand trial, they killed them. And in spite of all that, all you hear is how the Mormons railroaded them and framed them and tried to murder them. Now all those things are forbidden by the Mormon Church, so how could those men have set out to do them? It doesn't make any sense. They were tried and found guilty and sentenced, and now we're supposed to throw all that out and just turn them loose.

Informant Mo7 (Reconstructed Text)

Now I was a young girl when all that happened. My father and I ran a ranch just over the mountain from Klondyke, and I knew the Powers. I knew Granny and Ola, and they were all fine people. The stories that I've heard told about that poor girl! And not a word of truth to them. She was a beautiful, sweet young girl, just as proper as a girl could be. And they were very close, all of the family, except maybe Charlie. He just couldn't get along with his father, and so he was always going off somewhere to work.

I made it a point to go to Clifton and attend the entire trial, and when it was over, I came away with one question in my mind: "Where was the other side of the story?" It certainly wasn't told at the trial. John and Tom had that old Fiedler representing them, and most days he was so drunk he could hardly stand. Why they had him, I'll never understand, but he had done some work for their father years before when they lived over in New Mexico. So the trial only told one side of the story, and it was a story that I couldn't accept since I knew the people involved.

A lot has been made of the religious angle of this case, how it was all an organized plot on the part of the Mormons, but I've been a good Mormon all these years, and it never made me hate the Power family or tell lies about them.

Informant Mo8 (Reconstructed Text)

Well, I heard that one of the men who got killed was foolin' around with the sister. And the father found out and killed her. And that guy was goin' up there to kill the old man and the brothers to get revenge for them killin' her.

Informant Mo9 (Reconstructed Text)

My mother was raised with the Kempton family, lived with them for years, so she knows the true story and none of this goddam bullshit that everybody's talkin' all the time., They say that they was after their gold and their goddam worked out mine. Hell, they didn't have no gold. Where would they get it? That mine wasn't worth shit. And then they say they went up there and shot their father down like a dog, right on his doorstep and all that shit. That just ain't true; there ain't a goddam word of truth in it. The posse just went up there like good citizens and peace officers to do their job and bring them cowardly sons-a-bitches down 'cause they's draft dodgers. And then they had another good reason to go up there, because everybody in his right mind knew for goddam certain that they'd murdered their sister, broke her goddam neck. And when them officers got up there to that godforsaken mine, the Powers had an ambush all ready for them. They was just a-layin' there waitin' on them. And the posse walked right up to that cabin like men, not knowing that the cowardly bastards was waitin' for them. They walked right into it. And it was pitiful, awful. They showed 'em no mercy; they shot 'em down like dogs. They didn't have no chance 'cause the Powers had all the cover. And then what'd they do? Their father had got shot in the fight, and he was layin' there dyin', and insteada stayin' there to take care of him like they should have, they run off and left him to die like the goddam trash they was. Hell, that Tom Sisson was no good! He had been in prison before that ever happened, so you know he was no good. And the goddam governor let him out before he done his time, and he went right out and helped the Powers kill them lawmen. They shouldn't let nobody outa prison till they done the time they was sent there for.

And now the Powers want to get out of prison. I think they oughta let 'em out, and when they walk out the front gate, they oughta shoot them down just like they shot the officers. That's all.

Informant Mo10 (Tape Transcript)

I've heard fellas say that they was awful fine fellas, and everybody liked 'em. Well, Marion Lee had a cow outfit out here on Cottonwood Wash. And they was workin' Mesquite Flat country, and the oldest Powers boy was on the works. And Powers was ridin' a little old owl-headed pony. Nobody else carried guns, but the Powers boys always had their guns on. He's ridin' this little old owl-headed pony, and it bucked him off. Well, Marion started towards him, and Powers got up, so he just went and caught the horse. And he never said a word; he just come a-leadin' the horse back to Powers. And he just pulled out that gun, and he pointed it at Marion, and he said, "Just wipe that grin off'n your face, you Mormon son-of-a-bitch!" And Marion said that gun looked like it was bigger than a stove pipe.

And.... uh..... then .....Jim Kennedy ..... uh ..... owned what was supposed to been the best quarter horse in the United States, a horse they called Little King in Texas, and Jim named him Possum after he brought him out here. And he had about five stallions and some race horses in his barns and stables there, and the Powers boys come off down the creek with a bunch a little old ponies all had the distemper, and they started to water at Jim's trough. Jim looked out and seen them little old snotty-nosed ponies a-waterin' there, and he rushed out, and he said, "Don't water them horses here! Don't water them horses here!" Powers said, "Why you old son-of-a-bitch! Git back in the house!" He said, "I'll water my horses anyplace that I want to!" Jim told me, says, "I went to the house." Said, "That damn fool woulda killed me." And some of the other fellas there went out and talked to them, got 'em to leave.

Now them's the fine fellas they were. There was two fellas there, both of 'em different sides of the mountain, one of 'em a Mormon, the other one a non-Mormon ..... and ..... uh ..... they were both pretty well respectable kinda people. Everybody spoke well of both of 'em ..... and..... uh..... then the next thing. Doc Flatt come to the house there when the kids was sick. He come to the house there early one morning, and he told Dad: he said ..... about the killin'. They'd just got to town. We didn't have radio and everything then. And he told Dad about the killin'. And he said, "I reported the death of that girl to the sheriff's office. That girl that died of that mysterious ailment was a broken neck." And he said, "I reported it to the sheriff's office, and they went out there to ..... with the United States marshal..... the United States marshal on the slacker charge, and the ..... the sheriff's office to investigate the killin' of that broken-necked girl." Now that ..... that was what Doc Flatt told my daddy.

Well, they went out there. They say they shot the old man unarmed and all that. They walked right up the middle of a draw, not a one of 'em hid, right up a sand wash, right out in plain sight. And them fellas shot 'em from behind the ..... from inside the house. One of 'em got glass in his eyes, and they come back on this side a the border's the reason they got caught. And they give up to some soldiers down ......over in New Mexico.

About the reason they wasn't hanged, was that when this state was made a state, they abolished capital punishment. And ..... uh ..... the next election after that ..... uh ..... and..... uh ..... a rape case in Phoenix, where ..... down in the Salt River Valley, where an old kid killed a man and raped a woman, and he told her, "It don't do no good," he said, "They'll send me to the pen two or three years if I get caught, but I'll get out again." Well, he didn't git the pen; they lynched him. And ..... uh ..... the very next election they put capital punishment back in the state of Arizona.

Now if them fellas was fine fellas, I ..... I don't know ..... I ..... The only ...... people in those days ...... by the time the First World War, if a cowpuncher had a gun, he kept it in his bed; he didn't carry it with him. But those people never went unarmed in their lives. And a man that's always carryin' a gun is lookin' to do somethin' with it; he's carryin' it to use. So I'm ..... I was a good friend to Mart Kempton's family. Mart was a man about the age of my dad. I was a good friend ...... and then I worked with Hebe Kempton for a long time, a younger brother of Mart, an awful fine man if you ever met one. I knew Nate awful well, and they were .... they're an upstandin' family. And then you take Frank McBride's family; one of 'em is a senator now. And ..... uh ..... they ..... they were good people. They say they went over there to beat 'em out of their mine and one thing and another, the stories they put up. Them fellas didn't do anything only go over there as peace officers, as ..... uh ..... as sheriffs a-trying to do their duty. And that's the only way I can see it. I know the Wootans; they're still in the country, some of them. I know Wootan's kin folks, and ..... uh ..... I've worked with Wootans, and by golly, there wasn't a bloodthirsty one in the whole family. Of all these I've met: the McBrides, the Kemptons nor the Wootans. I don't know why they'd get three bloodthirsty ones over there after them fellas. I don't know.

Informant Mo11 (Tape Transcript)

My daddy told me all about the Powers and how they carried guns long after everybody else quit carryin' them and how they'd pull them every time they got in a little argument. They didn't have anything, and they had no respect for other people's property. Nobody liked them; Mormons and non-Mormons both had trouble with them, and yet people will try to tell you they were fine fellows.

They say the girl died of some mysterious ailment. Well, old Doc Flatt told my granddaddy that what she died of was a broken neck. Now that's not so mysterious.

They say they shot that old man down without a chance. That's a flat lie. They walked right up a draw, right in plain sight, and the Powers shot them from the house. That's the kind of fine fellows they were.

Then that Tom Sisson, now, he was a convicted horse thief. Matter of fact, my granddaddy bought one of the horses that he was convicted of stealing. So I think the facts of the case are pretty clear.

Informant Mo12 (Reconstructed Text)

The Powers killed those men, and they run off. They's gittin' chased, and they ran into that Colossal Cave, there outside Tucson, and they never did find them till they come back into the country from Mexico. They think they come out over in Carlsbad; them two caves is connected.[234]

Informant Mo13 (Reconstructed Text)

All I ever heard was about the girl and how she was screwin' her brothers and her father and that other guy. That really must have been

---

[234] "Manche Höhlen sind unergründlich und stehen durch unterirdische Gänge in Verbindung mit einem anderen Berg, mit einem entfernten Tale, mit einem See, mit einem Bach, mit einer Burg." *Handwörterbuch des Deutschen Aberglaubens*, 10 vols. (Berlin and Leipzig: Walter de Gruyter and Company, 1931-1932), Vol. 4, p. 177. Since the distance from Colossal Cave to Carlsbad Caverns is more than 350 miles, this may well represent the longest claim for an underground connection on record.

wild. No wonder they killed her. I don't see how anybody could do that. Ecch!

Informant Mo14 (Tape Transcript)

People from our church were the first people to come into this valley, and they settled and fought off the Indians and made this valley prosper. We've built houses and churches and schools. And in all that time I never heard of a good Mormon committing any crimes or going to prison or doing anything bad. So why would it be that in that one instance that those good church-going men would go up into that God-forsaken country to murder those Powers? It's beyond my understanding.

Now, on the other hand, I lived in this valley all my life, and I never heard one good word about the Powers. They never had anything. They drifted from place to place, and everywhere they went, they fought with people. And there wasn't a one of them up there that had the morals of an alley cat. That girl was an abomination to the Lord, and that old Sisson was an ex-convict. Now who would you expect to be in the wrong? This was all settled forty years ago to everybody's satisfaction, and I can't see a single reason as to why it should be dragged up again now.

Informant Mo15 (Reconstructed Text)

Them Powers boys was just flat mean .... like cruel. Mr. Claridge was chasin' cows up in that Galiuro country, and he come up on the Powers with a broke-down wagon. And ..... he was only gonna try and help 'em, and a packa dogs they had with 'em went after his horse, and the horse went crazy and threw him. (He was just a kid. I don't know how old, but a kid.) And the dogs come after him and bit him pretty good before the Powers pulled 'em off. And the next time his father seen old man Powers he said that somethin' should be done about them dogs. And Powers said he wasn't gonna do nothin'. And Mr. Claridge, old Mr. Claridge said then at least he could say he was sorry.

And old man Powers said, "Yeah, I'm sorry. I'm sorry my dogs didn't eat the damn kid up!"

Informant Mo16 (Reconstructed Text)

The Powers took all the gold they could out of that little shit-ass mine, and they hid it, buried it all around out there. And that's why they hung around here so long. They had enough time to get clean out of the country if they wanted to. Matter a fact, they did go to Mexico for a while. But where they made their mistake was they tried to sneak back after that gold, and that's when they got caught. They was lucky they didn't get strung up, too. They would have, but the soldiers protected them. Now they're talkin' about lettin' them loose. Shit! They'd just come back and get that gold and live like kings. That ain't right. They killed those good men, and they should have to pay for it.

Informant Mo17 (Reconstructed Text)

They say those men went out there to kill the Powers, and they shot their father. I don't believe that. That whole family was no good, always fightin' with everybody. And they would steal, too. That girl, Ola was caught several times stealing stuff from stores here in town. She'd hide stuff up under her dress and walk out with it.[235] She must have screwed like a mink too, because she was pregnant when they brought her down dead.

Informant Mo18 (Reconstructed Text)

My granmaw says that she remembers that Powers girl. She used to come to town every so often with her father or her brothers, and she'd go from one store to the other, stealin' stuff and hidin' it up under

---

[235] Similar allegations are made about another girl from a notorious family in George W. Walter, *The Loomis Gang* (Prospect, New York: Prospect Books, 1953), p. 23.

them long dresses they used to wear.[236] She'd take all that stuff back to the wagon, and then she'd walk up and down Main Street lookin' for somebody to take her out to the river bottom. It ain't no wonder that her brothers killed her. She was really no good.

Informant Mo19 (Reconstructed Text)

Well, what I heard these boys killed their sister. They brought her down with a broken neck and saying she'd been dead a lot shorter time than she really had, and the questions about that have never been answered.

Well, then their numbers come up in the draft, and they didn't come in, and Sheriff McBride and his deputies, Mr. Wootan and Mr. Kempton, and a U.S. marshal from Globe went up there to bring them out. And when they got there, the Powers was waitin' for them and bushwhacked them. The marshal got away. In the fighting the old man was wounded, and they just ran off and left him to die. Then they hid out all over the country here for a couple of months before the soldiers caught them. Now, they couldn't have done that without help. People were hiding them and feeding them and giving them fresh horses the whole time the man hunt was going on. And that was all done by the ones who hated and persecuted the Mormons all along. And they're the same ones who are making so much noise now.

Informant Mo20 (Reconstructed Text)

A lot of these Mexicans helped the Powers when they was tryin' to escape. And the Apache that they hired was a friend of theirs, too, and he kept leadin' the posses in the wrong direction. Some people say they shod their horses backwards, too, and that made them hard to trail, but I don't believe that.[237] I don't know why anybody would help them after what they done, but some people will sink awful low.

---

[236] See footnote 2.
[237] Motif K534.1. Escape by reversing horse's shoes.

Informant Mo21 (Reconstructed Text)

The whole thing is just a simple case of prejudice against Mormons. There was no way that they could have stayed loose that long with all those men after them. They had help and lots of it. And the very ones that helped them are the ones who to your face would say what an awful thing the Powers had done. They're the worst kind of hypocrites. The Mormons are the ones who have made this valley what it is, and they just won't forgive us for it. And then they'll make heroes out of hoodlums like that with no more morals than a mountain goat. And it's all pure jealousy.

Informant Mo22 (Reconstructed Text)

I know Kane Wootan's son, the highway patrolman that got shot a few years back. That really messed him up, you know. He ain't never gonna be the same. Well, I figure he ought a know the true story, being that it's his father that got killed, and he says it was straight-out murder. His father and Sheriff McBride and ..... those other fellas went up there to do their duty, and the Powers was layin' for them. The same fellas that was so chicken they couldn't fight for their country was able to lay there and shoot them men down like dogs. They say they shot their father with his hands up. Now why would they do that? They was lawmen doin' their duty, and the only reason they would have fired their guns was if they got fired at first.

And now people talk about paroling them. Why? They killed those men, and they've tried to escape a couple of times. The only way they should come out of there is feet first.

Informant Mo23 (Reconstructed Text)

I don't think it's right for you to go around asking people all these questions about the Powers. You people act like they was heroes or something. I think they ought to rot up there in Florence. They're cowards and murderers, and there's no way to change that.

They murdered their sister, too, you know. And you know why they killed her? Because she was pregnant by one of them or by the father or that old hired man, whatever his name was. And that's the kind of people you're trying to make heroes of! I don't understand it. Why don't you ask questions about what good men they killed and about all the orphan children that had to grow up without fathers? That's all I have to say.

Informant Mo24 (Reconstructed Text)

My grandfather used to talk about those Powers people. I guess they were really crude and uneducated. Like they had no respect for anybody, and the old lady, the grandmother, I guess it was, she shot her husband once, because he did something she didn't like. Just shot him. But I guess he got all right.

Informant Mo25 (Reconstructed Text)

Well, them Powers boys had a lotta gold they took out of that mine up there, and they hid it all, buried it and hid it in caves so nobody could get it. And when they killed them sheriffs, they had to run. Everybody wonders how they hid out so long. Well, I heard that they went over past Reddington to the big cave down near Tucson. Colossal Cave? And they went down in there. And there's a certain way that if you know it, you can keep right on goin' and come up way over in Carlsbad Caverns. Down below Hobbs? So that's why nobody ever found them for so long.[238]

Informant Mo26 (Reconstructed Text)

I just heard about the sister and how awful she was and how they killed her. And then I heard they put the shoes on their horses backwards to fool the posse.[239] And then they used to travel at night

---

[238] See footnote 1.
[239] See footnote 4.

and sleep in hollow logs in the daytime, and one time the sheriff sat down right on a log they were hidin' in.[240]

Informant Mo27 (Reconstructed Text)

I don't think there's really much doubt about what happened in that Powers case. The courts ruled on that at the time, and all this talk is just second-guessing. The men who were killed were good, God-fearing, churchgoing men, and that whole Powers family were of very low class, lower than Mexicans. Now, in a case like that, who would you believe? Certainly not the murderers.

Informant Mo28 (Reconstructed Text)

I've heard all the things that people say, all the terrible things they say about the lawmen, and I don't think it should be allowed. I mean, it's not right to talk about men that can't defend themselves like that. And I know the families of those men, and they're all good people, and it doesn't make sense that they would have done what they say.

I think it's just a case of cowardly, immoral people murdering innocent men, men who were just doing their job, and now, all of a sudden, there's this big fuss, and everybody's saying they're innocent and should be let go. If they were innocent, then why were they found guilty at the time? The only unfortunate thing is that they weren't ..... that the crime didn't take place at the time when they could have been executed. I never heard anything good about the Powers, and that old hired man had just gotten out of prison, so why are they supposed to be so holy?

Informant Mo29 (Reconstructed Text)

The reason the Powers were so hard to find was that they put the

---

[240] See William Lynwood Montell, *The Saga of Coe Ridge* (Knoxville: University of Tennessee Press, 1970), p. 103.

shoes backwards on their horses, and the posses were all going in the wrong direction. That's how it took so long to catch them.[241]

Informant Mo30 (Reconstructed Text)

Now, you're talkin' to the wrong man when you talk to me about the Powers. I'm related to both the McBrides and the Wootans, and I know that those men were shot down in cold blood. I think they should have been staked out on an ant hill. Woulda been too good for 'em.

Informant Mo31 (Reconstructed Text)

The Powers were crude people. The Ladies Aid Society had an oyster supper, and, of course, none of the Powers had ever ate an oyster, but Charlie plunked his dollar down and went on in. Well, he sat down at the table and was served. He took a forkful of food and bit into an oyster, and as soon as he did, well, he spit it all over the table in front of him. Everybody kinda stared at him, and he said, "You know, many a damn fool would have swallowed that."[242]

Informant Mo32 (Reconstructed Text)

I heard that all four of them, the two brothers, the old man, and that old hired man was all fuckin' that sister up there. And the old grandmother found out about it and raised hell, so they killed her. And then the girl had a boyfriend she was screwin', and she wanted to run off with him, and they got to fightin' about it, and they broke her neck. Then they thought the lawmen was comin' after them for that, so that's why they laid for them and killed them all.

---

[241] See footnote 4.

[242] This story is told about Sam Houston. See J. Frank Dobie, *The Flavor of Texas* (Dallas: Dealey and Lowe, 1936), pp. 6-7.

Informant Mo33 (Tape Transcript)

I don't know much about them Powers boys that got in trouble, but my dad used to tell me about the other brother, Charlie, and how crazy he was ..... all the crazy things he used to do. Like one time he was ridin' down the alley that used to run backa Main Street, and the Chinaman come out the back door of the restaurant to shake out a tablecloth. And Charlie's pony took one look at that tablecloth a-flappin' and commenced to pitchin' and buckin' and deposited old Charlie in the dust. And he jumped right up and pulled out his six-shooter and started firin' at that poor Chink. Tried to kill him, and probably would have if he hadn't run back in the restaurant.[243] He didn't care for nothin'. I guess none of them Powers did.

Another time he asked ol' Wiley Morgan for a job cowboyin'. And Wiley's crew was all filled up, but his cook had quit on him. So he asked ol' Charlie if he could cook for the crew, and Charlie said he could, and he took the job. Well, he went to it, and he was doin' a pretty good job, too. But there was a kid on the works, and he woke up early one morning and seen Charlie off in the brush a-takin' a piss. And then he come right back to the chuck wagon and started makin' biscuits. When it come time to eat, the kid wouldn't take no biscuits, and Charlie jumped him about it. They argued back and forth, and finally Charlie pulled out his six-shooter, and he was gonna make the kid eat the biscuits. The kid said he couldn't eat 'em 'cause Charlie had gone straight from pissin' to wallerin' his hands in the biscuit dough. Charlie said, "Well, hell! My hands ain't touched nothin' but my dick, and my dick ain't touched nothin' but my hands!"

Yeah, he sure was crazy and ignorant. All them Powers was ignorant. Kinda like hillbillies.

Informant Mo34 (Reconstructed Text)

I heard that Ola wanted to marry Kane Wootan's brother, and her father wouldn't let her. Then there was a young fellow here in Safford

---

[243] For a similar story see George D. Hendricks, *The Bad Men of the West* (San Antonio: The Naylor Company, 1959), p. 34.

who sold a claim for a lot of money, and he wanted to marry her. But her father said no. And so they tried to elope. But the old man shot the fella, and then had to poison his daughter to keep her quiet. They never did find that fella's body.

Informant Mo35 (Reconstructed Text)

I don't really think we should discuss it. Those men who were killed were all members of good standing in the Church. They didn't smoke or drink or steal, so why should they go up there and murder that old man? The Church is against murder just as much as those other things. Just look at the people involved. I don't see what purpose can be served now.

Informant Mo36 (Reconstructed Text)

That sister that the Powers boys killed was a real hell-raiser. She whipped a teacher in school over in Willcox because the teacher caught her stealing. And she was screwing some cowboy from over in the Sulphur Springs Valley. And her brothers and her father was screwing her, too. They broke her neck because she was pregnant. They wasn't none of them no good.

Informant Mo37 (Tape Transcript)

That Powers girl, Ola, was supposed to be so good and holy and all that .... Well, my aunt from over Willcox says that her brother went to school with Ola, and she used to use foul language all the time, and the teacher was always havin' to punish her. And one time she caught her in the cloak room stealin' gloves and hats and stuff and hidin' 'em up under her skirt.[244] And when the teacher called her on it, she whipped her. (She was a lot bigger than the teacher.) And they throwed her out of that school.

---

[244] See footnote 2.

Informant Mo38 (Tape Transcript)

Well, the story I'm going to tell is about the Powers brothers. It seems they had a mine out near Klondyke, and it wasn't very profitable. They lived a sort of low-class life, and they didn't have any education. For some reason they refused to register for the draft, and that made people very antagonistic towards them because everyone was so patriotic at that time.

Well, before anything could be done about it, they brought their sister's body down from the mountains, and they didn't say how she had died or anything. There are a lot of stories about that, but they aren't very nice, and I don't think I should go into that. But, anyway, it certainly focused attention on the Powers.

Sheriff McBride took two of his deputies, Mr. Wootan and Mr. Kempton, and another man who was connected with the federal government somehow and went up there to arrest the two young Powers on the draft charge and bring them in for questioning about their sister's death. Somehow the Powers found out they were coming and laid an ambush for them. They had such an advantage that it's a wonder that the fourth man in the group was able to escape and that the lawmen were able to kill the father of the boys.

It was certainly a terrible thing. I don't know how many children were orphaned by the Powers, but it was a significant number, and the men that they killed were comparatively young, with rich, full lives before them. They were all good, church-going men. It was a terrible, terrible thing.

Informant Mo39 (Reconstructed Text)

I really don't know anything except what I've heard. Is that what you want? Well, the Powers wouldn't register for the draft, and even after they'd been contacted several times, they refused to come down. So Sheriff McBride and three other men rode up there. The Powers heard them coming and were waiting for them, and in the fight that ensued the father of the Powers was killed as were the sheriff and two of his deputies.

They captured the three men down near the Mexican border, and they were brought back to Safford for trial. They would have been sentenced to death, I'm sure, but for a few years back then, Arizona didn't have capital punishment. So they were sentenced to life imprisonment.

Now, those are the facts as they've been told to me, and they don't seem to argue very well for releasing those men now. It seems to me the scales of justice were pretty well weighted in their favor. They received a fair trial, and it only seems fair that they serve the sentence which was imposed on them.

Informant Mo40 (Reconstructed Text)

I can't believe the Powers were any good or they would have gone to defend their country. Where would we be if everybody dodged the draft? And then that sister wasn't any good and had relations with her brothers, and they killed her. So it isn't hard to believe that people who lived like that and were so cowardly would shoot those men down.

Informant Mo41 (Reconstructed Text)

My Uncle M. knew all them Powers boys real well, and he says that the only one worth a damn was Charlie, and he was crazy. He was always doin' weird things and fightin' with people and gettin' the shit kicked out of him. Charlie tried to enlist in the army when the war broke out; but he couldn't pass the physical. But them other two boys was cowards, and they wouldn't go to fight. But they carried guns all the time and was always threatening people, and it ain't no wonder they finally killed somebody.

And then my Uncle told about them escapin' and how they was able to stay gone so long. Seems like the Apache they got to track them boys was a friend of John Powers. He used to fool around with them Indians and had helped this one out of a scrape or two, and the Apache never forgot it. So when he found out who it was he was hired to track, he just kept leadin' them posses on one wild goose chase after another. And that's how come it took so long to catch them. That and because some of the ranchers helped them. There was a lotta sick people when they got caught, but they never did tell who it was that helped 'em. They always claimed they was starvin' the whole time.

Informant Mo42 (Reconstructed Text)

The Powers! I'll tell you about the Powers! They're a goddam bloodthirsty bunch of cowardly bastards who should a been staked out on an anthill a long time ago! And so should all the people who're tryin' to get them off! Now get outa here and write that in your damn book!

Informant Mo43 (Reconstructed Text)

They was all fuckin' that girl up there, and they got her pregnant, so they killed her. And when they heard the law comin' after them, they knew they'd had it, so they killed the sheriff and his deputies and then tried to get away. Nothing complicated about that.

Informant Mo44 (Reconstructed Text)

There's certainly a lot of talk about the Powers today. Course, there always has been, but it's taken on a different tone in recent years. Seems everyone wants to forgive them for what they did. I guess you can tie it in with the general breakdown in morals and the increase in permissiveness. But it'll be a sad day for Arizona justice, if they ever let those men out of prison. It'll really be a justification of two men who shot down officers of the law in cold blood. I think if it does happen, it might be a good time for Judge Lynch to come out of hiding. And as far as there being some religious bias at work in this case, that's a lot of nonsense.

Informant Mo45 (Tape Transcript)

Now, some fellows say them fellows was drunk when they went up there, and I know that ain't the truth. They was good Mormon people, and there wasn't a one of them that drank. I know that for a fact. So anybody that says different just don't know what they're talkin' about. Now they was foolish .... it was a foolish play to go up there after them boys that way, and I heard my daddy tell Kane Wootan so right here on the place. Kane come by here just a week or so before the shootin' and was talkin' about goin' up there and bringin' them out. And my daddy told him, "Kane," he said, "a man could make a bad mistake goin' up there after them boys." Said, "You might better send somebody up there that knows them to talk to them." And ol' Kane said, "Hell, I know 'em! A man could go up there with a lightnin' bug on the end of a stick and bring them outa there." Said, "There ain't no fight in them boys." Hell, it wasn't but a couple a weeks we was packin' his body down outa there.

Course now, I don't blame them boys much either. I wouldn't have much to say for my boys if they'd see their daddy shot down right on the front steps and not do nothin' about it. There's two sides to everything, I guess, and you can't go on bein' bitter about somethin' till ya die. John's a cantankerous old bastard, but Tom's a pretty good old boy, and I don't see that a man gains much by goin' on believin' the worst about 'em and expectin' them to keep on payin' for somethin' that happened a long time ago.

But any man who says them officers was drunk is either spoutin' out of his bunghole or he's a flat-out liar.

Informant Mo46 (Reconstructed Text)

The Powers carried guns when nobody else in the country did. Nobody liked them; they fought with everybody. And they didn't seem to have any moral sense. Apparently they all used that girl and got her pregnant, and then they had to kill her. And that Sisson was a convicted horse thief. They were a sorry lot.

Informant Mo47 (Reconstructed Text)

Everybody knows the Powers were no good. I mean, they were the worst kind of white trash, and then to say that good, God-fearing men, good church-going Mormons, would go up there and murder their father ...... well, I don't know. What did they ever do that was any good? They fought with everybody. They couldn't read or write. They never set foot inside a church of any kind. Everybody knows they murdered their sister, and anybody can tell you why.

The doctor that examined her .....I think it was old Dr. Flatt ...... he knew she was pregnant. He just didn't see that it would serve any good purpose, so he didn't put it in his report, but everybody knew it. And how could she get pregnant way up there unless it was one of the men that lived there with her? And that's the kind of people that are involved in this thing. People like that are better off dead.

LEGEND TEXTS

NON-MORMON ANGLO TEXTS

Informant An1 (Reconstructed Text)

I heard that the sheriff had a hair trigger rifle, and he didn't mean to shoot the old man, but he did. So it wasn't really the Powers' fault, but that never did come out at the trial.

Informant An2 (Reconstructed Text)

That ol' Granny Powers was a tough old bird. I heard that one time she chased her husband up a tree, and when he wouldn't come down, she went and got an axe and chopped the damn tree down! And I know she wasn't afraid a nothin'. I seen her out ta Habys' one time, walkin' through the yard, and some of the boys was a-chousin' a big old range bull, and he come over that corral fence and was fixin' to run Granny over. Hell, she never missed a beat; she waited till he got up close, and then threw some bedclothes she was carryin' over his head. He stopped dead, shook his horns till he got loose of them sheets and blankets, and then took out for the high country. Old Granny never stopped walkin'. She was a tough one![245]

Informant An3 (Reconstructed Text)

The Powers took a lotta gold outa that mine up there, and they hid it in several places out there. That's why they stayed around here so long. They had lots of time to get away, but they were lookin' for a

---

[245] See William Lynwood Montell, *The Saga of Coe Ridge* (Knoxville: University of Tennessee Press, 1970), p. 59. As Montell points out, there is a strong resemblance here to Motif F618, "Strong man tames animals."

chance to get back and get that gold, and that's how they got caught. Now, I guess nobody'll ever find it.

Informant An4 (Reconstructed Text)

Well, I don't know much. Sometimes that's the way to be; it don't pay to know much ...... I'll tell you about Charlie. I run into old Charlie once over in Crazy Horse. And we'd had a hell of a rain shower, and Charlie was down there trying to build a little fire to dry off. So I lit, and between the pair of us we got a little fire going. Well, old Charlie thought he was quite a hand with a gun, and we was sittin' there, and a little bunch a turkeys come down the draw. And old Charlie out with his gun and emptied it into that herd. Well, every time he missed, his face got redder, till finally he was so mad he just run into them turkeys and pistol-whipped two of them to death. (Their wings was all wet and they couldn't fly, you know.)[246]

Then I heard one time he got troublesome over in a bar in Safford, and they took quite a little from him, and then they throwed him out in the street. He laid there for a minute and then he hollered, "That's a hell of a goddam way to run a saloon!"[247] That's all.

Informant An5 (Reconstructed Text)

I don't know much about them Powers boys. All I ever heard was that them cops shot their old man, and they just fired back. I did hear that when they was tryin' to escape, they come up to a ranch over in New Mexico and found a man beatin' his wife. And .... uh ..... they pulled out their guns and shot all around that guy's feet and run him off and told him he better not ever come back. And that woman cooked 'em a big feed and told 'em it was the best turn anybody ever

---

[246] See James A. McKenna, *Black Range Tales* (Glorieta, New Mexico: Rio Grande Press, Inc., 1971), p. 17.

[247] See Paul Patterson, "Cowboy Comedians and Horseback Humorists," in *The Golden Log*, Mody C. Boatright, Wilson M. Hudson and Allen Maxwell, eds. (Dallas: Southern Methodist University Press, 1962), pp. 102-103.

done her and give 'em a big bunch a food and stuff to take with 'em.[248] That's all I ever heard.

Informant An6 (Reconstructed Text)

Well, all I know is what I heard. There was a lot of talk a few years ago when they was gonna let them go. People seemed to feel that what they'd done was bad enough so that they shouldn't get loose. I don't know. They killed the sheriff and his men, and they killed the boys' father, and it's hard to know what really happened. But I can't see that they could be as bad as people say.

Oh, yeah. I heard that if you tried to stick somethin' in the hole in the old man's chest, it wouldn't go in without his arms was up over his head. So the police must have shot him after he surrendered.

Informant An7 (Reconstructed Text)

A man had to be a little soft in the head or drunk, one, to go up there after them Powers boys. They was all good shots up there at that camp, good enough to kill you, anyway. But I've seen a lot of men fire guns in my time, but I never have seen the beat of that John Powers. I was workin' for old Wiley Morgan (he was an uncle to the Powers) and me and him was ridin' up there by Four Mile, and we met John, and he rode along with us. And we come up there above Lackners', and we seen an old steer cross-canyon about 150 yards off, and he was et up with worms. Mr. Morgan said that we oughta catch him and kill him. And old John says, "Catch him, hell!" And before we knowed what was happenin', he pulled that old Colt of his and dropped that son-of-a-bitch right where he stood. Quick as lightning! He never aimed or nothin'.

And then down to Habys' once, I seen him shoot a hole through a quarter that the Haby boy threw up in the air. A hole clean through

---

[248] See George D. Hendricks, *The Bad Men of the West* (San Antonio: The Naylor Company, 1959), p. 110, for a similar story told of outlaw Al Jennings.

it![249] And then they got to hoo-rawin' him and sayin' it was a lucky shot, and nobody had another quarter. So he shot a hole through a fence board from about 20 yards and then put two more slugs into that board, and the hole wasn't a bit bigger.[250] I ain't see nothin' like it before or since. John was the best shot ever was in this country.

Informant An8 (Reconstructed Text)

That girl, the sister, was sneakin' out to see some cowboy that worked on a ranch up near there. And the old man didn't like it, and she tried to run away with him, and the old man sent the boys out to stop her, and they roped her off her horse and broke her neck. And when the sheriff went up there to see about it, they was afraid they wouldn't get a fair trial because there was bad blood between Wootan and them. So that's what caused the shootin'.

Informant An9 (Reconstructed Text)

All I know is about the lawyer, Fiedler. He was from over Silver, you know, and everybody knew he was a drunk. If he defended them, then they didn't have any kind of a show. They say he drank so much that the only time he staggered was when he was sober.[251] And he was crooked, too. They say on his tombstone it said: "Here lies Squire Fiedler, a lawyer and an honest man." And everybody said they musta buried two people in that grave.[252]

---

[249] See Frost Woodhull, "Folk-Lore Shooting," in *Southwestern Lore*, J. Frank Dobie, ed. (Austin: *The Texas Folklore Society*, 1931) p. 10.

[250] All of these feats would seem to fall under Motif X981, "Lie: Skillful Marksman."

[251] This same claim was made about the neighborhood drunk of my childhood whom we called Johnny Lush.

[252] See Hermes Nye, "Folksay of Lawyers," in *Singers and Storytellers*, Mody C. Boatright, ed. (Dallas: Southern Methodist University Press, 1961), p. 93.

Informant An10 (Reconstructed Text)

Well, I don't know a whole lot about what happened. It was a long time ago ..... long before I was born, and all I know is what I've heard. But anybody that had to live around these Mormon bastards very long would be lucky if all he wound up doin' was shootin' a few of the sons-a-bitches. I've waited tables here for a while, and I've seen 'em .... the world's biggest hypocrites. The same ones that are the biggest names in the Church are down at the cafe swillin' coffee all the time and claimin' that it's a sin. And booze .... I'll bet they drink more on the sly than other people do on purpose.

And I ain't even gonna say a word about how they figure that anybody that ain't a Mormon is fair game. They got their own wives knocked up all the time, and then they're down here sniffin' around any girl that ain't attached.

The way I see it, those poor boys didn't do a damn thing but shoot back in self-defense at the men that'd killed their father, and they had to spend their whole lives in jail for that. And that's the way they do anybody that's got the guts to stand up to 'em. They own everything worth havin' and begrudge us what's left.

Informant An11 (Reconstructed Text)

Well, I don't know that I really know a hell of a lot about it. But there's a lotta talk, and I guess there must be some truth in it. Course, it all depends who you talk to. Seems like all the Mormons tell one story, and that's a lot different from the stories you're likely to hear from somebody else. 'Pears like that's the way it always is. You tangle asses with a Mormon, and sooner or later, you gotta fight the whole mess of 'em, and even if you was to whip 'em, you still come out in the wrong. Course, what do I know? I'm just a goddam no-good, half-breed Apache. (Laugh) Not to be trusted.

Well, anyway, my grandmammy (she's a full-blood) she claims she knew them Powers, and I've heard her talk about that old lady, the granny. She says she was real tough, wouldn't take no shit from nobody and always ready to back it up with an old shotgun she had. Said she pulled it on more than one. But she liked her. She was .... like ..... fair.

She didn't care who you were; she treated everybody the same. And the boys was just like everybody else; some good, some bad. So I figure they got in some Mormon's way somehow, and they paid the price.

Informant An12 (Reconstructed Text)

They say that Kane Wootan killed old man Powers because he had borrowed a rifle from somebody, and he didn't know that it had a hair trigger. It was cold that morning, and he shot him by accident.

Then the Mormons say that they .... that the sheriffs didn't shoot him with his hands up. But after he was dead, the only way you could stick something in the bullet hole was to raise his hands up ..... like .... over his head.

Informant An13 (Reconstructed Text)

One time Charlie Powers bought a horse from an old fellow who was passing through the valley, and the old fellow guaranteed the horse to work cattle. Well, Charlie took the horse over to the livery stable and left him over night, and when he come back in the morning, the horse was dead. Well, the old fellow had left town, so old Charlie lit out after him, and he caught up to him in Pima. He told the old man that the horse he'd guaranteed had died. And the fellow said, "I'm sorry, son. I guaranteed him to work cattle, not to live."[253]

Then another time he lost a big bunch a money up on the reservation to some Indians that had a sway-backed pony that could run like a deer. Charlie figured that anything that looked as poor as that Indian pony couldn't outrun nothin', and he lost a pile. He went crazy anytime anybody mentioned the word Indian to him after that.

---

[253] I cannot find this story in print, but I'm sure it is a common horse-trading story. It was part of the repertoire of Jim Winne, the recently deceased blacksmith at the Farmer's Museum, Cooperstown, New York, and I also heard it told of a used car dealer in Mullica Hill, New Jersey, in 1966.

Informant An14 (Reconstructed Text)

Kane Wootan wanted that mine that the Powers had, and he wanted it bad, and he wasn't one to let anybody stand in his way. I heard that he tried to buy them out, and when they wouldn't sell, he bought the Upchurch ranch to put a little pressure on them. And then he went ahead and claimed that their water belonged to him. But they wouldn't be pushed; they wouldn't back off, and so he trumped up that slacker charge and figured that when the posse went up there, he'd see to it that they was all wiped out. He was gonna murder all the Powers. He just didn't figure on them bein' as tough as they was. I'll tell you right now they wasn't to be fooled with. Old John had killed a lotta people before that shootin' up there ever was, and you didn't wanta fool with him. And Tom neither; he would fool around and josh a lot, but you better believe that he wouldn't stand for nobody leanin' on him.

Informant An15 (Tape Transcript)

Well, you wanna know then about where the Morgan .... er .... uh ..... the Powers boys come in. They come into the country ...... they had brought in about sixty head a cattle, some wagons, a buggy. There was the old man Powers, Tom, John, and Charlie, the boys. They were pretty good cowboys, too. They moved their cattle up in the Galiuros and they had a place down on the creek below the store, where they made their headquarters. Later they sold that and got a hold of the old mine up in Rattlesnake. Who they got it from I don't remember, but I know that it was ..... had been ...... had been some trouble up there before. A man by the name of Tucker was killed up there at that mine, and I don't remember who his partner was. But evidently the Powers got that mine from him or jumped it or some way. I don't know how they got it, but anyway they had it..... had the old mine. And they built a road to that mine. Started to build at the Haby ranch, right back of the .... on a ridge back of the ranch. Built that road on up to the mine, moved in a stamp mill. They got that old stamp mill from a company that had gone broke over in Four Mile. And then they were moving in a boiler into there about the time the war was started, and they didn't get the boiler across the divide from the Gila to the Aravaipa. They broke a wagon down. That old boiler set there for many years before it was finally moved. Don't know where it went, but it disappeared anyway.

And they used to come down to my father's place. That was .... usually they stopped there. I Iad a Model T that they left there. They'd come down horseback, leave the horses there in the pasture, take the old Model T to the Gila River, to town, to Safford.

And they were .... they were pretty good boys. They were never any hands to mix much with anyone, and consequently the general public knew very little about them ...... which was kind of a drawback when they did have troubles. But they caused no one any trouble when they were in this part of the country until the shooting took place up at their mine. They were illiterate, and I don't think they actually realized what a war really was and why they should have to go. Anyway, they failed to register and not being registered, why there was some friction brought up by some of the ...... their .... acquaintances that was more or less hostile toward them. But as far as the boys were concerned, one of them would have been over draft age, the other was under ..... er ...... was of draft age, and I don't think one of them would have had to register anyway. Charlie, the older one, wouldn't have had to gone anyway. He wanted to enlist, but when he went to enlist, why they told him he wasn't physically fit. Aw, there was nothin' wrong with him: he had a leg broke, his chest set over on one side a little where a horse fell on him, a few ribs outa place there, and his nose was smashed over on the other side of his face. But when they told him he wasn't physically fit to enlist, why he insisted that he could whip any man on the board if they'd try him. He'd prove his physical ability. But evidently they didn't want to carry the European war that close to home so they let him go. (Laugh)

And the other two boys, I really don't believe they knew what it was all about. They had pressure brought on them, and I guess they'd been pushed a time or other, and they wasn't gonna be pushed any more. And I really believe if somebody had gone to them ...... gone up there, talked to them, reasoned the thing out ...... I don't believe they'da had any trouble. But when men like they were raised ...... in the mountains. They were rough; they weren't men who would take a bluff at any time, 'cause if you did, they'd call it. And I have an idea that they ..... uh ....

they were just pushed a little too far.

You know ...... and before the thing come to a head, why their sister and their grandmother were going down to Klondyke in a buggy. The horse run away and uh .... the horse run away, turned the buggy over; it killed the old lady and hurt the girl ..... hurt her neck. She'd been going over to a doctor in Pima, a Dr. Dryden. He was treating her for an injured neck and supposedly it was all right. At least the doc thought it was getting better. And then later why the boys brought her down to my father's place. And they said she'd been killed. Well, after examining .... Dryden then come over and examined the body. At least I think it was Dryden or it could have been Dr. Platt at that time that examined the body. Anyway he could find no evidence of any foul play, but in those days, why uh ...... there was not an autopsy made ...... partly, yes, but the cause of it he couldn't determine ...... how she died. But, anyway, the boys were blamed with killing her. At least that's the way the story built up, not from within but from without. The neighbors knew the boys and knew that that would not be the case because those boys thought the world and all of the girl and always treated her that way. But, anyway, I think that is one of the main factors that contributed to the Powers killing, as it is now called through the country.

Then instead of sending somebody up that knew them, let them talk it over with the boys, why they went in force. I think that was a mistake by the officers ...... by doing so, because as a rule you can talk pretty near the toughest kind of a man into an agreement of some kind, if you will give a little ground as well as try to take some ground. But, anyway, it didn't work. They went up .... went up to stage a fight, surrounded the place and from all evidence that we know of, why the officers fired the first shot, killing the old man and shooting one of the boys through a window ...... a splinter knocked his eye out. But then the boys returned the fire. After returning the fire, they killed the sheriff and two deputies. And the third ..... a man by the name of Haynes, he was a United States Deputy Marshal from Globe. And from all accounts that I know of, why Haynes tried to talk them out of the procedure they were going through ...... going to ...... when they ...... when they tried to take the boys ..... talk to them. He figured that ...... he told them, "This looks more like an ambush ...... a killing procedure than an arrest." But that was voted down, I guess. Anyway, they had the killing.

The boys took off to old Mexico, were gone quite a while and then come back. But, anyway, I can't say that the boys were altogether wrong; can't say that they were all right either. But I think the solution was brought on by a little hasty judging and underestimating the boys if they did get them on this thing. I think that's the main thing, because those boys'd fight. And they'd been pushed; they'd been pushed many times. And you can't just keep pushin' a man around. Pretty soon he's not gonna take it. I think that's just exactly what happened there. Of course, that's ..... that doesn't help the orphan kids, all right, that was left, but that's an old thing, the sins of the fathers will descend on the future generations. That should be understood, and if you wanna take care of your family, why don't go pickin' any trouble because you might not live to take care of that family. So I don't approve of too much violence, but sometimes that seems to be the only thing that settles anything even though it does make a poor settlement. That's as far as I know on the Powers boys, they were honest; they were truthful; they were good neighbors, never bothered anyone; and they were workers.

When they come back for trial, why they had an old lawyer that they had known for years back. And I guess maybe he'd been in his day ...... a man by the name of Fielder, I believe. Anyway, I believe that Fielder was quite a spiritualist, that is with the spirits that soar downward, and I think that he was pretty well spirited up when he tried their case, so that he didn't have much of a defense. And even if they had, public opinion at that time was entirely against them. And so I don't know much to say about the trial. Anyway, at that time, why ..... they didn't have much council on their ...... for defense. And it seems like there was a lotta prejudice ...... more prejudice used than horse sense. I think .... I don't care what a person gets into, there's usually two sides to a case, and it should be examined.

Informant Anl6 (Reconstructed Text)

Well, our ranch was about twenty-five miles south ..... southwest of Fort Thomas, and I can just barely remember, at least I think I remember, when John Powers used to come by there. I don't know why he was up that way so often; some business on the reservation, I guess. But I can remember my folks talkin' about him even if I don't remember him. And then when we moved in here to town, I remember Ola. She was such a pretty girl and sweet. She used to come in here with her father and her brothers to shop, a couple of times a year, and she always had a smile and a kind word for everybody. Then when she got killed, there was all this awful talk about her and what a terrible person she was. And that just wasn't so. There wasn't a word of truth in it. And it seems as though they just went out there to kill her brothers on the strength of those stories. I think it's terrible the way that family has had to suffer, and I hope something can be done to get those poor men released from prison.

Informant An17 (Reconstructed Text)

The Powers was all fine people, hardworking, honest; I never knew a one to tell a lie. I've heard it said that their daddy was against the draft and wouldn't let his boys go in and register. That's a bald-faced lie. His name was Thomas Jefferson, you know, and he was proud of it and as patriotic as ever a man was. Them boys was going in to register just as soon as ever they got the mill set up there in Kielberg. They wasn't none of them against the war, and not a one of them that wouldn'ta died for his country. But they'd worked hard on that old mine; everybody else had give up on it, but old man Powers seen ryolite layin' around in there, and he knew there was gold. And they was just about to make it pay when all this happened.

Kane Wootan knowed what they had, and he figured to get it. He'd bought the Upchurch ranch up there, and he figured if he went up there and wiped the Powers out, it'd be easy to file on their mine. But he didn't figure on the kind of men he was dealin' with. If they were cowards like people said, he mighta got away with it. But they was real men, and they fought him and killed him, and then they was railroaded into the pen for it.

Informant An18 (Reconstructed Text)

First of all, I'm not a Mormon so you can't say I'm against the Powers because of that. They say those lawmen went out there and killed their father. I don't believe that. And even if that did happen, they still had no right to kill those lawmen. They should have surrendered no matter what. And then if they loved their father so much, why did they run off and leave him dying? Why didn't they stay there and take care of him? No, all they thought about was their own skins. And that old Tom Sisson he had already been to prison once for stealing horses, so he couldn't have been too innocent.

And then, how did they stay loose for so long? They couldn't have hid out from all those posses and all those soldiers for that long without help. People hid them and fed them and gave them fresh horses, and they did it just because they were jealous of all the successful people here in the valley. Pure spite was what it was. I think they got just what they deserved. It makes me sick to hear all the fuss that's going on now. They should die right where they are.

Informant An19 (Reconstructed Text)

I don't really know anything about the Powers, and neither does my brother. Don't believe what he tells you; it's a lotta shit. He'd say anything that would get him in good with the LDS. He wants to marry J., and he'd swear that bulls give milk if that's what the Mormons were saying.

I figure the Powers were pretty good old boys that did something the Mormons didn't like and paid for it. There's a whole lotta people it don't pay to fuck with.

Informant An20 (Tape Transcript)

I knew all the Powers, but I remember John and Tom the best. Tom was just full of fun, and John was awful quiet. Seemed to me like he didn't care for people near as much as animals. He was always talkin' quiet to horses and dogs, and he'd never say a word to a person.

And they loved him; horses and dogs would follow him around whenever he'd come on to the place. He had a little bay mare, what the Mexicans call *retinto*,[254] real pretty; Maudie he called her. My dad always said she was the best cow horse he ever seen. Said many times he'd give John any ten head on the place for her. Well, anyway, John had her trained to come when he called her. I don't care where she was or who had a-hold of her, when he spoke her name, she'd bust a gut to get to him. Even in a corral full of horses, he'd just open the gate and speak her name, and she'd come right to him.

Informant An21 (Reconstructed Text)

John and Tom come to stay with us for a while when they got out of jail. Mom had knowed them when she was a little girl, and she was glad to have them stay here. They sure got a rough deal. They didn't do a thing that I wouldn't do in the same place. It was proved that their father was shot down with his hands up. The only way you could put anything all the way in the bullet hole was to hold his arms over his head, and then it would go in. So we know that part of their story is true, and then they never knew who it was who killed him until the shootin' was all over. They're good people and I'll help them all I can.

Informant An22 (Reconstructed Text)

My dad supervised the prison farm up at the prison when I was a little boy, and I spent all my time playing out where John and Tom were working. There never were two men nicer to a boy than they were. My mother never worried if she knew I was with them. They never talked about their case to me, but they couldn't have done what they were supposed to do. I know that. Since I've been grown, I've heard all sides of the story, and I think the state of Arizona owes these men a great debt. It's one of the great injustices of all time.

---

[254] Bay, with a pronounced reddish tint, according to this informant.

Informant An23 (Reconstructed Text)

My grandma knew the Powers when they lived up here in the canyon. She said they was all fine people. The women folk went to church regular even after they moved up to Rattlesnake. I figure it was a put-up job. The Mormons got them. Them kinda things will happen around here.

Informant An24 (Reconstructed Text)

Well, I think everybody was scared to death of them, from what I've heard. They come in here from Texas; they was different; they was rough, and everywhere they went, they pretty soon give out the notion that they wasn't to be fooled with. Now, that didn't sit too well with some folks hereabouts, and something had to be done. So it was.

Some people can't live with the notion that a man don't want nobody messin' with him. So they keep pickin' and proddin' at that fella till they make him mad. And then their feelings get hurt when he comes back at them.

The Powers wasn't sociable; they wanted to stay to themselves, and right away people said there must be something wrong with them. So they made up stories about what kind a people the Powers was, and their own stories scared them silly, till they got so skittish they went on up there and forced them boys to blow their brains out.

There ain't a bit a doubt in my mind, that if folks had left that family alone, let them come and go, and do what they wanted without pickin' and pryin' at them, that shootin' never would a happened.

Now, some people around here ain't first class at mindin' their own business, especially if it looks like the other fella might have a little dust in his poke, and that mine that the Powers was workin' had somethin' to do with what happened.

Informant An25 (Reconstructed Text)

The Powers was pretty slick. They knew all the country around here, and that Sisson had been a scout with the army. So they led them soldiers and posses a merry chase. They bushed up mostly in the daytime and traveled at night, and they would circle back on their own trail, and the soldiers never really had any idea where they were. I believe they had some help; I mean, some people give them food and stuff, but they didn't need much. That old John had been trackin' horse thieves ever since he was a little kid, and he knew every trick there was to know. They'da got clean away if they hadn't come back from Mexico.

Informant An26 (Tape Transcript)

Well ..... I was around Willcox and went to work for the Mule Shoe outfit. It was operated by Mabe Lawson. At that time, it was ..... I'd imagine it was around February sometime of 1918. I'd been workin' there about a week or ten days, I suppose, or a little longer, and we got up to wrangle our horses one morning before daylight, myself and a partner named ..... uh ..... Tom Doody, and when we got out in the pasture by the horses, we saw three animals standin' in the corner by themselves and went over to see what they were.

It was two horses and a mule. They'd evidently been rode pretty hard; they was still wet with sweat. And we didn't know what to make of it because they was in the pasture with our horses. And we taken them on in, and we still didn't know what had happened, but we was short some horses. And some time that day Mr. Lawson went into town, Willcox, and reported this and found out then that what happened. It was the Powers boys had got into some trouble down the Aravaipa country, Rattlesnake Canyon. They had killed a sheriff and a couple of his deputies. And so then we knew what was goin' on, and the big hunt was on.

These fellas evidently were headed for Mexico, but they changed their mind and didn't go to Mexico; they went to ..... back towards the Graham Mountains and then to the Chiricahuas. And they had out ..... I imagine ..... fifteen hundred soldiers or more for a period of about a month's time lookin' for them. And they couldn't find them. The snow was pretty deep up in the mountains yet; they lost their tracks. Those boys musta stayed up there about thirty or thirty-five days in that range of mountains, and they never did find them. They found them when the case was about gave up. They decided they didn't know what to do with them. They came out of the mountains then and crossed across the valley by Hachita, New Mexico. And just before they got to the border, they came to a ranch house there, and there was a woman alone. They were hungry, and they stopped to see if they could get somethin' to eat. And she did feed them, according to Mr. Brink Schreiber, the man who captured the boys. And he got his direction and followed them to the border ..... line fence, and their tracks went through all right. So they let the fence down and went on in. And they trailed 'em, as I remember, eight or ten miles inside till they came to a small mountain. He had three soldiers with him, and part of them went around the hill, and he, himself, went over the hill. And when they got over where they could see down the next canyon, why they seen a little smoke down the canyon, and it was these boys, all right. They had a campfire. So they slipped up pretty close and really ..... they got the drop on the boys all right. But the boys offered no resistance at all, so he says, although they all had guns and plenty of ammunition. And they were around this little campfire roastin' some jackrabbits; they'd shot jackrabbits somewhere. And that was the breakfast they was a-havin'.

So then ..... they brought 'em back to Duncan, and at that time ..... by that time I'd went back to Duncan. And they put 'em in jail there and held 'em for a few hours, decidin' what to do. And I got to see the boys and also Tom Sisson. One of the boys had a pretty bad eye. Said that he was layin' behind a pack saddle, and one of the bullets hit the pack saddle and shot hardwood into his eye and put his eye out.

So then they taken them from there to Clifton to hold 'em over because they were afraid if they taken 'em to Solomonville, that they'd surely be lynched. And then after the trial they were all convicted, sent up for life, I didn't hear much more about the boys; only just maybe every eight or ten years I'd get some word of what they was doin' down in the big house. And at one time, I understood, they ..... the boys got out and made a run for it, but they got them back in short order. And then when ..... the last account I had is when they let them out here lately and pardoned 'em. So that's about all I know about it right now.

Wait, there is a little more to say. After this had happened, another week or so, the boss hired a cook, and he was a Dutchman from over in the Aravaipa country, and he lived right in near where these Powers boys lived, and he told me quite a bit about the life they lived and how it all came up. And he said that there was quite a bit of talk goin' back and forth that they wouldn't come out for the draft law, and the law had sent them word if they didn't come in, they was gonna come out and get 'em and bring 'em in feet first, if necessary. So no doubt the boys was all prepared for just that kind of a thing. And the Dutchman said that the boys could see the fellas comin' in before they got there, and that actually he thought they had a bead on all the officers by the time they got settled down. So that was why the killin' was so quick and sudden.

Informant An27 (Reconstructed Text)

My father never had a chance. He stepped out that door, and they shot him down like you'd shoot a deer. He'd just got outa bed; it wasn't full light yet. My Maude mare come runnin' down past the house with my sister's colt, and they run right over a bitch and her pups, and they put up a squall, and my dad stepped out with a shotgun, and they shot him like you'd shoot a deer.. Showed him no mercy. He had his hands up, and they shot him, killed him.

Roberts: What was the fight like?

There was a lotta lead thrown. That house was peppered with bullets. They almost killed Tom Sisson in his bed. I grabbed a rifle and looked out the window and got hit right away. Tore the bridge of my nose away and blinded me in the left eye. Before I knew what was happenin', I was wounded, hurt bad. I had trouble seein', but I fired back the best I could.

Roberts: Did you hit anybody?

Yeah. I killed McBride and Kempton. I didn't know who they was when I shot them, but the two I killed turned out to be McBride and Wootan ..... er ..... Kempton. My old pardner that I buried last week killed Kane Wootan. Wootan was sneakin' around the side of the cabin, and he didn't know that Tom could see him through the logs. Tom just stuck his gun barrel through the logs into Kane's belly and pulled the trigger. That son-of-a-bitch grunted like a pig when that bullet hit him. Old Tom never fired a shot; never even picked up a gun, and they sent him to prison for the rest of his life.

Roberts: It was a terrible thing. Did you see your father put his hands up?

Didn't see him, no. But I was buildin' up the fire in the stove when he stepped out the door, and I heard somebody yell somethin', and right after that they shot him with his hands up. They meant to kill all of us; they didn't come out there to take any prisoners.

Roberts: Why do you say that? Didn't they come to take you in to register for the draft?

That's what they want you to believe. The draft had nothing to do with it. It was the mine they wanted. If I hadn't lost Tom, we'da opened that mine up and showed how rich it was. That was what they were after, the mine.

You've heard of the Mountain Meadows Massacre?[255] Well, that's what this was, a little Mountain Meadows Massacre. The Mormons knew how rich that mine was, and they come out here to kill us and get it. Wootan was the ringleader; he had it in for us because none of us was afraid of him. And then they called us murderers. They come out here in the dark, surrounded the house, killed my father, and shot my eye out before any of us fired a shot, and then they call us murderers.

I didn't have to go in the draft anyway. I was workin' for the Forest Service at that time, and they told me that I couldn't go. A bunch of Apache bucks jumped the reservation and come down through the Aravaipa, and everybody was scared of 'em. Well, I never met the man or the Indian who could scare me, so I went up there to talk to 'em, and they listened and the next mornin' they went back up to San

---

[255] In September, 1857, a company of emigrants from Missouri, Arkansas, was attacked by Indians and Mormons dressed like Indians. One hundred and twenty of the emigrants were killed; only seventeen children were spared. Twenty years later, John Doyle Lee, a son of Brigham Young by the principle of temple adoption, was convicted at Beaver, Utah, of having led the massacre and was returned to that site and shot.

Carlos. And the Forest Service office said that he wanted me on the payroll. So I couldn't have gone if I wanted to. They needed me here.

They come out to murder us all, but they didn't figure on us fightin' back. They got my father; he never had a chance. They poisoned my sister, too.

Roberts: They did?

Sure they did. I think they meant to get us all. I never figured out who did it or how they did it, but I think they meant to get us all. My sister cooked for us all, you know. But that morning she was fine, and then later on my dad went down there, and she wasn't feeling good. And then Tom went down there, and she was having convulsions, and right after that she died. They poisoned her. They wanted to get us all so they could get our mine. That's what they wanted. It's a terrible thing.

Roberts: It certainly was. Just awful.

Nobody knows how awful it was except Tom and me, and now he's gone. You ever been shot?

Roberts: No, I haven't. I guess it hurts pretty bad.

Hurt? Yeah, it hurts. It's like somebody hit you with a sledge hammer. But what does mostly is make you mad. Nothin' makes you madder than gettin' shot. I been shot several times.

Roberts: Several times?

Yeah. I was shot a couple times before the shooting up at the mine, and it don't tickle.

Roberts: How did you come to get shot?

Oh, that was when I was just a kid, over in New Mexico. Some horse thieves come through and run off some of my dad's horses, and my mare, old Maude, was in that bunch, and I liked her awful well. I just figured I wasn't gonna let them take her. So I got an outfit together and trailed them. I tracked them all the way over to near Clifton. I come up on their camp, and I picked a good spot and waited until they started stirrin' in the morning. I called down to them and told them to give up. They went for their guns, and I killed the one, and the other one run off. I got all our horses back, and I got their whole outfit, and it come to a lot of money. And it seemed to me to be a pretty easy way to make money, so for the next few years I took to chasin' horse thieves. Did pretty good at it, too.

Roberts: Was that horse thief the only other man you killed?

Oh, no. Countin' Mexicans, I guess I've killed right around twenty-five men, but none that didn't need it.

Roberts: Oh .... How did you get away from here?

I don't remember much. My eye was givin' me a lotta trouble, and I just depended on the two Toms. I remember being awful cold, and finally I told my brother that if he didn't build a fire for me to get warm, I was gonna die. So we stopped and camped. I guess it was my fault we didn't get away. They had to wait for me so often. They got awful close to us a few times, close enough so we could hear them. One time Tom hid in a log and Wheeler and some of his men come and sat right on that log, and Tom heard their plans.[256]

Roberts: Did you think a lot about giving yourselves up?

We never would have give ourselves up to the law, because we knowed they'da killed us. We finally give up to the soldiers because we figured they wouldn't kill us. I never would have give up. We coulda killed them soldiers like pickin' tin cans off a fence, but Tom thought we oughta surrender and go back and straighten things out. He thought we'd get a fair trial.

Roberts: Did you?

---

[256] See footnote 7.

Hell, no! First off, they tried to kill us. Would have, too, if it hadn't been for the soldiers. They got a mob of them Mormons outside the jail, and they was makin' a lot of noise, and that captain told us not to worry. And he went out there and said, "Listen, you Mormon sons-a-bitches! If anything happens to them men, I'm gonna start my men firin' in Solomonville, and they won't stop till they get to Geronimo." And that was the end of the trouble from the crowd. Course, they blinded me in that jail. I was just beginning to see light out of this bad eye, and the doctor come in, and he put carbolic in it. That was the worst pain I ever felt, and I never seen anything out of it since. I believe they done it on purpose.

Then at the trial, they bought off our lawyer. He didn't do nothin' for us. We'da been better off without a lawyer. I heard the Mormon Church spent $300,000 to get us convicted. That's how bad they wanted our mine.

We never had no chance. I'm the last one. They've killed us all and locked us up for our whole lives, and all of our work went for nothin'. Folks that tells that we got a raw deal, tells the truth.

Informant An28 (Reconstructed Text)

I don't hold no grudge against nobody. I figure that just makes you old before your time. (Laugh) We're outa jail now, and we plan on stayin' out. Nobody can pay us for the time we did there, though.

The whole thing was a nightmare. We'd just got up in the morning. I hadn't got outa bed yet. Dad was up and had his pants on. John was runnin' around in his longhandles gettin' the fire goin'. I was awake but layin' in bed, and I don't believe old Tom was awake at the beginning. The first thing I knew, John's mare, Maude, and a colt that my sister had hand-raised come a-gallopin' through the yard, and they run right through a bitch and a litter a pups that she had there in the yard. They set up an awful howl! Dad grabbed a shot gun and stepped out the front door. I'll always believe he thought a lion was after the horses. As soon as he stepped out, I heard a voice shout, "Throw up your hands!" Well, I commenced to come outa that bed, but before I hit the floor, a shot rang out. I hurried over to the door. Dad hadn't closed it, and through it I could see that he was down and hurt. I tried to get to him, but when I showed myself in the door, I drew a lot of fire. I jumped back, grabbed a rifle, knocked a pane out of the window, and started firin' back.

It wasn't full light yet, but I seen somebody right up close in front of the house, and I took a bead on him, but before I could fire, he went down. John got him. Then I seen somethin' through the logs of the cabin. The chinking had fallen out in some places, and I could see somebody movin' along the side of the cabin. I just stuck the barrel of my gun in his belly and pulled the trigger. He grunted like a pig when that slug hit him! I turned back to the window just in time to see another man go down in front of the cabin. The firing stopped then. Old Tom had never got outa bed. Matter of fact, I'm not sure he ever woke up till a slug hit into a log right over his head.

Well, then we stepped out to see about Dad. He was shot awful bad, and we could see there wasn't much to be done for him, but we got him up and got him into bed, made him as comfortable as we could. It wasn't until we finished with that, that we got a chance to see who'd been shootin' at us. I turned the man right in front of the house over, and as soon as I seen it was McBride, I knew we was in trouble. Turned out the one I shot was Kane Wootan, and the one farther from the house was Mart Kempton. We didn't know nothin' about the government man they say was there. Well, before we got things sorted out, Jay Murdock and Henry Allen rode up. They'd heard the shootin' and come over to see about it. John had been hit in the eye and nose, and he was in considerable pain, so we tried to doctor him.

We knew we was in a real jackpot, but we didn't know what to do about it. I kinda wanted for us to give ourselves up, but John was against that, and Jay Murdock said that he thought the Mormons would lynch us. I was worried about my dad, too. He was conscious now and then, and he told me, "Son, I put my hands up, and they shot me." Jay Murdock said he didn't think Dad would last long, and if we was goin', we'd better ride out.

John was in rough shape, bleedin' and in a lotta pain. We didn't have any horses caught up, so I looked around and found their horses tied down in a wash, and I brought them back. Old Tom said that he was goin' with us, said he knew the country south a lot better than we did, and said he could help with John. I tried to talk him out of it, but he wouldn't have it anyway but what he'd go along. So we took their horses and some of their guns and ammunition and headed on out of there.

John slowed us down pretty bad. He had trouble stayin' in the saddle and a couple of times he begged us to go on and leave him, but I couldn't do that. He kept complainin' of the cold, and he finally said if I didn't stop and build him a fire, he couldn't go on. We stopped and made camp, and old Tom did what he could with John's wound. It was a terrible lookin' thing. That bullet had taken the piece of bone in his nose that's right between his eyes out and then had run right across his left eye. He said he could see light out of it but that the pain was awful bad. I kinda knew how he felt, 'cause I'd run a Spanish bayonet[257] in my eye comin' off a bank, and I couldn't see much out of mine either. I still don't see much.

A lot of people was good to us while we was on the run. We changed horses a few times, and some people give us food. They all told us our only chance was to get to Mexico because the Mormons was after us. Runnin' kinda went against my grain; I'da lot rather gone in and tried to explain what happened, but John wouldn't hear of it, and most everybody we talked to seemed to think he was right.

They come close to us several times. We could hear them movin' through the brush behind us lots of times, but old Tom was pretty cagey, and he always seemed to know someplace we could bush up and fool 'em. One time I crawled out on a little ledge and looked down, and there was Wheeler and some other fellas not forty feet from me, a-talkin' about how they missed us and where we was headed. They figured we was headin' due south, so that's why we swung over east. Another time east of San Simon, I backtracked a little to see if there was anybody on our trail, and I had to hide in the brush by the side of the trail while three of them rode past. If they'da spit, I'da got wet, but they never seen me.[258]

One time Tom Sisson rode in to scout a little ranch and see about gettin' some grub, and he met a young fella who was ridin' to join up with the posse. That fella told Tom what bloodthirsty critters we all was, and Tom told him if we was as fierce as he said, he'd have to be awful brave to go after us. The boy agreed with him, and old Tom

---

[257] A species of Yucca with spine-tipped leaves.
[258] Contrast Tom's accounts of these events with the legendary ones. (An27, Mo26, Mx1)

never let on who he was.[259]

It wasn't no fun though. We was hungry and cold a lot of the time, and both my brother and me was in a lotta pain. We finally got to the border and crossed over near Hachita. We stopped and ate at a little ranch house below the border and then rode off a mile or two to rest. We didn't think they'd come after us, but after a couple hours we heard some horses comin'. We spread out and had them pretty well covered. There was nine of them, all soldiers, and we could have killed them easy, would have, too, if John had his way. But I was tired a runnin', and I didn't see no future for us in Mexico, and I figured the soldiers wouldn't kill us, and we could get a fair trial. So we just walked down and give ourselves up. Lieutenant Hayes was the officer's name, and he guaranteed us that we'd get fair treatment, and he done all he could to see that we did.

They brought us back to Safford and put us in jail. There was a lotta talk about lynching us, but the army put a stop to that. I never did know a lawyer but old Squire Fiedler over in Silver, so I sent for him. I guess that was a mistake; he never did give us a chance to tell our side a things and didn't seem to much care.

I don't think we got anything like a fair trial. Old Tom never fired a shot, and he still got life. He died up there in prison. It wasn't none of it no picnic.

Informant An29 (Tape Transcript)

I live in Safford, Arizona, and history's been my hobby for .... oh .... a good many years, and the story which has particularly intrigued me in this area is the Powers story. It's the story of a family that is a most tragic one; one that's .... well, their lives were filled with violence. And it's a story that's.... I think that it's Arizona's best story outside the Graham-Tewksbury feud, the Pleasant Valley story which took place in central Arizona. And it's a story in which there's a great deal of controversy. A story which has engendered a great deal of hate. And what I did when I became interested in it, I contacted a great many people, and they commenced tellin' me their versions, and I found out

---

[259] This story was in my grandfather's repertoire of stories about Jesse James.

... seemed like everybody had an uncle who had a friend who knew the Power family. So what I tried to do was contact parties involved in this Powers story. And ..... in the course of my research, why I learned that the Power family were from the Kimball County area, deep in the heart of Texas up above San Antone, in that area. And it was here in this region that ..... around Fredericksburg, Kimball County, Junction County, Texas, that the old man Power (his name was actually Jeff Power) well, this is the region where he met Martha Power and..... (Martha's often referred to as Matty) and she was the daughter of Mr. and Mrs. C. B. Morgan. Jeff Power and the Morgans were engaged in the cattle game, and the old man has told stories of his marriage to Matty, and it seems as though they evidently had a wedding license, and they were going into Junction, Texas, to get married, and on their road into Junction, why they met a minister, and the old man ...... evidently there were witnesses around, 'cause he told how the group dismounted from their horses, and how he and Matty were married in the center of a dusty road.

And it was in this area .... why .... the Power family, Jeff and Matty, had a son born to their union. That was .... uh .... name was Charlie. And in the year of 1890, why .... the Power family .... Jeff, Matty and Charlie, why they followed the C. B. Morgans into western New Mexico, into the Mogollon region, northwest of present ... of Silver City. And here the Power family, why they hunted a great deal. There's some dandy stories connected with their stay in this area, particularly the Bearbit Brown story. That's my favorite. It seems as though this Brown was a gentleman who was quite wealthy, and with other wealthy Chicago businessmen he came into this Mogollon region to hunt. And they said that while this Brown was separated from one of ..... from his companions, why he encountered a bear, and the bear came at him, and Brown used his knife, and the bear clawed Brown. It was a ferocious fight, and when Brown was found by his companions, he was lyin' alongside this bear. The bear was dead, and the tracks plainly showed where this bear had dragged himself to water, returned to Brown's side and died there. And at any rate, well, Brown was taken to Silver City, and ..... I forget the number of stitches that was taken in his face, but it was around 140. They say he was terribly mutilated, and so .... in time, why he returned to his Chicago home, and he made such a .... such a .... well, he was just grotesque. And they say that it affected his business life, and his wife divorced him. So Brown why he just sold out his business and returned to this Mogollon region, and he commenced livin' the life of a herbet .... er .... of a hermit, and it was told how the Power family, they befriended him. They ..... how the old man Power used to bring him food, and how he ..... this Brown loved to read, so the old man would bring him .... oh .... newspapers and books, and he was rarely seen, but he was one of the Powers' neighbors.

And another move made by the Powers took them to the present Gila, New Mexico, region; in fact, just about a mile north of the present Gila, New Mexico, store. And their house, it sits on the brow of a hill ..... oh ..... possibly a mile from the Gila River ..... why it still stands. It's been remodeled recently, and it was here that three more children were born to the Power family. John was born in '91, and Tom was born in '93, and Ola was born in ..... Ola was born in ..... I know that date, but I believe it was in '97.

At any rate, why it was here that tragedy first sought out and found the Power family. Matty had taken this baby, Ola, and they were visiting a family named Neal, who lived on the Power .... family .... had rented a small picket-type house, had a dirt roof, a very crude affair. And while Granny (and I will identify Granny as being the mother of Jeff Power; I know her by no other name; she was a small, trim woman with a fiery tongue) ..... And while Granny and Matty and the baby, Ola, was visiting these Neals, why this roof caved in. One of the large limbs that they had supporting this dirt roof, why, broke and struck Matty on the head (she was pregnant at that time) and it caused her death. So she was buried just a short distance from the Power home; there's a marble marker there today. And it's said that the old man wept bitterly at her grave. I know that he did mourn the loss of his Matty, that he never remarried.

And there's a lotta stories connected with the Power family while they lived in this particular area. And a great many centered around the Lyon-Campbell Cattle Company. And this Tom Lyon and Angus Campbell, why they combined in the early days to create one of the really large cattle domains in the west .... and after Angus Campbell died in the White House in .... I believe it was '92, why, Lyon married his widow. Later they established a big ranch headquarters at Gila. In fact, that building still stands. It has thirty-six rooms, and all of the floors are hardwood, and it has one immense fireplace. And at any rate, why, this Lyon was noted as sort of a ruthless fellow. He was very domineering, arrogant, and he was warring with the nesters up there. And as a result of this trouble with these nesters, why there was a great many killings. The story I particularly have in mind is the time that Jeff and this Tom Lyon had been quarreling over water rights. See, the Power family were neighbors to Lyons, and .... so the old lady, Granny, why she tired of hearin' her son and Tom Lyon quarrel over this water, so one day she took a shovel and a gun up to a certain headgate, and she turned some water loose, and she thought that'd bring Lyon there, and it did. So they quarreled, and Granny, she wins the argument by snatching a shotgun from behind a tree, and even today she's known by old timers up in that region as Shotgun Sal.

There's other stories about Granny. For instance, one of the parties that knew her best, a Mrs. Reynolds from Pima, has told me the story that Granny related to her, how back in Texas her husband had been spendin' too much time in the saloon, and so she went into the saloon after him. One time she took ... she had a whip, and she whipped him out of the saloon; she whipped him home; and he climbed up a tree. And I know Mrs. Reynolds said, "What'd ya do next?" Says, "I didn't do a consarn thing but chop that tree down!" So that was Granny for you.

Now in the year of 1905 they left this Gila, New Mexico, region, and they made their way over into Doubtful Canyon which is near present-day San Simon, Arizona. They lived there about a year and had a little trouble about fire. Fire destroyed their home. They weren't satisfied with this country, and about the year 1906, why they moved to the Willcox area. And there about seven or eight miles northwest of Willcox, about 160 acres of land there. And they're still in the cattle game. And it's while they're here that Ola goes to school. And while she's attending school, why she becomes angry with the teacher. Seems as though she didn't have too much education, and this Willcox teacher would chide her and make remarks such as, "Why even the Mexican children know more than you do." So one of those days, she made some remark that particularly infuriated Ola, and so Ola, she pounces on her with the fury of a wildcat and gets her down on the floor and pummels her with her fists. And that little incident ended Ola's education.

So from this Willcox region, why the Powers' next move is into the Aravaipa, and they're located at Stowe's Gulch, not too far from where Mae Davidson now lives. And, undoubtedly, they went into that region because Charlie, he'd found work there, and they had relatives there, the Wiley Morgans. He'd be Jeff Power's brother-in-law; he'd established himself there in the canyon not far from where the present Klondyke store is now located. So while they was livin' at Stowe's Gulch, why Charlie learned that a ranch, the Rattlesnake Ranch, located deep in the heart of the Galiuro Mountains, could be purchased, and I understood it was for a very small sum of money. I forget that sum right now, but it was for like $100. At any rate, why, the party that they bought it from was named Branson, and it was a widow and two sons that had been runnin' goats there, and originally, why this ranch had been started by a party that plays a most important part in the Tombstone story. I'm a little vague on his name right now. At any rate, why this is the ranch that the Powers settle on, and they commence running their cattle in this area. It's located … oh … possibly twenty-five miles north of Klondyke. I mean south … sort of southeast …. a little southeast of the present Klondyke store. And it's very difficult to get into this region. I know that for a long period of time they just literally had to pack in and out for supplies. And it was while they were here that they ran their cattle. I was tryin' to remember their brand. At any rate, why, they had one main brand and a lotta other brands. And they lived in a world of themselves, and they were self-reliant. They … had a lotta abilities. For instance, they were all good blacksmiths. I was told that the Power boys' father was a top blacksmith, and they were very good at leatherwork, and they was excellent shots and good cowboys. I know that Tom in particular said that he could go anywhere that a cow could go. Their country was very rough and brushy, and. they needed to be good cowhands. And the reason they called this rough place the Power Garden Place was they diverted water from Rattlesnake Creek, and they raised some alfalfa and a little grain and had a garden patch, hence the name.

So they're living in this area when they become involved in a mine. This mine is located uh …. this mine was located over in Kielberg Canyon. Now I'll try to briefly explain, when you're in Rattlesnake, if you continue about seven miles south, why Rattlesnake bends sharply to the southeast, and instead of bending with the canyon, if you climb right over the mountain, there's a trail that leads right into the bottom of Kielberg, and it's here that there's a mine. And this mine had quite a background. It's a story in itself, and I won't try to go into it. It's sort of a jinx mine, and for a long time it'd been called the abandoned claim, so many miners had looked it over and decided that it wasn't a paying mine. They'd find gold, just traces .... sometimes they'd find a fair amount, but not in what they thought was paying quantities. So the Powers become involved in this mine, and it's kind of a roundabout story. I was trying to remember the name of the man. There was a man named Al .... There was a fella named Al ..... I'll think of his name in a minute, and with a Mexican, they'd been working in the Jackson country, which is down south of this mine in Kielberg Canyon which I'm tellin' you about. So they looked it over one time, and they decided to see what they could do, and they were tunneling high up on top of this mountain, and one day while they was sharpening tools, why this Al (I'll still say his name in a minute) he uh accidentally hit this Mexican on the head, and the Mexican thought that it wasn't an accident. So he thought that this Al was trying to kill him. So he sold his share of this mine to a man named Tucker, Perry Tucker. And these two ..... this fellow's name was Al Bauman, B-A-U-M-A-N. And so Tucker and Bauman, they finally quit the tunnel at the top of the mountain, and they run short of funds, and they both left that country and worked at various places. And then they come .... when they returned, why they erected a log cabin, which still stands, known as the Power cabin, among other things, let's see, they were interested also in building a trail. They improved that .... they was the first ones that did much towards establishing a better .... uh ...... not so much as a road but a trail leading down into the Aravaipa Canyon. At any rate, why one of the trips that these two men had made into Klondyke for supplies .... why .. one night they were camped near the Klondyke store, and they met a fellow there named Kirby. And this Kirby, Lee Kirby, why he was a forest ranger. He was a new one; he'd been over in the Roosevelt area for a short time, and then he was transferred to this Klondyke station. And this Bauman had .... I mean this Kirby had been, he was a very fine fellow from what I understand. And incidentally, he's still living today in Phoenix, and he reached a very high rung in the Forest Service ladder. At one time he became supervisor of the Tonto National Forest (that's our largest here in Arizona) and then he went to the regional office in Denver. At any rate, during the course of the conversation near the Klondyke store one evening, why this Kirby remarked that he'd attended a dance in Safford, and Tucker remarked that only fallen women ever attended these dances. And he also made remarks about Mrs. Greenwood, the wife of the proprietor of the store, and the girl that worked for her. And Kirby knew this girl, and he stoutly defended their honor, and the two men quarreled. And this Kirby …. er .. this Tucker told Kirby, said, "Don't you ever come near the mine." But he did, he said, "I'm gonna go there. If I have business there, I'm gonna go there." And one time he did have business there, and so …… at any rate, Tucker comes out of the mine, and the two quarrel, and uh …. Tucker, he ……. according to Bauman's later testimony, he started this whole affair, and Kirby shot and killed him. He was buried just outside of the mine, in fact, in a little canyon just below the mine. This was all …. this occurred in … oh, let's see ….. on the third of January, 1912.

Well, the reason I'm telling you this story, it plays a part in the Power family story. And the Power family then …. in a roundabout way ….. they had the Powers doing work …. well, they acquired an interest in this mine, and to make a long story short, at one time there's five different parties who have ownership in this mine. So in the end the Power family starts buying them out, and they acquire complete ownership of the mine. One of their first acts is to start building a road, trying to construct a road from the Haby place out to their mine. And while they're engaged in this particular activity, they're camped … oh … three, four, five miles north of the ….. er … rather south of the Haby place, and they were visited there by Ola and Granny. Now Ola and Granny at this particular time were living in the Aravaipa Canyon, near what is the Sanford place. There was a house that burned down there recently, and they were almost across the wash from this Sanford place. And the way they'd acquired this place, why Charlie, why he had homesteaded it. But they never did acquire too good a rights. But at any rate, that's why the Power women are living there at the time that they make a trip to where the men are one Sunday. They're goin' out there and have Sunday dinner with them. And they had borrowed a horse; it was called Old Rose (it was a roan) from a cowboy out in that region named Jeff Clayton. And uh …. in their buggy they made this trip. They had the meal, and they had a very pleasant meeting. I might explain at this time also helping with this road work is a man named Tom Sisson. Sisson had been ... he was a native of Minneapolis, and as ..... he left home at an early age and joined the army, and then in '92, I believe it was, why he was mustered out of the service at Fort Grant. He was a wheelwright and remained in that general Fort Grant-Klondyke-Willcox area for a great many years. And he was a constable; he was an officer out to Klondyke at one time. At any rate, why he was sent to prison for stealing a horse off the reservation, and he was pardoned, and at this particular time, he had joined with the Powers in this road activity, and I've been told that they supplied him with his food and lodgings, tobacco and so forth, and if they were to profit in the mine, well, then they would compensate him. So these are the parties that Ola and Granny visited, and when they started home .... it was fairly late when they arrived at their pasture gate, and for some unaccountable reason at this time, well, this roan seemed to go wild, and Ola was driving. She was a strong girl, but she couldn't hold this roan, couldn't manage it, and it made for the Power house, and it swerved right before it got to a woodpile .... before it reached a woodpile, and the buggy overturned. Ola and Granny were thrown from this buggy, and both were hurt, Granny seriously so, and as a result of her injuries, why Granny died. She was buried .... she was attended, incidentally, by Dr. Parker, who used to live not too far from where the ranger station is located. But Granny was buried in the Klondyke cemetery which is located not far from the Newell Weathersby's home, present home. And at that time it was explained to me by old-timers, there was no road leading up to this cemetery, and the parties were carried up the hill. And there's a little story connected with Granny's death. She had a little Mexican hairless dog named Frijole that she prized very much, and the reason she had this dog, it was in accordance with the superstition in the Southwest that if you had a Mexican hairless dog, and if you slept with it ... for instance, if you had rheumatism, why your rheumatism would be transferred to the dog. So Granny always claimed that she .. her rheumatism left her, and apparently Frijole had it.[260]

---

[260] This is a widespread contemporary belief. Tom McCahill, auto columnist for *Mechanix Illustrated*, has published numerous testimonials to the efficacy of this cure for asthma. Jan Brunvand reports its appearance in a health column

So the Power boys continue their road work, and their next project is to erect a mill. They were trying to erect a mill at what was called Gold Mountain, and Gold Mountain was right near where I told you that this Rattlesnake took a sharp turn to the southeast. The reason they located there is that there is no water in Kielberg Canyon, and so … I understood they paid … I think … $450 for this mill. They dismantled it, packed it in there, and was in the act of erecting it at the time that war was declared. This was 1917, of course, and the time when Tom and John received summons to go in and register. Charlie, by that time, why he had pulled out and left the Power family. He had come into Safford. They told he had bought an old automobile, a Michigan automobile, which he .. uh …. well, it was a lemon, and the Powers rode him so about it, why they claimed it angered him, and he went into Safford, stayed for a while, traded it for a motorcycle, and started for Silver City. This motorcycle broke down, and so he remains in the Silver City region, and I know he loses a hand in a well-digging accident. He died in that area just north of Silver City some four or five years ago. So much for Charlie.

Back to the Powers, now, who were engaged in this .. erecting a mill, and at the time the war had broken out, and the boys don't go in and register as they're required to do, and they become slackers. Well, it was during this period that tragedy again visited the Power family. This time, why Ola dies, and there's a world of stories connected with Ola's death. And she dies at Gold Mountain. The coroner's report tells that she died from causes unknown. And there's a great deal of mystery attached to this particular story. Just to be brief, why, these general stories are that somebody killed Ola in the … in the Power .. uh … killed Ola to conceal the fact that she was pregnant. Now that's one story. Another story is that she had a lover named Red. He was a cowboy from the Willcox area. She was tryin' to contact him, and they roped her off a horse, and this fall from the horse injured her neck. Another story is that she was roped in play. Another story is that the old man, that uh .. (that's quite a psychological thing) the old man was extremely jealous of her, and couldn't stand to think … you know .. of any man having her. And there's just a maze of stories connected with this. I

---

in the *St. Louis Post Dispatch* in *The Study of American Folklore* (New York: W.W. Norton and Company, Inc., 1968), p. 182.

remember Henry Allen, who's one of the few parties left who really knows this story well, and I said, "Well, what do you think, Henry?" And he said, "Well," he said, "I think that perhaps she got some cyanide pellets that the Powers kept around their home .... they would put these pellets in the carcass of a dead animal, cow, and hope to .... that they could poison a lion." And still living is a Mrs. Mel Bosco, and she was the first party outside that immediate family that was there, and I asked her what she thought, and she said, "Well ...." It amounted to this: that she thought Ola had been dead much longer than Power ..... the Powers claimed. And Joe .... uh ... Joe... let's see ... I'm trying to say ..... he was a Justice of the Peace at the time, and I know him well ..... I can't recall his name. But at any rate, he told me that in a conversation with Dr. Platt, that Dr. Platt estimated Ola had been dead three to five days. Now all the other parties I know that know the Powers well claim that the Powers loved Ola very much, and that they wouldn't harm her. So very frankly, I just don't know what did happen to Ola. That's just some of the stories connected with her death.

At any rate, why, the Power boys, it's told, why they watch the proceedings of this coroner's jury, and then there was an autopsy performed on Ola's body at the Haby home. And they're in the hills just back of the Haby home while all this activity is going on. They watch the funeral procession as it wends down the canyon, and Ola was buried beside her former friend ... uh ... Granny.

Well, again the Powers, why they're back in this country; they didn't attempt to leave there, but were hiding out. And at that time .... let's see .... it's in February of 1918 that there has been correspondence from a Deputy U.S. Marshal named Haynes and he's contacted the sheriff of Graham County ... uh ... McBride. And so .... this group .... this group .... uh.... let's see .... well, I better identify this group. There's Sheriff McBride and U.S. Marshal Haynes, and there's Deputy Sheriff Mart Kempton and Deputy Sheriff Kane Wootan. And this group .... uh........ Haynes deputized Kane Wootan as a... Now I just remembered the name of this justice of the peace; his name was Joe Blaek, B-L-A-E-K. And at any rate, why, these officers then, they leave Safford in Sheriff McBride's car (it was a Model T) and they stop at the Haby place. Mr. Haby advised these people that they'd better proceed with caution in attempting to arrest these boys. And they go on to Al Upchurch's ranch. Incidentally, Al's place actually was .... he'd just sold it to Kane

Wootan, but he'd remained on the particular ranch. They arrived there about suppertime, and Al Upchurch, who (incidentally, he died at the Pioneer's Home several years back) .... uh ... well ..... they ... the officers, they asked for mounts, and they got them there. And so they had supper, and after supper they started into this Rattlesnake country. And they went up .... let's see .... what's the name of that canyon? At any rate, why .... I might tell that Kane Wootan had uh .... Kane Wootan had loaned Deputy U.S. Marshal Frank Haynes his rifle, and he had borrowed Al Upchurch's rifle, and I think this is a very important point, and I'll explain why in just a few minutes. So these men ride through the night, and they stop at the Bosco place. No one was there. Stop at the Power Garden place. No one was there. And then they come to Gold Mountain; no one was there. And it was early in the morning when they started down this long trail that leads to this cabin, which is right near the Power mine. They surround this cabin, and John had two pet mares, Connie and Maude, that he had raised from the time that they had been little colts, and they were pets, and they ran through the yard, and the old man appeared .... uh ..... stepped outside the door with gun in hand, and I believe that he thought perhaps that they were a mountain lion outside. So when he comes outside, well Kane Wootan tells him to throw up his hands. And this is a very controversial point, because the old man is shot, and the controversy rages around whether Kane Wootan did shoot him with his hands up or whether bullets were fired first from the house, which Haynes later testified in the trial held there in Clifton, that the first shots in the battle that followed were fired from the house. But at any rate, why, the old man was shot, and I just mentioned a while ago about Kane Wootan having Al Upchurch's gun. Now this is what Al Upchurch told me. He said that this gun had a hair trigger. He said it was cold out there that morning, and he said perhaps Kane Wootan was nervous. He said, "I believe that Kane shot the old man, but I don't believe that he meant to." And I just don't know. That's just one of the many stories and versions that you ... that we have connected with this fight. But in the battle that followed, why, Kane Wootan, Martin Kempton, and Frank McBride were killed. And Tom, John, and Tom Sisson that participated in this battle, they were all in the house. Why, they come out when they deemed it safe to do so. They get the officers' mounts and guns, and they start towards Mexico. And in the meantime, this Haynes, they haven't seen him, he starts toward Safford. They .... this group .... these three men, the two Powers and Tom Sisson, they start southward, and they go to the Murdocks. Jay Murdock and his brother, John Murdock, and Henry Allen, and Ed Knote, and a cowboy .... let's see ... a Mule Shoe cowboy .... uh ..... well, at any rate, those men are all gathered near the Murdock place. They'd heard the shooting, and they sorta guessed what'd happened. At any rate, why these .... uh ... the two Power boys, they requested that these men try to take care of their father. When they'd left him, why, he was still alive. And these men asked them where they're goin'. Well, they were going down into Mexico, or if I remember correctly what Jay Murdock says, they didn't know where they were going. That's the way ... Jay's version. At any rate, why, Murdock and these other men that I named, they went to the cabin, found the three officers dead. They found the old man just outside the door. They took him inside and put him on the bed, but he wanted to be moved for some reason .... I don't know, but they took him to the mine tunnel, placed him inside there. During the afternoon, why, he died.

Well, shortly after they'd arrived there, though, this Henry Allen, he'd been dispatched by Murdock to go in and tell what had happened. See, they didn't know that Haynes had viewed this fight. So when Henry Allen arrives at the Upchurch place, there's Haynes, and already a few of the Aravaipa ranchers had gathered at this spot. And ... but Haynes is very vague about what had happened. He .... about all he'd say was that McBride was down. According to Allen, why, he didn't know, for instance, that Mart Kempton and Kane Wootan was dead. So these men go in to .... let's see ...... Henry Allen and the supervisor named Quinn and another boy, they ride into Safford, and the word is spread about .... what happened.

And soon a gigantic man hunt is underway ... they have told that more than 3,000 people have participated in that hunt. A great many were soldiers from Fort Bliss and Camp Jones and Fort Huachuca. And then there were officers, of course, from all over the Southwest, a great many possemen. It looked like, though, that these men had eluded the officers and reached the safety of Mexico. And uh .. let's see ..... just about a month later they were captured near ..... they were captured across the line from Hachita. It's called the corner country of New Mexico. And the party that was responsible for this capture ....

led the group that captured these men was a Lieutenant Hayes, and this Lieutenant Hayes described how later he crossed the line into Mexico. He actually wasn't supposed to, but he did, and how they .... he felt that the Power boys actually could .... had a chance to kill all of them ..... his group, but they didn't do it.

And they were in bad shape physically, and they surrendered and was taken to the Safford courthouse. And they secured the services of a lawyer named Fielder, James Fielder, from the Deming-Silver City area, and he secured a change of venue for these boys, so their trial was held in Clifton, the county seat of Greenlee County. It's located about forty miles northeast of Safford. And this trial commenced in May of 1918, and I'm a little vague on the time, but I think it lasted just about a week. And once the jury went out, they was only out about a half an hour, and they rendered a verdict of guilty. And most of the parties that .... familiar with this story believe if Arizona had had capital punishment, the Power boys would probably have been executed in some manner.

So they were taken to prison in May of 1918. And they ... while they were there, Tom along with another party ..... let's see .... what was his name? He was involved in an escape, and then still later .... I believe it was in '39 that Tom and John and another prisoner .... uh .... convict, they also escaped. Tom and John was found along the river bottom near Yuma, and the officers, they didn't seem to care whether they got them or not, decided they were in Mexico and let the boys go. And they were in there for several months, and they caught them trying to enter .... re-enter the United States at Eagle Pass, Texas. And they were returned to prison, and then this .... let's see.... in May of 1960, why, they were released from prison. And John, at the present time, is in the Silver City area, and I understand that Tom is now living in Mesa. At first he was up near .... located near Payson on some ranch.

Informant An30 (Reconstructed Text)

The old man Powers used to keep a pretty close eye on Ola, and she didn't like it none too well. I mean like when they came to town, she was always givin' some old boy the eye. And there was a Mule Shoe cowboy, a lanky, ugly fellow, name a Red. I disremember his last name.

He was always sniffin' around her. And I'll always believe that she got to sneakin' off to see him, and he got her pregnant. Now whether the old man found out and killed her, or the boys tried to keep her from runnin' off with him and killed her accidentally, I don't know, but I believe one a them two things happened.

And then about the shooting, I believe Kane Wootan was the cause of it. He was a real hot shit, always a-soundin' off and leanin' on people, and he had it in for them Powers for some reason or another. It may a been because they was leaned .... wouldn't take leanin' on, and it may a been because they had somethin' he wanted. I heard that he bought a ranch up there in that Galiuro country not long before the shootin'. It may a been somethin' that come out a that. But anybody that got in Kane's way was liable to get hurt. That don't mean that the Powers was angels; they had their faults like most. Yeah. Maybe more than most.

Informant An31 (Reconstructed Text)

All I ever heard was about the old man's wound, how you could stick something in it if you put his arms up over his head, but if you put his arms any place else, nothing would go in. And I guess that proves that they musta shot him when he had his hands up. That's all I know.

Informant An32 (Reconstructed Text)

Well, now, I'll tell you what I know about it, and it's quite a lot. I can remember the things that happened back then real good; it's what happened ten minutes ago that I have trouble with. (Laugh) One day back just after the war started, I was down at the court house, and Kane Wootan come out and flagged me down. And he says, "Hey, take a ride with me." Well, I didn't have nothin' else to do, so I went along. And he was goin' out on the Willcox road to look at some calves he was thinkin' about buyin'. He'd just bought the Upchurch ranch, and he wanted to put a little better stock on it. Well, we talked about the war, and Kane said he'd go in a minute if it wasn't for his family. I told him I didn't have to go that far to find a fight. Well, then he started in on McBride and what a horse's ass he was and said he'd like to give the county a good sheriff.

Well, that was that. Well, then in the fall, I seen him again, and he got me aside and told me about the Powers and how they wouldn't register for the draft, and he looked over there at the Galiuros and he said, "The man that brings them outa there is gonna be the next sheriff. How about goin' up there with me and helpin' me get 'em?" I told him I hadn't lost nothin' up there on Rattlesnake, and besides the Powers hadn't done nothin' to me. And I told him that the man that went up there to bring them out at gunpoint was likely to come back dead. And he laughed and said that whole bunch up there didn't have balls enough to fill a teacup. And I told him I'd leave that kinda investigation to somebody else.

To tell the truth, I never cared a lot for old Kane. He was a little bit screwy, always on the prod. I guess you'd say he was ambitious. And I liked the Powers. The old man was a little funny, but Tom was a helluva fine guy, pleasant and a lot of fun to be around. John was a different proposition. He didn't like to talk or joke around either one. I never seen him mad, but I never seen him glad either. And Tom told me that John had killed a bunch a people back in New Mexico, mostly Mexicans, and all of them horse thieves. Hell, anybody up at that camp could shoot the eye out of a gnat.

Now, about that girl, the terrible stories you hear about her ... well, there ain't no truth to 'em. I've sat at the table with her, and I knew her real well, and she was one fine girl. And the boys and the old man were foolish about her, and there wasn't nothin' dirty about it neither. They just thought she was the finest thing ever drew breath. And till Granny got killed, she lived in the cabin with Ola, and man nor beast better not look cross-eyed at that girl or they'd have Granny to deal with. Now, I've thought a lot about how she died. What I know for sure is that nobody up there, neither the Powers nor old Tom Sisson, woulda harmed a hair on her head, no matter what she done. She was in that accident with Granny, and from then on she doctored for her neck. Now maybe it was that. I've heard it said that her neck was broke when they examined her at the inquest. Maybe it had been broke all along. I don't know. Then old Tom Sisson told me before he died that she went into convulsions, and I got to thinkin' that maybe she'd somehow got some strychnine. They always kept a lot of it for poisonin' coyotes. But I just don't know.

Informant An33 (Reconstructed Text)

I talked to Jay Murdock and to Lee Solomon about this business, and I think I've got the straight of it. They say that Kane Wootan wanted that old shitty-ass mine the Powers had. Well, I don't believe that. Nobody in his right mind woulda give a bull's tit for that thing. A dozen different men worked that claim, and none of them made enough to pay for the sugar in his coffee. They all thought there was gold up there, but enough of them had worked themselves broke to prove different. Kane had been around enough and talked to enough people to know that that mine wasn't worth nothin'. Kane wanted to get ahead, and if the mine was worth anything, he might a gone after it, but that wasn't so. But I do think that Kane had a hard-on for the Powers because old John had made him pull in his sails a little bit over at the Klondyke store. Kane was a-spreadin' his tail feathers over there one time, mouthin' off and sayin' a lotta things he shouldn't, talkin' about the Powers none too favorable, and he made the bad mistake of thinkin' that old John was just about like his brother, Charlie. Now, Charlie was a silly old fuck, and he'd make a lotta noise, and maybe even pull his pistol and scatter a little lead, but he really didn't have the balls to kill a white man, and he kinda showed it. But ol' John wasn't cut from the same piece a goods. He'd kill ya if you gave him cause, and more than one had made that mistake. Well, anyway, when ol' Kane found out he had a stud horse by the whangerdoo, he had to back and fill a little bit, and he come off lookin' a little silly. And anybody done that to old Kane had an enemy for life.

That's what put Kane on the Powers' ass, and he tried to get several people to go up there with him and get them. Billy Whelan and Lee Solomon both told me he'd tried to get them to go up there. And they both told him the same thing: anybody that'd go up there fixin' to bring them out by force would have to be a certified jackass. But he wouldn't listen.

Now, I don't say he shot the old man on purpose. Jay Murdock told me that Kane had a rifle that he'd borrowed from Al Upchurch, and that rifle had a hair trigger. I believe Kane shot the old man without meanin' to, and that was all she wrote.

Informant An34 (Tape Transcript)

Well, I came to Arizona about 1930 and eventually wound up in Graham County, over in the Aravaipa Canyon. And one of the stories that intrigued me after coming to this part of the country was the old Powers story. Now the story as it was told to me occurred like this. The sheriff and two of his deputies from Safford came to the Aravaipa Canyon and made it known that they were going up after the Powers boys. Now ..... it seems that not only one, but more than one man prevailed upon these men not to go up as a posse to bring those two boys out, but rather to send somebody up who knew them to reason with them, and they could be talked into coming out. But they were going in at night and arrive at the Powers property in the very early morning hours, perhaps before daylight. And as circumstances turned out, that's exactly what happened. They did arrive there and were stationed around the cabin as daylight broke. And the teller of the story gave this version. That the dogs started barking, and Mr. Powers, the boys' father walked outside to see what the commotion was about. But as was customary in that lonesome, high country, he picked up a rifle as he walked out the door, and as he did walk out the door, he thought he saw a figure out in the underbrush, and he hollered, "Who's there?" or "Who's out there?" not thinking actually that it was a person .... that actually there might have been an animal out there. But the customary call was to holler, "Who's there?" And he took a few steps toward the corral, and as he did so, somebody hollered to him to throw up his hands, which he did. He had no more than gotten his hands in the air than a shot rang out, and Mr. Powers was struck in the chest .... and uh .... fell to the ground. Then there was another shot fired. Well, the two boys, Tom and John, who were in the cabin, ran to the window to look out to see what all the shooting was about, and they saw their father lying on the ground. So they each grabbed a rifle, and one of the boys broke the glass and stuck his gun out. And a shot went off right near him, and a remaining piece of the glass hit him in the eye and blinded him in that eye. Well, as he fell backwards, the other boy jumped to the window to try to see what was going on, and another shot was fired, and bits of glass sprayed his face. Now, I was always under the impression that this boy was not immediately blinded. But he did see where the shot came from, and he called to his brother and told him where he'd seen the rifle fire come from. So they put up a front; one of them fired a shot over the window sill while the other ran to an opening, and the fight was on.

Well, these boys were expert shots, as everyone well knows, and after a short series of firing on the parts of both parties, the posse and the boys, three of the men were killed. The fourth man, who was the government man, was not out in the open, and when he saw what had happened to the sheriff and his deputies, why he backed on out in the brush, got away, and left.

Now my informant claims to have appeared on the scene shortly after this took place. He lived in the mountains not too far from these boys, and when he got there, Mr. Powers was still alive. He said he took old Jeff in his arms and asked him what happened. And he told him that this was exactly the way it had happened. That he'd walked out, somebody had told him to throw up his hands and he did, and somebody shot him. "And I just don't know why they shot me."

So the boys decided to pull out. They didn't know whether there would be another posse following that one, and my informant helped lay Mr. Powers out on a cot and stayed with him until he died. The boys left this part of the mountain, went out of the Galiuro Mountains into the San Pedro Valley, crossed the valley and went over into the Chiricahuas, where they were eventually captured.

After the boys were captured, they were brought back to Safford, and the feeling was so high in the town over what had happened that they were eventually removed to Greenlee County, to the Clifton jail. And it was at Clifton where they were tried. And they were given a life sentence, and this life sentence was almost carried out. Three men, old Tom Sisson, who was convicted of assisting the boys in the shooting, was tried with them and found guilty and also sentenced to life and did die in the Arizona State Prison. The two boys, Tom and John, served some forty years in the Arizona State Prison.

As I recall they had three hearings before the Parole Board, all of which were blocked by relatives and friends of the Kempton, McBride and Wootan families. And the circumstances surrounding this made it impossible for the boys to get out. There was one time at the second hearing that I know of ..... they were to have gone before the Parole Board, when one of the survivors, a son who was a highway patrolman at the time, received a bullet wound in his arm by a couple of car thieves, a couple of colored boys that he'd stopped merely for an inspection. One of them shot him in the arm, and with all the attending publicity and ballyhoo about this incident, the opportunity for the Powers boys to be released was automatically killed right there. And as time proved ..... uh .... sentiment began to sway in favor of the Powers boys, but two of the families fought them to the last, refused to let them out of prison. That was the Wootan family and the McBride family. But eventually a son and brother of Mr. Kempton went before the Parole Board and said that they could see no further purpose in the boys staying in prison. They were old men, and he thought that they had served their time. And in the third hearing .... uh ... the third hearing to my knowledge, that is, they were finally released from the Arizona State Prison with the understanding that they were not to return to Graham County, and especially to the Galiuro Mountains where all this had taken place.

One of the points of interest pertaining to this case was brought out by my informant as to whether or not Jeff Powers had thrown up his hands at the command as he related to the informant. When the doctor was examining Mr. Powers after his death, the only way a pencil could be inserted into the bullet hole the full length was by completely raising his arms above his head. There were those who interjected that this could have been made possible by throwing his rifle up to his shoulder in a firing position. So his arms were raised to a half position, as might have been encountered by holding a rifle at shoulder position and at that point the pencil would continue to hit leaders and would not penetrate to its full depth. And then when the arms were raised full length overhead, again the pencil could be inserted to its full length.

Informant An35 (Reconstructed Text)

I came here from Oklahoma about five years ago, and since I've been here, I've heard a lot about the Powers. It's very interesting the different things you hear; it all depends on who you talk to. It all seems to hinge on whether or not the father was shot with his hands up or not. The Mormons that I've talked to claim that when he was told to put his hands up, he opened fire, and they had to shoot him. But I've also heard that the wound that he received could only be fully probed if his arms were raised over his head. I don't suppose there's any way to learn the truth now.

Informant An36 (Tape Transcript)

I forget what year that was now. All ready? ...... I used to live along the San Pedro River. One morning I .... I had come off of the ranch down there. I just went off to feed my horses, in the mornin', about four o'clock in the mornin', and I heard the gate open up there, and I didn't know who was comin', so I just stood there and waited till they rode up. And I said, "Howdy, fellers!" And when they spoke, I recognized Kane Wootan's voice. So I asked them to git down and put their horses up. We'd have coffee. Got to talkin' and I asked them what they was doin' there, and they said they was followin' some fellas that stole some burros over near Safford headin' for the border. So I told them, "Well," I said, "they passed here two days ahead of you. I guess they're over ... over the border now, but if the burros is tired, they may stop up here in this brush." So McBride said, "The burros is pretty well worked-down so we might overtake them."

"Well," I said, "I got an old Model T here. We can take that and go on up." And right sure enough, where I knowed that they'd stop in this brush, they'd went in there. So McBride, he got out. And I said, "Hold on, Mac," I said, "we'll go on to the upper end. They've got to come out on the road up there." They did. They'd come out there that morning. So I kept lookin' up south, knowed that they couldn't be far off up there. So, first thing you know, before we'd got to Benson, well, I seed these burros comin' off of a hill goin' in to Benson. I says to Mac, "There's your burro train comin' in now." He said, "Well, that's all a that. Somebody's beat us to 'em."

So they talked to 'em there a while, and then we started back. Got down below Benson there about ten miles, and Kane pulled out his six-shooter and shot into a buncha quail, and the gravel killed a few quail. So he got out and picked 'em up. Rode around and had to go around a hill to get back into the river bottom, and another buncha quail come out, and McBride pulled his six-shooter out and shot. Gravel killed a couple there, so he picked 'em up, took 'em in. So goin' on down the road, why he looked up on the mountain up there, and he says to Kane, he says, "Kane, if I knowed them Powers boys was up there, we'd take Bill and get ... take them boys in." And I says, "Mac," I says, "them Powers boys is up there, but," I says, "you're not takin' Bill." I says, "Now, you fellas go on back to Safford and," I says, "notify them boys, and if they don't surrender, why then come up here and get 'em." But they made a foolish break. They went up there to fight it out, and that ended the officers. And there shouldn't a been no such thing as that fight ... with anybody. They coulda got them boys without havin' a bit a trouble. I knowed them boys for a number of years. But when a man's a little crowded, well, he's bound to fight. And they put up a fight and lost out.

Well, when the Powers boys ... when they started out, well, I come off of the mountain there down to the ranch on the San Pedro, and a fella by the name of Haggs told me, he says, "You're just in time for the posse." "Well," I says, "Haggs, I'm more than in time." "No," he says, "sure enough," he says, "the posse's out here after the Powers boys, and you're right in the posse."

Sure enough, the sheriff, Ned Wheeler, drawed me into the posse, and I had to get out and scout around. I could see the tracks, but never could locate the boys. So my wife was about to have a baby, and she was gettin' pretty excited, so I told Mac ... er ... Wheeler, I says, "I've got to take my wife to Benson." "Well," he says, "we need you here because you knew ... know the country." "Well," I says, "my wife's gettin' pretty nervous." So Mac said, "Well, take your wife to Benson and come right on back."

That night they lost the tracks entirely. They'd come out through a lane, and the cattle had covered up the tracks. So I told him, I says, "I'll go out here east. They're bound to went out over the hills east." Sure enough, I found the tracks out there, and I was to shoot when I found them ... the tracks. So I fired one shot. So the fellas headed off and come up there. By the time they got there, there was shootin' down on the river, callin' us back to the river. So we lit out for the river down there, and a fella from Johnson mine down there had notified them that they just run by there that morning. They stole some horses from the Cross X ranch, left their wore-out horses there and took fresh horses and headed out for the Chiricahua Mountains. And they was captured in Mexico; the soldiers of Mexico captured them.

Informant An37 (Reconstructed Text)

The Powers got their sister pregnant, and because of that they killed her. And when the lawmen went after them, they laid for them and killed them. They escaped into Mexico, but then they come back for some reason, and the soldiers got them. They got life imprisonment, and now they're tryin' to get out.

Informant An38 (Reconstructed Text)

The Powers was awful thick with the Apaches, and when they was chasin' them, they got the Apaches to trail 'em. And they kept leadin' the soldiers in the wrong direction. Then they went down in a cave or somethin' underground, and they come up over in New Mexico, and the soldiers didn't know about that cave.[261] I don't know how they caught them.

---

[261] See footnote 1.

LEGEND TEXTS

MEXICAN TEXTS

Informant Mx1 (Reconstructed Text)

One time when they was chasing the Powers boys, they picketed their horses for the day pretty far from where they hid out. And they dug out a little ditch to hide in, and it was up under a big fallen-down log. And they was in there sleepin', and the sheriff who was leadin' the posse came and sat down on that log with some of his men, and they talked about their plans and which way they was gonna go. And the Powers just laid there, holding their breath, and they heard all about the posse's plans and which way they was gonna go, and so they got away.[262]

Informant Mx2 (Reconstructed Text)

I guess I shouldn't say this, but the Mormons are different from other Anglos. It doesn't seem like they think that anyone else is really human. They are the only ones who matter, and anyone else is some kind of animal.

I think they wanted the Powers' gold mine, and that's why it all happened. I heard that the Powers were nice; they gave money to poor Mexicanos and helped them and all.[263] So I don't think they did what the Mormons said. I don't believe that.

---

[262] See footnote 7.

[263] Motif Q46. Reward for protecting fugitives. See Homer Croy, *Jesse James Was My Neighbor* (New York: Duell, Sloan and Pearce, 1949), pp. 9-10, 122-123, and 156-157.

Informant Mx3 (Reconstructed Text)

I don't care what these Anglos do to each other. I wouldn't care if they all killed each other. But I heard the soldiers went into Mexico to get the Powers. They had no right to do that. If the Mexican army did that, these *chingados* would scream bloody murder.

I don't know, but I heard the Powers was good to some Mexican people, and that's more than any of these Mormon bastards ever was. You didn't record that, did you? (Laugh)

Informant Mx4 (Reconstructed text)

I heard the Powers was dirty people. Like they was screwin' their sister, even the father was. And then one time, one of them was workin' as a round-up cook, and they caught him pissin' in the biscuits or somethin' like that.

Informant Mx5 (Reconstructed Text)

Oh, I know those Powers buried gold up there! I knew a man, he was a *bracero*, a wetback, and he worked out there in that country. And he told me himself that he saw treasure lights out there in lots of places around that Powers' cabin.[264] And he said that he was gonna get it. Now, you know, you just can't dig up treasure when you see those lights. If you do, something bad will happen to you.[265] But there's a religious medal you can wear that will protect you.[266] I don't know which one it is, but he said he knew. Well, anyway, shortly after that, that man disappeared, and nobody knows what happened to him. Maybe he found the gold and went back to Mexico, or maybe something happened to him. I don't know, but I hope those poor men get out of prison and get it for themselves. They've earned it.

---

[264] Motif N532. Light indicates hidden treasure.
[265] Motif N591. Curse on treasure. Finder or finders to have bad luck.
[266] Motif D1380. Magic object protects.

Informant Mx6 (Reconstructed Text)

I don't see what all the fuss is about; everybody arguing about what happened with the Powers. I don't think you can ever sort it out, because all you Anglos are crazy. You're always fighting and killing each other for money. Now Mexicans fight and they kill each other, but it's because they're drunk or they're fighting over a woman or because one of them insults the other. But you can insult an Anglo or even his wife, and that won't make him as mad as doing something that costs him money. It's like money is the only thing that matters. And the Powers had a gold mine, and somebody else wanted it. So they just naturally started killing each other. That's the way Anglos are. I don't mean you. You're not from around here. But the ones around here, it's like money's all they care about, and they'll do anything to get it. And the more money they have, the worse they are.

Informant Mx7 (Reconstructed Text)

Perhaps I shouldn't say this, but the Mormons are very difficult to get along with. Like, they look down on everybody. Like, if you're a Catholic, they look down on you. When I was in the low grades, I used to ride the school bus, and they used to tell me that my religion was the religion of the devil, and it used to make me cry. And it's not just Mexicans they look down on; anybody who isn't a Mormon is inferior.

Mr. S. out in the Aravaipa knew the Powers real well, and he says they were killed because they stood up to Kane Wootan and wouldn't let him bully them. And he says there was no doubt that they shot the father down, because he was wounded in the chest, and after he was dead, they tried to put something in the wound and nothing would go in unless you put his hands way up over his head. So that means they shot him with his hands up, and that's not right. I guess I would want to kill somebody if they shot my father like that.

A lot of people say that there's a lot of gold buried out there that the Powers hid, but I don't believe that.

Informant Mx8 (Reconstructed Text)

I don't think the Powers got a fair chance. They wanted to stay up there in the mountains and mind their own business, but the law wanted to send them over to Germany or Japan to kill people. That's not right. People shouldn't have to kill people if they don't want to. And nobody should be able to make them. That's not right.

And then they tell all the stories about their sister and how bad she was, and they say they killed her. I don't believe that. If they killed her, why didn't they arrest them? People always say things like that about ... when somebody does something they don't like. Like if a Spanish boy gets into trouble, right away Anglo people start talking about how bad he was and how bad his family is, and with a lotta people no Spanish people are any good. And that's not right. People shouldn't do that, but they do if they don't like the people they're talking about.

I think those poor men have suffered enough. They should let them out.

Informant Mx9 (Reconstructed Text)

I heard that them Powers boys found a lotta gold up there in that mine and then didn't keep their mouths shut about it. And then when the sheriff and them other fellas heard about it, they figured on some way to get it away from them. Some people say that them Powers never got the word on the draft, and that somebody seen to it that they didn't, so they didn't have no suspicion about anybody comin' after them.

The only mistake they made was on not figuring how tough those Powers boys were. They weren't to be fooled with. And that mistake was what killed them. I heard that them Powers had killed lots of men. I think they killed another man up there at that mine before the fight. And they say that one of them, I don't know whether it was John or Tom, was just like Tres Dedos Yaqui;[267] he liked to kill just for the fun of it. They were crazy to go up there and try to bring them boys out,

---

[267] Three-Finger Jack, a member of the Joaquin Murietta band, famed for his senseless acts of cruelty and very well-known among adolescents in the area.

they were too tough. And people who knew them told them that, too, but they wouldn't listen. Crazy!

Then Mike V. told me that they must have got most of the gold out of the mine and buried it. And they couldn't get back to get it, and nobody else could find it. And there was a wetback out there in Klondyke, workin' for Mr. H. And they say that where there's treasure buried, lights come at night and hang over it.[268] And this wetback seen them lights, and he went up there to try and find the treasure, and nobody ..... he never was seen again. I wouldn't go up there to that place for anything.

Informant Mx10 (Reconstructed Text)

There was this fella from Safford, and he had a lotta money, and he wanted to get together with that Powers girl, and she thought it was a good idea. But her father didn't want her to mess with nobody; he just wanted her to stay up there and cook and clean and everything. So this guy got some horses and went up there to get her to run off with him. And nobody ever saw him again. And right after that they brought her body down and I guess they're the only ones that know what happened, and they're not tellin'. I think they caught 'em runnin' off, and they killed the guy and hurt her somehow, and then she died. But I don't know.

Informant Mx11 (Reconstructed Text)

The Powers were a very sad family. It's almost like someone got a *brujo* to work on them. Their lives were filled with death and sorrow. I think the mother was killed when they were very small when a roof fell in. And then their grandmother was killed in an accident when a horse ran away with the buggy she was driving. And then their sister died very shortly after that. And then the shooting of their father took place. It was all very tragic. And then they've had to spend all of their lives in

---

[268] See footnote 31.

prison. You know, it's funny, but I wonder if there was a *brujo* involved?

Informant Mx12 (Reconstructed Text)

My grandfather knew all the people involved in that case, and he says the Powers were good people. They never used bad language or cursed or anything, and they worked real hard, and seemed to have a lot of respect for other people. He doesn't believe they would kill anybody without a good reason. You know sometimes you just have to kill somebody. He says the other men were all right too, but he didn't like Kane Wootan. He says he was mean and like pushy with anybody that would let him get away with it. He was real mean to Mexicans and would laugh and make fun. My grandfather says it was his fault.

Informant Mx13 (Reconstructed Text)

I heard that after they got the Powers, all the Mormons wanted to lynch them. But the officer in charge told them that if anything happened to the prisoners, he'd kill every Mormon son-of-a-bitch in the valley. (Laugh) That's what I heard.

Informant Mx14 (Reconstructed Text)

I lived in Los Angeles for a while, you know, and I never heard about the Powers till I came back this time. But I've heard a lot about it since then.

Seems the Powers had a gold mine, and Wootan wanted it. And he wanted to be sheriff, too. And he figured if he went up there and killed them, he could get their claim, and he'd be such a big hero he could get elected sheriff. But he didn't figure on how tough the Powers were, and after he shot their father down, they killed the three sheriffs.

And after they run off, lots of people seen 'em, and some of them helped them, like gave them food and a place to sleep and stuff. And everybody that helped them they gave them a big bunch a money.[269] And one place, they found a man beatin' his wife, and I think they killed him or maybe beat him up pretty good. But, anyway, his wife was grateful to them.[270]

Informant Mx15 (Reconstructed Text)

This is just another incident in the history of Anglos in this country. Time after time they kill each other, and it's always over money. Money is more important to Anglo people than their families or anything else. And then they just keep it in the bank and never spend it or have a good time or anything. They don't know how to live like civilized people. The only good thing I heard was that when the Powers were escaping, a lady fed them, and they gave her a whole lotta money for it. She was a Mexican lady.[271]

Informant Mx16 (Reconstructed Text)

When the Powers ran away, and the soldiers were chasing them, they came to my grandmother's ranch over near Bowie, and they wanted to have ... to trade horses for some fresh ones, but she didn't have any. And none of her sons were home, just her daughters, my mother and her sisters, and they were real little. And they asked her if she could give them something to eat. Well, she was scared because she knew who they were, but she didn't know how to tell them no, so she got some food for them. She didn't have much, just some beans and tortillas, and while she was fixing it, they gathered up a whole lot of wood for her, and when they finished eating, they gave her twenty dollars and told her to buy something nice for the girls. Then they thanked her and rode out.[272] And after that some soldiers came and asked about ... whether she had seen them, and she wouldn't tell them anything. She always said that it wasn't any of our business.

---

[269] See footnote 30.
[270] See footnote 10.
[271] See footnote 30.
[272] See footnote 30.

Informant Mx17 (Reconstructed Text)

My godfather, he used to go out in those Galiuro Mountains back in the twenties and thirties, and he found a little cave not far from Powers Garden. And he said in the cave there was a stone wall that somebody had built. And he thought it was a place where the Powers hid some gold. So he tried to tear down the wall. But he said that every time he touched the stone, he would hear sounds like of shots and screams and horses running. And it scared him so bad he never would go back again and try to get it. Several men was with him when it happened, and they all say the same.[273]

Informant Mx18 (Reconstructed Text)

The Powers had lots of gold from their mine, and they buried it up on those mountains. And they never came back and got it. And if you go up there, you can see lights where they buried that treasure.[274] But if you tried to get it, something bad, very bad, would happen to you because they're still alive.[275]

But they didn't leave all their gold; they took some with them. And every place they stopped and the people were nice to them, they left those people some gold.[276] And it was usually Mexican people they stayed with because they knew they wouldn't turn them in.

Informant Mx19 (Reconstructed Text)

Uncle L. knew all those guys. I guess they all tried to push him around if they didn't know any better; he never would take any of that crap. They all tried to push him around, but he's still up there on the Aravaipa. Well, anyway, he says that Kane Wootan was out to get the Powers and kept bragging about how he was gonna go up there and get

---

[273] Motif N576.1. Voice of ghost scares away treasure seekers.
[274] See footnote 31.
[275] This notion would seem to be related to Motifs N551, Who may unearth a treasure, and N543, Certain person to find treasure.
[276] See footnote 30.

them. Uncle L. tried to tell him that they weren't to be fooled with, but he wouldn't pay any attention. He went right up there and got himself and those other guys killed. That's the way these people are. They fight over anything. They're greedy, and they won't listen to reason. All those people got killed over a gold mine, and I guess nobody got any good out of it. They're always trying to get what somebody else has, and they don't know how to enjoy what they got. I think they all got just what they deserved.

Informant Mx20 (Reconstructed Text)

I don't know ... I think the Powers should be let free. They were very kind. I heard that one time they helped a woman that her husband was beating her.[277] And another time they gave a woman a whole lotta money just for some frijoles and tortillas.[278] So they must have been good men. I think they should get out.

Informant Mx21 (Reconstructed Text)

Well, I heard a lot about them Powers, but you can never tell everything you know. Right? Well, I'll tell you about Charlie. Old Charlie he got hurt. A horse fell on him and hurt his chest so he couldn't ride, and he got a job as a cook on the works. And, hell, he didn't know nothin' about cookin'! He'd just stick his hands, dirty as hell, right in the biscuit dough. And one a the fellas didn't like that, and he told the boss that Charlie didn't wash his hands, and old Charlie said, "Like hell I don't! How you think I get the flour off them?"[279]

Then another time a fellow'd complained there was dirt in his food, and Charlie said, "You got to eat a peck a dirt before you die." And the fellow said, "But, hell! Not all to once!"[280]

---

[277] See footnote 10.
[278] See footnote 30.
[279] See Eric Thane, *High Border Country* (New York: Duell, Sloan and Pearce, 1942), p. 75.
[280] See Stan Hoig, *The Humor of the American Cowboy* (New York: The New American Library, 1960), p. 111.

And then another time he burned up most of the stuff he was cookin', and there wasn't much for supper. Nobody cared much because the grub was so bad. But there was one fellow, he was a hog; he'd eat anything. So he kept complaining that he needed something to eat. And finally Charlie got mad, and he slapped a big old jar a mustard on the table and said, "Here, help yourself. I got three more jars in the wagon."[281]

Yeah, he sure was crazy.

Informant Mx22 (Tape Transcript)

Well, the Powers boys, that's what I said, come down to vote, and they didn't let 'em vote because they wanted them to read the constitution. See? And the boys didn't git ..... they got probably sore, and they wouldn't vote. They wouldn't read the constitution. And when this registration come for the army, they wouldn't ..... they said if they couldn't vote, they couldn't fight. See? That part of it. And then when they went over to ..... the officers to git 'em, you know, why .... I told Mr. Wootan, Kane, if I was him, I'd be sick or be gone some place. And he shook his head and said, "No fightin' blood in them boys." Well, I told Kane, said, "I'd sure hate to go up there and find out if there's any fightin' blood in them boys." And they went on.

And then when the boys ..... they was dead over there, Mr. Upchurch come down here and tried to get me to go to pack 'em out. And I didn't go. There's lotsa people up there, and I didn't think I should go up there. That's the way I felt about it. See?

I heard how they was killed up there. The Powers boys killed 'em up there. They surrounded the house is what I heard. I didn't see none of this, but that's what I heard. And when the boys .... well, that's what they told me ... they even run the horses by the house. The dogs was barkin', and when his dad come out, why ..... outdoors .... daylight come, why ... they asked him to throw his hands up, and he was gonna throw his hands up when they shot him. And then the shootin' took place. You oughta see that house! Man! They say .... well, I seen it; they

---

[281] See Mary Jourdan Atkinson and J. Frank Dobie, "Pioneer Folk Tales," in *Follow de Drinkin' Gou'd*, J. Frank Dobie, ed. (Austin: The Texas Folklore Society, 1928), pp. 72-73.

don't say; I seen it, that house, the way it was shot up, you know. I don't know how in the world them bullets went through there and got the boys. And then one a the men, they say, come around the house .... and .... you know ..... went through the window, you know, fell. He got up, poked a gun through the window and pulled the trigger on another one of the sheriffs. And then Tom said when they got outside, things didn't last no time at all. It didn't last no time.

When the father was shot, he didn't die. They took him to the tunnel ..... that's what ... they left him there and went by and told Mr. Jay Murdock about it, and they took care of him. And they pulled out.

Informant Mx23 (Reconstructed Text)

My brother used to ride for Mr. Haby and for Carl Bott, too ...... and he used to ride that Rattlesnake country, and he said that when you're way off up there by where the Powers had the mine, well, you can see a whole bunch of .....lights ..... like ..... lights like there is a treasure buried there.[282] But he never would go and see because the father is in ...... he's ..... well, he wasn't buried or anything. They just threw his body in a wash up there, and his spirit is restless, like, because he didn't get buried.[283] So he never would go down and look. I don't blame him. I wouldn't go near there for nothing!

Informant Mx24 (Reconstructed Text)

The Powers want to get out of jail so they can come back and get their gold. They took all the gold out of that little mine because they knew there was people who wanted it, and they buried it all around in places up there. I've heard that if you ride up there at night, you can see a whole lot of lights shining all over where they buried it.[284] But nobody can take it because the people who buried it are still alive.[285]

---

[282] See footnote 31.
[283] Motif E235.2.2. Ghost returns because corpse was not properly buried.
[284] See footnote 31.
[285] See footnote 42.

But they can get it, and if they should die, then somebody else can go and dig it up, and nothing will happen to them.

Informant Mx25 (Reconstructed Text)

Well, they were very dangerous men. That John looked so mean! I wouldn't go near him for nothing. I wasn't surprised when I heard what had happened, because they were men who weren't afraid; they would shoot you or anything. But still those sheriffs had no right to go up there and shoot their father. Anybody would fight the men who killed their father. They should. I think it was Mr. Wootan's fault. He was always pushing at people, and if you didn't take his pushing, he got very angry.

And I always heard that Mr. Upchurch said that Wootan had gave his rifle to the man from Globe. And he borrowed a rifle from Mr. Upchurch, and Mr. Upchurch warned him that it had a hair trigger. And I think maybe he shot that man by accident.

Informant Mx26 (Reconstructed Text)

Well, I know they murdered them boys' father. Mr. M. told me. When he got up there, the old man was still alive. He was in real bad shape, but he was still alive. And Mr. M. told me he was an awful mess. And after he died, they tried to put things in the hole where the bullet was, and nothin' would go in unless he raised his arms up over his head. And then they say that the Powers ambushed them. Well, the old man was in his drawers. Now nobody would go out to pull an ambush on a cold morning in his drawers, would they?

Informant Mx27 (Reconstructed Text)

Those Powers boys had a real good gold mine up there in the Galiuros, and people knew about it. That was their mistake; they should have kept quiet about it. But these Mormons over here found out about it, and they just went up there to kill all the Powers so they could get the mine. That's one thing about you Anglos, especially Mormons: you'll do anything for money. I don't mean you, yourself; I mean Anglos as a rule. They just went up there to murder them boys and their father, and the only thing went wrong was them Powers wouldn't hold still for it, and they killed them lawmen.

The only thing I can't figure is why they didn't hang them. If they'da been Mexicans, they would have lynched them right when they caught them. No mercy. One thing you have to understand: these people have all the power, and they won't stand for anybody crossin' 'em. Look at what happened in Solomon in March.[286] They'll get everybody that was involved in that before they're finished, and that's just the way they done the Powers.

Informant Mx28 (Reconstructed Text)

The Powers boys were real tough. John had killed a lotta men over in the Mogollons before they ever came here. And there was one time a bunch of Apache bucks jumped the reservation and was comin' down through the Aravaipa, and John was up there doin' some work for the Forest Service. And he had spent some time up there on the reservation and knew a lotta them Apache boys. So he rode on up to where they was and talked to them, and the next morning they went back to San Carlos. He wasn't scared a nothin'.

He was the best shot I ever seen. He could hit anything with a rifle or a handgun. And when he got crossed, he went right away for his gun. He wasn't much for fightin' with his fists. But he never started no trouble; never bothered nobody. He was more like his father; quiet and didn't like to bother much with people. Tom liked people a lot, and he was always laughin' and jokin' around. John didn't mess around. He was awful good with animals, though. He always had a bunch of pups underfoot, and he had a mare, old Maude, that he'd had for a long time, that would follow him around like a damn dog. She was a real good horse, too, lots a bottom. He could push her around these hills all day, and she was still right there under him. I never did know what

---

[286] The reference is to a school board election in which a Mexican candidate was successful for the first time.

happened to her. They didn't ride her outa there; they took the posse's horses. I guess one of these Mormon son-of-a-bitches got her; they got everything else.

Now I was old enough to know that whole family. Charlie was kind of a silly old shit. He'd fight at the drop of a hat, but there wasn't no harm in him. I've heard stories about the old lady, and people used to laugh and call her Shotgun Annie, but when I knew her, she was a real nice old lady. And I know these stories you hear about Ola aren't true. I've heard terrible things said about her, and I know better. She was as nice a girl as you'd ever wanta meet. She was a big girl, pretty as a picture, and just as pleasant and nice as could be. She had a smile for everybody. She only used the finest language, and she wouldn't stand for any other kind being used around her. The Powers and old Tom Sisson talked pretty salty, but not around her. And she didn't live with them, you know. She and Granny had their own cabin down at Powers Garden, about a mile from the mine. She used to come up there and cook their meals, but she never spent one night under the same roof with them. Besides that, they all loved her. I mean, she was the pet of all of them, and so anybody that says she was pregnant or that her brothers killed her is talkin' a lotta shit. She wasn't that kind of girl.

If you ask me, it was Kane Wootan that caused the whole thing. He was always kind of a hot shit, always bullyin' them that'd let him and chasin' women. It ain't no secret that he wanted to be the next sheriff. McBride himself knew that, and he was worried. Old Lee ... Lee, ... hell .... Lee .... I can't call his name .... He lives up there in Globe now .... Well, anyway, he told me that Wootan propositioned him and told him that if he could bring the Powers down, it would give him the election. And he told old Lee that if he'd go up there with him, he'd make him a deputy when he got to be sheriff. Old Lee told him that he wasn't gonna go up there even if Wootan made him president. Kane laughed and said that those boys talked a lot better than they fought. And Lee said he'd just as soon keep 'em talkin'. Now, that fella told me that hisself.

Kane had bought the Upchurch ranch not long before the shooting, you know, and that ranch has always had a water problem. And I know that Kane saw the old man Powers when he went in to town to arrange for that stamp mill that they bought and tried to get him to sign some of that water over to him. The old man told him to go chase hisself. So Kane had good reason to be on the prod for the Powers.

Informant Mx29 (Reconstructed Text)

I heard that Kane Wootan was down at the Klondyke store one time, and he was talking about Ola Powers. He was sayin' some pretty bad things about her because she wouldn't marry his brother. And John Powers was down at the Morgan ranch, visiting, and somebody told him what Kane was doin' down at the store. And John went down there, and he was nobody to fool with, and he made Kane apologize and admit he was lying. And that's why Kane was so down on the Powers.

Then some people say that the Powers buried their gold up there, so they wouldn't get robbed taking it to town, you know. And after the father got killed and the brothers went to jail, everybody looked for it, but they never could find it. And then like where there's buried treasure, there's supposed to come a light at night. Like if you bury money or jewels or something, and you die and nobody can find it, then a light will shine at night where you buried it.[287] Well, my dad told me there was a wetback or a *bracero* who was riding up in that Galiuro country, and he saw those lights, like. And he told everybody that he was gonna go back up there and find it. And he went up there, and nobody ever saw him again. Now I don't know if that's true, but that's what my dad says.

I don't think they ever shoulda gone to jail, and I hope they let them out, because I don't think anybody woulda done any different if they had their father shot down like that.

Informant Mx30 (Reconstructed Text)

My father and my uncles knew them Powers boys, I guess. Anyways they talk about 'em, and I know L. knew them real well. He used to go see them in prison all the time, and he thinks it wasn't their fault. He

---

[287] See footnote 31.

thinks that it was Kane Wootan that caused all the trouble. He was a real .... like a loudmouth and a bully, especially with Mexican people, and like he wanted to be sheriff. And he thought if he went up and got the Powers, he could get elected. L. says that Kane tried to get him to go up with him. L. was a tough old bird, I guess. Anyway, he was always tryin' to get him to go up there or askin' him about the best way to go up there and stuff like that. And L. told him not to go up there, but he went ahead.

And then L. went up there and helped to pack the bodies out. And he said that the old man Powers had a bullet hole in his chest that killed him. And if you tried to put a stick in that hole, it wouldn't go in. But if you raised his arms up over his head, then the stick would go all the way in. So that proves that he had his hands up when they shot him. And them Powers boys wouldn't take nothin' from nobody, so when their father was shot down, well, they wouldn't stop till they'd killed everybody that did it. And you can't blame them, you know. I think if somebody killed my father, I'd go after them. Wouldn't you? So I don't think it was their fault.

And then they really got away, you know. They were across the border in Mexico, and them soldiers went over after them. They didn't have no right to do that. If the soldiers of Mexico came across the border after somebody we'd go to war on 'em, drop atomic bombs, probably. But it's okay for these soldiers to go over there into another country and bring them back, and nobody says nothing.

Informant Mx31 (Reconstructed Text)

This is the story of the Powers boys as I heard it. They had a gold mine up on Rattlesnake, and they were doing very well. Then the war came, and they were drafted. And some time before that they had gone down to Klondyke to vote, and they wouldn't let them because they couldn't read the constitution. And they said if they couldn't vote, they wouldn't fight. So the sheriffs went up there to get them.

It was early in the morning when they got to the Powers' place. And the father, he heard them, and he stepped out on the porch with a shotgun and asked who was there. And somebody told him to put his hands up. And he did and they shot him. I know he put his hands up because Mr. Jay Murdock said that the only way a pencil would go into his wound was to raise his arms over his head. Well, anyway, them boys and old Tom began to shoot back, and it wasn't long before they were all dead.

When they caught them and brought them back, they tried to hang them .... lynch them, but the soldiers wouldn't let them. They gave them an old drunken lawyer who didn't do anything to defend them. And then they sent them to prison for life. That's all I know.

Informant Mx32 (Reconstructed Text)

Well, I'm not from around here, and I haven't been here too long, but I have heard my uncle and ...... well ..... other people talk about it ..... and ..... well ..... I guess I have an opinion.

It seems to me that they probably did something that the people in power didn't like and had to pay for it. It's still very much that way here. We have those prayers in the schools even though it's not constitutional and you know what happened in the school board election in Solomon. It seems as if you belong ..... if you belong to the right church, you can do anything, and if you're against them, they're out to get you. You should know that. Those poor men stood up to them about something, and they made them pay for it. I don't know how or why anybody who's not a Mormon lives here.

APPENDIX III

LIST OF INFORMANTS

Because of the sensitive nature of much of this material to tellers of one or another of the versions of the legend, I have deemed it advisable to withhold the names of most of the informants from the body of this study and to refer to most of them only by code designation. The exceptions to this procedure are the Power boys, John and Tom, whose testimonies are referred to by code designation throughout this work, but who are identified in this list. The ages given for the informants are in every case their ages on the date when the text was collected.

Mormon Informants

Informant Mo1 is a cattleman, 59 years of age. This text was collected on December 12, 1962.

Informant Mo2 is a male, 48 years old. He has always lived in Safford and is employed as a butcher in a local supermarket. This text was collected on January 12, 1963.

Informant Mo3 is a male cotton farmer. He is 63 years old. A life-long resident of the area, he now lives in Lone Star. This text was collected on May 10, 1963.

Informant Mo4 is a 24 year old male. He was born and raised in Mesa, but has been attending Eastern Arizona College in Thatcher for the past two years. This text was collected on October 13, 1962.

Informant Mo5 is a female, 18 years of age. She attends the local high school. Her family is obviously prosperous. This text was collected on March 4, 1963.

Informant Mo6 is a female, 20 years old. She is the sister of Informant Mo5. This text was collected on November 15, 1962.

Informant Mo7 is a female, 65 years of age. She is a successful business woman and an important political leader. She worked doggedly through the years to effect the parole of the Power boys. She resides in Central. This text was collected on October 6, 1962.

Informant Mo8 is a female, 17 years of age. She attends the local high school. Her family moved to Safford five years ago. This text was collected on January 17, 1963.

Informant Mo9 is a male, 30 years of age. He has always lived in the area. This text was collected on April 7, 1963.

Informant Mo10 is a male, 58 years of age. He has always lived in Safford. This text was collected on November 10, 1962.

Informant Mo11 is a male, 20 years old. He is the son of Informant Mo10. This text was collected on December 9, 1962.

Informant Mo12 is a male, 19 years old. He lives in Safford and is a senior at the local high school. This text was collected on November 9, 1962.

Informant Mo13 is a female, 19 years old. Her family moved to Safford five years ago. She is studying to be a cosmetologist at the local beauty school. This text was collected on April 6, 1963.

Informant Mo14 is a female, 90 years of age. She belongs to one of the pioneer Mormon families in the valley and has lived in Safford for seventy-five years. This text was collected on November 9, 1962.

Informant Mo15 is a male, 16 years old. He is the great-grandson of Informant Mo14. This text was collected on February 9, 1963.

Informant Mo16 is a male, 22 years old. He has lived in Eden all of his life. This text was collected on December 1, 1962.

Informant Mo17 is a male, 22 years old. He attends Brigham Young University. This text was collected on December 19, 1962.

Informant Mo18 is a male, 20 years of age. He is the brother of Informant Mo17. This text was collected on March 1, 1963.

Informant Mo19 is a male, 27 years of age. His family was one of the first to settle in the valley. This text was collected on April 10, 1963.

Informant Mo20 is a male, 19 years old. His is another pioneer family. This text was collected on December 1, 1962.

Informant Mo21 is a male, 23 years of age. His family is an old one in the valley. This text was collected on October 6, 1962.

Informant Mo22 is a male, 30 years of age. He came to Safford twelve years ago. This text was collected on October 12, 1962.

Informant Mo23 is a female, 17 years of age. She has always lived in the area. This text was collected on January 12, 1963.

Informant Mo24 is a female, 15 years old. Both of her parents were born and raised in Graham County. The family has just moved back to Safford. This text was collected on May 27, 1963.

Informant Mo25 is a male, 18 years of age. He is the great-grandson of the first president of St. David Stake. This text was collected on October 13, 1962.

Informant Mo26 is a female, 18 years old. She has always lived in Safford. This text was collected on October 3, 1962.

Informant Mo27 is a male, 21 years of age. This text was collected on December 5, 1962.

Informant Mo28 is a male, 18 years of age. This text was collected on September 15, 1962.

Informant Mo29 is a male, 17 years of age. He has recently moved into the area and attends Safford High School. This text was collected on December 3, 1962.

Informant Mo30 is a male, 21 years of age. His family is one of the oldest in the valley. This text was collected on April 14, 1963.

Informant Mo31 is a male, 35 years of age. This text was collected on November 7, 1962.

Informant Mo32 is a male, 18 years of age. His is an old family in the area. This text was collected on April 9, 1963.

Informant Mo33 is a male, 55 years old. He is the father of Informant Mo32. This text was collected on May 17, 1963.

Informant Mo34 is a male, 19 years of age. He has lived in Safford for seven years. This text was collected on October 10, 1962.

Informant Mo35 is a female, 18 years old. Her family moved into the area three years ago. This text was collected on December 9, 1962.

Informant Mo36 is a male, 17 years of age. This text was collected on April 14, 1963.

Informant Mo37 is a male, 18 years of age. He has always lived in Safford and is the brother of Informant Mo36. This text was collected on January 17, 1963.

Informant Mo38 is a female, 18 years old. She has lived in Safford for ten years. This text was collected on April 10, 1963.

Informant Mo39 is a male, 21 years of age. His family is one of the old, prosperous ones. This text was collected on December 10, 1962.

Informant Mo40 is a female, 20 years old. She has always lived in Safford. This text was collected on November 11, 1962.

Informant Mo41 is a male, 23 years of age. His mother's family is a very old one in the valley. This text was collected on January 12, 1963.

Informant Mo42 is a male, 54 years of age. My relationship with him was quite cordial until I posed the formula question. This text was collected on April 17, 1963.

Informant Mo43 is a male, 19 years of age. He has always lived in Safford and attends Safford High School. This text was collected on February 16, 1963.

Informant Mo44 is a male, 57 years of age. He is a native of Safford and the father of Informant Mo43. This text was collected on March 15, 1963.

Informant Mo45 is a male, 55 years of age. His family has been on the Aravaipa for seventy years. This text was collected on November 5, 1970. I had asked this informant the formula question eight years before, but at that time I received a negative response.

Informant Mo46 is a male, 35 years of age. This text was collected on February 15, 1963.

Informant Mo47 is a male, 21 years of age. He is a native of Safford. This text was collected on November 10, 1962.

Non-Mormon Anglo Informants

Informant An1 is a 26 year old male. He resides in Safford and has been in the area about three years. This text was collected on February 10, 1963.

Informant An2 is a 72 year old male. He spent his working life as a cowboy in the Safford area. This text was collected on November 27, 1962.

Informant An3 is a male, 61 years old. He has been in the area for about two years. This text was collected on January 11, 1963.

Informant An4 is a 67 year old male cattle rancher from the area. He is now quite prosperous, but spent his youth cowboying in the area. This text was collected on June 7, 1963.

Informant An5 is a 17 year old male high school student. He lives in Safford and has been in the area for six years. This text was collected on November 7, 1962.

Informant An6 is a male, 23 years of age. He has lived in Safford for eleven years. This text was collected on October 11, 1962.

Informant An7 is a male, 70 years old. He now lives in Willcox but was a cowboy in the Klondyke area during the time the Powers lived there. This text was collected on November 9, 1962.

Informant An8 is a male, 21 years of age. He has lived in Safford all of his life. This text was collected on December 5, 1962.

Informant An9 is a male, 35 years old. He lives in Silver City, New Mexico, and is employed as a liquor salesman. He has been visiting the Gila Valley for about ten years in this capacity. This text was collected on February 20, 1963.

Informant An10 is a female, 25 years old. She has lived in Safford for three years. This text was collected on February 22, 1963.

Informant An11 is a male, 19 years of age. This text was collected on May 6, 1963.

Informant An12 is a male, 19 years old. He is the son of Informant An13. This text was collected on March 9, 1963.

Informant An13 is a male, 60 years old. He has lived in the area all of his life. This text was collected on March 15, 1963.

Informant An14 is a male, 30 years old. He is distantly related to Informants Mo14 and Mo15, but his branch of the family long ago gave up the practice of Mormonism. This text was collected on November 1, 1962.

Informant An15 is a male, 70 years old. He operates a large cattle ranch in Klondyke. His father owned the ranch to which the body of Ola Power was brought after her death and at which the posse stopped before they went to the Power cabin. The informant was present at both of these times and knew the family quite well. This text was collected on July 11, 1961.

Informant An16 is a female, 58 years old. Her father moved to Safford when she was quite young. This text was collected on December 27, 1962.

Informant An17 is a male, 75 years old. He spent his life cowboying in the area and knew the Power family well. This text was collected on April 17, 1963.

Informant An18 is a male, 22 years of age. This text was collected on February 19, 1963.

Informant An19 is a male, 20 years old. He is the brother of Informant An18. This text was collected on February 19, 1963.

Informant An20 is a female, 57 years old. She was widowed while very young and left with two small sons to raise. She has managed the large cattle ranch that her husband left her with notable success. She knew the Powers in the old days, and they have lived on her ranch in Klondyke for extended periods of time since their release from prison. This text was collected on October 9, 1962.

Informant An21 is a male, 30 years old. Since the release of the boys from prison, this informant has become very close to them and is probably John's best friend. He was a pallbearer at Tom's funeral. This text was collected on January 10, 1963.

Informant An22 is a male, 47 years of age. He lives in Tucson. His father was the manager of the state prison farm while the Powers were there. He remembers them then and has been extremely friendly to them since their release. His son was a pallbearer at Tom's funeral. This text was collected on October 7, 1962.

Informant An23 is a male, 51 years old. He lives in the Aravaipa Canyon on the family ranch. This text was collected on May 10, 1963.

Informant An24 is a male, 54 years of age. His is an old family in the area. His son was a pallbearer at Tom's funeral. This text was collected on January 13, 1963.

Informant An25 is a male, 67 years old. He has been a prospector in the mountains of this region for his entire working life. This text was collected on November 9, 1962.

Informant An26 is a male, 70 years of age. He had been a cowboy all of his life, working all over the state of Arizona. This text was collected on July 27, 1961.

Informant An27 is a male, 79 years old. This informant is, of course, John Power, one of the principals of the legend. I have known John since 1961, when he and his brother first came back to the Aravaipa country. There were serious difficulties in persuading the Powers to tape their story, for they were convinced that it had economic potential for them either as a book or a motion picture. At one point they actually signed a contract with a writer from San Diego, and they refused even to tell the story for a short period of time. When no money was forthcoming, however, they went back to telling the story freely to anyone who would listen, but still refused to tape it. The story was always related by Tom, who was gregarious and articulate. John remained in the background, toying with his crutches, and occasionally punctuating a statement of Tom's with a grunted curse. A question directed at John would usually be answered by Tom. When Tom died, I was intrigued by the thought of John without a spokesman, and so I made a trip to Arizona expressly for the purpose of interviewing John directly, and the text which appears in this study was gathered over the course of two days, November 6 and 7, 1970. This time was spent almost entirely in the Klondyke cemetery working on the graves of Granny, Ola, and Tom. John still refused to record any material for me, but for the first time he spoke freely and even allowed me to photograph him. In this interview he offered confirmation for the first time of those texts that claimed he had a previous history of killing. During this interview he broke down again and again at the mention of Tom or Ola or his mother. He greatly resents the treatment given his father's remains, and when in a discussion of the impossibility of ever discovering them, I let slip that I knew the location of his mother's grave and had even visited it, he became what I can only describe as dangerously excited. His memory is beginning to fail, and he is a very bitter man with marked paranoid tendencies, but in his case paranoia may represent the only intelligent approach to life.

230

Informant An28 is Tom Power. Tom was 77 years old when he died in 1970. I heard Tom tell his story twenty-two times. It varied little from telling to telling, and the version presented in this study is as faithful as hastily scribbled notes and a faulty ear can make it. Tom was an amazingly light-hearted human being, who very seldom showed any bitterness at the way in which his life had unfolded.

Informant An29 is a male, 55 years old. He is an excellent amateur historian with magnificent files of documents, photographs, and interviews that he has painstakingly collected over the years. This text was collected on July 21, 1961.

Informant An30 is a male, 72 years old. This text was collected on December 5, 1962.

Informant An31 is a male, 22 years of age. He has lived in Safford all of his life. This text was collected on October 23, 1962.

Informant An32 is a male, 78 years old. He has spent his entire life as a cowboy in the state of Arizona. He knew the Power family from the time they moved onto the Aravaipa and worked assiduously to effect the release from prison of John and Tom. This text was collected on April 7, 1963.

Informant An33 is a male, 66 years of age. He was a cowboy in the Klondyke-Willcox area for forty years. This text was collected on April 12, 1963.

Informant An34 is a male, 54 years old. He came to Arizona in the thirties and has lived in the Fort Grant-Klondyke area ever since. This text was collected on July 14, 1961.

Informant An35 is a male, 27 years old. He has lived in Safford for two years. This text was collected on January 11, 1963.

Informant An36 is a male, 93 years of age. He lives on a small ranch outside Willcox. He was apparently a very able lawman, and stories about his tracking ability are still told in the area. This text was collected on August 3, 1961.

Informant An37 is a male, 43 years old. He has lived in Safford for two years. This text was collected on April 8, 1963.

Informant An38 is a male, 62 years old. He has been a life-long resident of the Gila Valley. This text was collected on April 16, 1963.

Mexican Informants

Informant Mx1 is a male, 29 years old. He works as a farm laborer. This text was collected on October 5, 1962.

Informant Mx2 is a female, 18 years of age. She has always lived in Safford. This text was collected on October 12, 1962.

Informant Mx3 is a male, 22 years old. He was born and raised in Safford. This text was collected on November 11, 1962.

Informant Mx4 is a male, 19 years of age. He lives in Safford. This text was collected on November 14, 1962.

Informant Mx5 is a female, 47 years old. She has lived in Safford for forty years. This text was collected on February 9, 1963.

Informant Mx6 is a male, 19 years of age. He graduated from Safford High School last year. This text was collected on March 7, 1963.

Informant Mx7 is a female, 18 years old. She attends Safford High School. This text was collected on March 7, 1963.

Informant Mx8 is a female, 24 years old. Her father claims that his family was in the area long before any Anglos arrived. This text was collected on November 1, 1962.

Informant Mx9 is a male, 20 years of age. This text was collected on February 10, 1963.

Informant Mx10 is a male, 19 years of age. He has lived in Safford for eight years. This text was collected on December 7, 1962.

Informant Mx11 is a male, 22 years of age. This informant is the most tradition-oriented person that I interviewed in the area. This text was collected on January 6, 1963.

Informant Mx12 is a female, 21 years old. She has always lived in San Jose. This text was collected on February 18, 1963.

Informant Mx13 is a female, 20 years old. She lives in San Jose. This text was collected on January 12, 1963.

Informant Mx14 is a male, 19 years of age. This text was collected on October 6, 1962.

Informant Mx15 is a male, 20 years of age. He has lived in Safford most of his life. This text was collected on October 13, 1962.

Informant Mx16 is a female, 22 years old. She moved to Safford three years ago. This text was collected on November 7, 1962.

Informant Mx17 is a male, 24 years of age. His family has always lived in this area. This text was collected on January 6, 1963.

Informant Mx18 is a male, 23 years of age. He has been in the valley for about five years. This text was collected on March 14, 1963.

Informant Mx19 is a male, 20 years of age. He now lives in Safford, but when he was a child, he lived in Klondyke. This text was collected on November 7, 1962.

Informant Mx20 is a female, 19 years old. She lives with her family in Solomonville. This text was collected on January 31, 1963.

Informant Mx21 is a male, 52 years of age. He has lived his entire life, with the exception of a few years in the army, in the Aravaipa Canyon. This text was collected on March 16, 1963.

Informant Mx22 is a male, 78 years old. He has lived his entire life on the same ranch in the Aravaipa Canyon. He is the father of Informant Mx21. This text was collected on July 18, 1961.

Informant Mx23 is a female, 20 years old. She lives in San Jose. This text was collected on October 7, 1962.

Informant Mx24 is a female, 38 years of age. She has lived in Safford for twenty years. This text was collected on November 5, 1962.

Informant Mx25 is a female, 60 years old. This text was collected on April 18, 1963.

Informant Mx26 is a male, 85 years of age. He lives in the Aravaipa Canyon on a small ranch. This text was collected on February 9, 1963.

Informant Mx27 is a male, 21 years of age. He lives in Safford. This text was collected on May 8, 1963.

Informant Mx28 is a male, 80 years old. He has worked all of his life as a cowboy and still rides regularly. This text was collected on January 8, 1963.

Informant Mx29 is a male, 31 years old. He is a cowboy and has always lived in the area. This text was collected on April 23, 1963.

Informant Mx30 is a male, 21 years of age. He was raised on ranches in the Klondyke area where his father worked as a cowboy. This text was collected on October 1, 1962.

Informant Mx31 is a female, 27 years old. She lives in Solomonville. She is the sister of Informant Mx30. This text was collected on October 5, 1962.

Informant Mx32 is a male, 19 years of age, who came to Arizona last year. This text was collected on May 12, 1963.

SELECTED BIBLIOGRAPHY

A. BOOKS

Allport, Gordon W., and Postman, Leo. *The Psychology of Rumor*. New York: Henry Holt and Company, 1947.

Andersson, Theodore M. *The Problem of Icelandic Saga Origins*. New Haven: Yale University Press, 1964.

Asch, Solomon E. *Social Psychology*. New York: Prentice-Hall, 1952.

Atkinson, Mary Jourdan, and Dobie, J. Frank. "Pioneer Folk Tales," in *Follow de Drinkin' Gou'd*, ed. by J. Frank Dobie. Austin: The Texas Folklore Society, 1928.

Bancroft, Hubert Howe. *History of Arizona and New Mexico, 1530-1888*. San Francisco: The History Company, 1889.

Bartlett, Frederick C. *Remembering: A Study in Experimental and Social Psychology*. London: Cambridge University Press, 1932.

Blegen, Theodore. *Grass Roots History*. Minneapolis: University of Minnesota Press, 1947.

Brunvand, Jan Harold. *The Study of American Folklore*. New York: Norton and Company, 1968.

Calvin, Ross. *River of the Sun*. Albuquerque: University of New Mexico Press, 1946.

Cannon, John Q. *The Life of Christopher Layton*. Salt Lake City: The Deseret News Press, 1911.

Chadwick, H. Munro, and Chadwick, Nora K. *The Growth of Literature*. 3 vols. Cambridge: Cambridge University Press, 1932-1936.

Clark, Thomas D. *The Rampaging Frontier*. Bloomington, Indiana: Indiana University Press, 1964.

Croy, Homer. *Jesse James Was My Neighbor*. New York: Duell, Sloan and Pearce, 1949.

Dégh, Linda. "Processes of Legend Formation," in *IV International Congress for Folk-Narrative Research in Athens: Lectures and Reports*, ed. by Georgios A. Megas. Athens, 1965.

Dobie, J. Frank. *The Flavor of Texas*. Dallas: Dealey and Lowe, 1936.

Dorson, Richard M. *America in Legend: Folklore From the Colonial Period to the Present*. New York: Pantheon Books, 1973.

---. *American Folklore*. Chicago and London: University of Chicago Press, 1959.

---. "The Debate over the Trustworthiness of Oral Traditional History," in *Volksüberlieferung, Festschrift für Kurt Ranke*. Edited by Fritz Harkort, Karel C. Peeters, and Robert Wildhaber. Göttingen: Otto Schwarz and Company, 1968.

---. "Defining the American Folk Legend," in *American Folklore and the Historian*. Chicago: University of Chicago Press, 1971.

---. "How Shall We Rewrite Charles M. Skinner Today," in *American Folk Legend: A Symposium*. Edited by Wayland D. Hand. Berkeley, Los Angeles and London, 1971.

---. *Peasant Customs and Savage Myths*. 2 vols. Chicago: University of Chicago Press, 1968.

Georges, Robert A. "The General Concept of Legend," in *American Folk Legend: A Symposium*. Edited by Wayland D. Hand. Berkeley, Los Angeles and London, 1971.

Gomme, George L. *Folklore as an Historical Science*. Detroit: Singing Tree Press, 1967. Reprint of the London, 1908, edition.

Gottschalk, Louis. *Understanding History: A Primer of Historical Method*. New York: Alfred A. Knopf, 1965.

Hartland, Edwin Sidney. "Folklore: What Is It and What Is the Good of It?" *Popular Studies in Mythology, Romance and Folklore, No 2*. London: David Nutt and Company, 1899.

---. *The Legend of Perseus*. 3 vols. London, 1894-1896.

Hendricks, George D. *The Bad Men of the West*. San Antonio: The Naylor Company, 1959.

Hockett, Homer C. *Introduction to Research in American History*. New

York: Macmillan, 1938.

Hoig, Stan. *The Humor of the American Cowboy*. New York: New American Library, 1960.

Hunter, Milton R. *Brigham Young, the Colonizer*. Salt Lake City: The Deseret New Press, 1940.

Hyman, Herbert. H. *Interviewing in Social Research*. Chicago: University of Chicago Press, 1954.

Johnson, Allen. *The Historian and Historical Evidence*. New York: Charles Scribner's Sons, 1926.

La Piere, Richard T., and Farnsworth, Paul R. *Social Psychology*. New York: McGraw-Hill, 1936.

Liestol, Knut. *Origin of Icelandic Family Sagas*. Oslo: H. Aschehoug and Company, 1930.

McClintock, James H. *Arizona, the Youngest State*. Chicago: S.J. Clarke Publishing Company, 1916.

---. *Mormon Settlement in Arizona*. Phoenix, Arizona: Manufacturers and Stationers, Inc., 1921.

McCulloch, W.S. "Why the Brain Is in the Head," in *Cerebral Mechanisms*. Edited by L.A. Jeffress. New York: Wiley, 1951.

McKenna, James A. *Black Range Tales*. Glorieta, New Mexico: Rio Grande Press, 1971.

MacRitchie, David. "The Historical Aspects of Folklore," in *The International Folk-Lore Congress, 1891. Papers and Transactions*. Edited by Joseph Jacobs and Alfred Nutt. London: David Nutt, 1892.

---. *The Testimony of Tradition*. London, 1890.

Mathews, John Joseph. *The Osages*. Norman, Oklahoma: University of Oklahoma Press, 1961.

Montell, William Lynwood. *The Saga of Coe Ridge*. Knoxville: University of Tennessee Press, 1970.

Moore, Daniel G. *Enter Without Knocking*. Tucson: University of Arizona Press, 1969.

Nevins, Allan. "Conversation," in *Interpreting American History: Conversations with Historians.* Edited by John Garraty. New York: Macmillan, 1970.

---. *The Gateway to History.* New York: Anchor Books, 1962.

Nordal, Sigurdur. *The Historical Element in the Icelandic Sagas.* Glasgow: Peter Hallberg, 1957.

Nye, Hermes. "Folksay of Lawyers," in *Singers and Storytellers.* Edited by Mody C. Boatright. Dallas: Southern Methodist University Press, 1961.

Osgood, Charles E. *Method and Theory in Experimental Psychology.* London and New York: Oxford University Press, 1953.

Paredes, Américo. "Folklore and History," in *Singers and Storytellers.* Edited by Mody C. Boatright. Dallas: Southern Methodist University Press, 1961.

---. *With His Pistol in His Hand: A Border Ballad and Its Hero.* Austin: University of Texas Press, 1958.

Parker, Donald D. *Local History: How to Gather It, Write It, and Publish It.* New York: Social Science Research Council, 1944.

Patterson, Paul. "Cowboy Comedians and Horseback Humorists," in *The Golden Log.* Edited by Mody C. Boatright, Wilson M. Hudson, and Allen Maxwell. Dallas: Southern Methodist University Press, 1962.

Peuckert, Will-Erich. *Deutsches Volkstum in Märchen und Sage, Schwank und Rätsel.* Berlin: Walter de Gruyter, 1938.

Postman, Leo. "The Experimental Analysis of Motivational Factors in Perception," in *Current Theory and Research in Motivation.* Edited by J.S. Brown. Lincoln, Nebraska: University of Nebraska Press, 1953.

Raglan, Lord Fitz Roy Richard Somerset. *The Hero.* New York: Vintage Books, 1956.

Robinson, Will H. *Story of Arizona.* Phoenix: The Berryhill Company, 1919.

Sherif, Muzafen. *The Psychology of Social Norms.* New York: Harper, 1936.

Shibutani, Tamotsu. *Improvised News: A Sociological Study of Rumor.* New York and Indianapolis: The Bobbs-Merrill Company, 1966.

Smedslund, J. *Multiple Probability Learning.* Oslo: Akademisk Forlag, 1955.

Stern, William. *Zur Psychologie der Aussage.* Berlin: J. Guttentag, 1902.

Sydow, Carl Wilhelm von. "Kategorien der Prosa-Volksdichtung," in *Selected Papers on Folklore.* Copenhagen: Rosenkilde and Bagger, 1948.

Thane, Eric. *High Border Country.* New York: Duell, Sloan and Pierce, 1942.

Vansina, Jan. *Oral Tradition: A Study of Historical Methodology.* Translated by H.M. Wright. Chicago: Aldine Publishing Company, 1965.

Vitaliano, Dorothy B. *Legends of the Earth.* Bloomington, Indiana: Indiana University Press, 1973.

Wake, Joan. *How to Compile a History and Present Day Record of Village Life.* Third Edition, revised and enlarged. Northampton, England, 1935.

Walter, George W. *The Loomis Gang.* Prospect, New York: Prospect Books, 1953.

Weech, Hyrum. *Autobiography.* Hollywood, California: Lee Publishing Company, 1931.

Westermann, Diedrich. *Geschichte Afrikas.* Cologne, 1952.

Wiener, Norbert. *Cybernetics.* New York: Wiley, 1948.

Wilgus, D.K., and Montell, William Lynwood. "Beanie Short: A Civil War Chronicle in Legend and Song," in *American Folk Legend: A Symposium.* Edited by Wayland D. Hand. Berkeley, Los Angeles, and London: University of California Press, 1971.

Wood, Elizabeth Lambert. *The Tragedy of the Powers Mine.* Portland, Oregon: Binfords and Mort, 1952.

Woodhull, Frost. "Folk-Lore Shooting," in *Southwestern Lore.*

Edited by J. Frank Dobie. Austin: The Texas Folklore Society, 1931.

Woodworth, Robert S. *Experimental Psychology*. New York: Henry Holt and Company, 1938.

Wyllys, Rufus Kay. *Arizona, the History of a Frontier State*. Phoenix: Hobson and Hur, 1950.

Young, Kimball. *Social Psychology*. New York: F.S. Crofts and Company, 1936.

B. ARTICLES IN JOURNALS

Attneave, Fred. "Some Informational Aspects of Visual Perception." *Psychological Review*. LXI (1954), 183-193.

Bartlett, Frederick C. "Some Experiments in the Reproduction of Folk-Stories." *Folk-Lore*. XXXI (1920), 30-47.

Breckenridge, R.T., and Ratroff, O.D. "Pulmonary Embolism and Unexpected Death in Supposedly Normal Persons." *New England Journal of Medicine*. 270 (1964), 298.

Bridges, J.W. "An Experimental Study of Decision Types and Their Mental Correlates." *Psychological Monographs*. XVII (1914), 37-44.

Buchan, David D. "History and Harlaw." *Journal of the Folklore Institute*. V (June, 1968), 58-67.

Campbell, Donald T. "The Indirect Assessment of Social Attitudes." *Psychological Bulletin*. XLVII (1950), 15-38.

Campbell, Donald T., and Gruen, W. "Progression From Simple to Complex as a Molar Law of Learning." *Journal of General Psychology*. LXIX (1958), 237-244.

Carlson, Jessie B., and Duncan, Carl P. "A Study of Autonomous Change in the Memory Trace by the Method of Recognition." *American Journal of Psychology*. LXVIII (1955), 280-284.

Cash, McKinley. "On the Track of the Power Boys." *Journal of Arizona History*. VIII (Winter, 1967), 248-255.

Chapanis, Alphonse. "The Reconstruction of Abbreviated Printed Messages." *Journal of Experimental Psychology*. XLVIII (1954), 496-510.

Clarke, R., and Campbell, D.T. "A Demonstration of Bias in Estimates of Negro Ability." *Journal of Abnormal and Social Psychology*. LI (1955), 585-588.

Coffin, T.E. "Some Conditions of Suggestion and Suggestibility." *Psychological Monographs*. LIII (1941), No. 241.

Crosland, H.R. "A Qualitative Analysis of the Process of Forgetting." *Psychological Monographs*. XXIX (1903), No. 23.

Dalen, James E., and Dexter, Lewis. "Diagnosis and Management of Massive Pulmonary Embolism," *Disease-a-Month*. (August, 1967).

Dégh, Linda, and Vazsonyi, Andrew. "The Dialectics of the Legend." *Folklore Preprint Series*. I (December, 1973), No. 6.

---. "Legend and Belief." *Genre*. IV, 281-304.

Dorson, Richard M. "Oral Tradition and Written History: the Case for the United States." *Journal of the Folklore Institute*. I (December, 1964), 220-234.

---. "Traditional History of the Scottish Highlands." *Journal of the Folklore Institute*. VIII (December, 1971), 147-184.

Dupree, Louis. "The Retreat of the British Army from Kabul to Jalalabad in 1842: History and Folklore." *Journal of the Folklore Institute*. IV (June, 1967), 50-74.

Fife, Austin E. "Folklore and Local History." *Utah Historical Quarterly*. XXXI (Fall, 1963), 316-323.

Gould, Richard A. "Indian and White Versions of 'The Burnt Ranch Massacre.'" *Journal of the Folklore Institute*. III (June, 1966), 30-42.

Gunnerson, Dolores A. "The Southern Athapascans: their Arrival in the Southwest." *El Palacio*. LXIII (1956), 346-365.

Hand, Wayland D. "Status of European and American Legend Study." *Current Anthropology*. VI (October, 1965), 439-446.

Heidbreder, Edna. "Toward a Dynamic Theory of Cognition." *Psychological Monographs*. LII (1945)

Henderson, E.N. "Memory for Connected Trains of Thought." *Psychological Monographs*. V (1903), No. 23.

Hochberg, Julian, and McAlister, E. "A Quantitative Approach to Figural Goodness." *Journal of Experimental Psychology*. XLVI (1953), 361-364.

Hösch-Ernst, Lucy. "Die Psychologie der Aussage." *Internationale Rundschau*. I (1915), 15-33.

Jansen, Wm. Hugh. "The Esoteric-Exoteric Factor in Folklore." *Fabula: Journal of Folktale Studies*. II (1959), 205-211.

Jordan, Philip D. "The Folklorist as Social Historian." *Western Folklore*. XII (July, 1953), 194-201.

Klein, Barbro. "The Testimony of the Button." *Journal of the Folklore Institute*. VIII (1971), 125-146.

Krech, David, and Calvin, Allen D. "Levels of Perceptual Organization and Cognition." *Journal of Abnormal and Social Psychology*. XLVIII (1953), 394-400.

Lewis, F.H. "Note on the Doctrine of Memory Trace." *Psychological Review*. XL (1933), 90-96.

Lovibond, S.H. "A Further Test of the Hypothesis of Autonomous Memory Trace Change." *Journal of Experimental Psychology*. LV (1958), 412-415.

Lowie, Robert H. "Oral Traditions and History." *Journal of American Folklore*. XXX (April-June, 1917), 161-167.

---. "Oral Traditions and History: Discussions and Correspondence." *American Anthropologist*. XVII (1915), 598-600.

McGinnies, Elliot M.; Comer, P.B.; and Lacey, O.L. "Visual Recognition Thresholds as a Function of Word Length and Word Frequency." *Journal of Experimental Psychology*. XLIV (1951), 65-69.

McGregor, John C. "Burial of an Early American Magician." *Proceedings of the American Philosophical Society.* LXXXVI (1943), No. 2.

Meighan, Clement W. "More on Folk Traditions." *Journal of American Folklore.* LXXIII (1960), 60.

Michael, D.N. "A Cross-Cultural Investigation of Closure." *Journal of Abnormal and Social Psychology.* XLVIII (1953), 225-230.

Myres, John. "Presidential Address." *Folk-Lore.* XXXVII (1926), 12-34.

Nutt, Alfred. "History, Tradition and Historic Myth." *Folk-Lore.* XII (1901), 336-339.

Pendergast, David M., and Meighan, Clement W. "Folk Traditions as Historical Fact: A Paiute Example." *Journal of American Folklore.* LXXII (April-June, 1959), 128-137.

Raglan, Lord Fitz Roy Richard Somerset. "Folk Traditions as Historical Facts." *Journal of American Folklore.* LXXIII (1960), 58-59.

Robinson, D., and Rohde, S. "Two Experiments with an Anti-Semitism Poll." *Journal of Abnormal and Social Psychology.* XLI (1946), 136-144.

Shute, G.W. "Tragedy of the Grahams." *Arizona Cattlelog.* (April, 1960), 32-37.

Tillhagen, Carl Herman. "Was ist eine Sage?" *Acta Ethnographica.* XIII (1964), 10.

Vitaliano, Dorothy B. "Geomythology." *Journal of the Folklore Institute.* V (June, 1968), 5-30.

Wagoner, J.J. "Development of the Cattle Industry in Southern Arizona, 1870's and '80's." *New Mexico Historical Review.* XXVI (1951), 54-58.

Wells, Merle W. "History and Folklore: A Suggestion for Cooperation." *Journal of the West.* IV (January, 1965), 95-96.

Wishner, J.; Shipley, T.E., Jr.; and Hurvick, M.C. "The Serial Position Curve as a Function of Organization." *American Journal of Psychology.* LXX (1957), 258-262.

C. UNPUBLISHED MANUSCRIPTS

DeCaro, Francis Anthony. "Folklore as an 'Historical Science': The Anglo-American Viewpoint."

D. CENSUS REPORTS

United States Bureau of the Census. *United States Census of Population, 1960. Detailed Characteristics, Arizona.* Final Report PC (1)-4D. Washington, D.C.: United States Government Printing Office, 1962.

E. INDEXES

Aarne Antti. *The Types of the Folktale; a Classification and Bibliography:* Antti Aarne's *Verzeichnis der Märchentypen* (FFC No. 3). Translated and enlarged by Stith Thompson, 2nd revision. Helsinki: Suomalainen Tiedeakatemica, Academia Scientiarum Fennica, 1961.

Baughman, Ernest W. *Type and Motif-Index of the Folktales of England and North America.* The Hague: Mouton and Company, 1966.

Cross, Tom Peete. *Motif-Index of Early Irish Literature.* Bloomington, Indiana: Indiana University Press, 1952.

Handwörterbuch des Deutschen Aberglaubens. 10 vols. Berlin and Leipzig: Walter de Gruyter and Company, 1931-1932.

Thompson, Stith. *Motif-Index of Folk Literature.* Revised. Bloomington, Indiana: Indiana University Press, 1955.

Thompson, Stith, and Balys, Jonas. *The Oral Tales of India.* Bloomington, Indiana: Indiana University Press, 1958.

F. NEWSPAPERS

Arizona Daily Star. Tucson, Arizona. February 12, 1918; February 13, 1918; February 14, 1918; February 15, 1918; February 16, 1918; February 17, 1918; February 19, 1918; February 20, 1918; February 21, 1918; February 24, 1918; February 28, 1918; March 9, 1918; March 10, 1918; March 19, 1918; April 28, 1960.

Arizona Republic. Phoenix, Arizona. December 29, 1939; April 17, 1940; January 26, 1969.

Arizona Republican. Phoenix, Arizona. December 18, 1923; January 16, 1924.

Deseret News. Salt Lake City, Utah. Volume XXXII, p. 574.

Eastern Arizona Courier. Safford, Arizona. September 16, 1970.

Graham Guardian. Safford, Arizona. December 14, 1917; February 15, 1918; February 22, 1918; March 1, 1918; March 15, 1918; May 17, 1918.

Tucson Citizen. Tucson, Arizona. February 12, 1918; February 13, 1918; February 14, 1918; February 15, 1918; February 16, 1918; February 18, 1918; February 19, 1918; February 20, 1918; February 21, 1918; February 22, 1918; February 23, 1918; March 9, 1918; March 13, 1918.

APPENDIX IV

ADDITIONAL NEWSPAPER ACCOUNTS

The following newspaper accounts were not included in the original manuscript and the author was probably not aware of them. They have been added now to provide more examples of reporting from the time, including a humorous article about the "man hunters." The name Power is misspelled as Powers so many times that we have refrained from inserting [sic] every time.

Bisbee Daily Review, Feb. 12, 1918, courtesy of Arizona State Library, Archives and Public Records, obtained from http://adnp.azlibrary.gov/, p. 1 and 6.

3 MURDERERS ARE REPORTED SURROUNDED BY DEPUTIES
Men Who Killed Officers In Graham County Said to Be Surrounded by Posse of Officers and Cowmen.

(By Review Leased Wire)

GLOBE, Feb. 12. Tom Powers, John Powers and Tom Sisson, slayers of Sheriff Frank McBride and Deputies Mark Kempton and Kain [sic] Wootan in a battle between officers and draft evaders in the Klondyke district of Graham county are within reach of three combined posses early this morning. That a battle will be fought before the fugitives are stopped is the belief of federal and county officers here. The men have been run down a mile from Reddington, twenty-five miles south of the sene [sic] of the murders.

Jeff Powers, father of two of the fugitives, died this afternoon at 4 o-clock. He was shot by the officers when they attempted to take the two Powers boys at 7:30 o'lock [sic] Sunday morning. The bullet entered his body a short distance below the heart.

Deputy United States Marshal Frank Haynes, former sheriff of Gila county, sought the two Powers boys, aged 26 and 28 years as draft evaders under the federal draft law. The Graham county officers who were killed were attempting to investigate the mysterious death of a sister of the youths who was alleged to have been assaulted and murdered by unknown persons.

A battle followed the approach of the four officers to the Powers cabin resulting the death [sic] of the three Graham county officers and of the elder Powers. Haynes escaped and made his way back to Safford where he gave an alarm that resulted in numerous posses being sent into the field. The capture of the fugitives, who include Tom Sisson, a "nester" and ex-convict paroled by Governor G. W. P. Hunt, after conviction on a charge of stealing cattle from an Indian, is anticipated this morning.

That the fugitives are well supplied with food is indicated by a telephone report from Reddington that two wagon loads of supplies were taken into the hills today. Officers are on the trail of this food now in order to ascertain its destination.

(By Review Leased Wire)

SAFFORD, Ariz., Feb. 11. Sheriff R. F. McBride and deputies Mark Kempton and Kane Wootan were killed Sunday morning about 6:30 o'clock in battle with Tom Powers and John Powers, slackers, and Tom Sisson, horse thief, at the home of the Powers boys in Raulenake [sic] Canyon, Galiuro mountains.

Deputy U. S. Marshal Frank Haynes of Globe, Sheriff McBride and Deputies Kempton and Wootan left Safford Saturday afternoon at 4 o'clock for Galiuro mountains by way of Klondike [sic] to get Tom Powers and John Powers, two slackers. They reached a house near the mine of John [sic] Powers, father of the Powers boys, about daybreak on Sunday morning and surrounded the place. Powers, the father, came out of the house with a gun and was ordered to hold up his hands. As one of his boys opened the door and started firing at the officers, the elder Powers dropped, shot through the right shoulder. About 25 shots were fired by the officers. McBride was shot by Tom Powers and Kane by John Powers. Kempton, as he kicked in the door, was shot by Tom Sisson, a horse thief sentenced to the penitentiary 5 years ago and paroled by Governor Hunt. He lived with the Powers' [sic].

Marshal Haynes escaped unhurt and went to Klondyke for help. A posse from Klondyke started Sunday afternoon for the Powers camp to bring back the bodies. Haynes arrived at Safford at 4 p.m. Sunday with news of the killing.

The murderers took the officers' horses and ammunition and started for the border to go into Mexico. They stopped at Hot Springs, one mile from the Powers house and told a man named Allen they had killed the officers and that their father was shot and for him to go to the Powers home and take care of him. Allen and a man named Murde went to the house and found the wounded man. They took him into a tunnel of the mine and placed him on a cot.

Allen then came to Safford, reaching here about 4 o'clock Sunday afternoon. Posses left Safford, Thatcher, Pima, Fairview and Ft. Thomas Sunday night heavily armed for the Galiuro mountains to get the slackers and Tom Sisson.

The bodies of the dead officers are expected to arrive in Safford tonight.

A report from Reddington, in the San Pedro valley today, states that the Powers boys and Sisson reached there Sunday night.

Advices of the killing were received in Bisbee Sunday evening about seven o'clock and a bulletin posted on the Review board was read by hundreds.

(Continued on Page Six)

Al Kempton, who's [sic] brother was killed was notified by Sheriff Wheeler on the phone first and then received a telegram from Safford. He left early yesterday morning by auto for Safford.

Sheriff Wheeler, after he received the news, called up all his deputies in the county and posses were sent in every direction in hopes of heading the murderers off. He, with a posse, is watching the pass between the Galliuros [sic] and the Little Dragoons where a trail leads from the Arivaipa [sic] Canyon by way of the Hot Springs into the Johnson country. Jess Moore and posse from Willcox are watching the east end of the Arivaipa [sic] Canyon and along the south slope of the Grahams in the vicinity of Ft. Grant is another posse. Deputy Sheriff William Bennett of Benson and a posse are watching the lower San Pedro to prevent them from crossing into the Catalinas. Deputy Sheriff Brakefield and Joe Hodges are watching the point of the Huachucas in the vicinity of the Palominas Custom House to head them off from going into Mexico in that locality. Deputies from Douglas are watching the Mud Springs and Mulberry Pass in the Chiricahuas, while others are watching the pass going into the Swisshelms and into Rucker Canyon.

Other Posses Out

From Tucson comes advices [sic] that Sheriff Rye Miles has several posses out, two of these are in the lower San Pedro country in the vicinity of Mammoth and Reddington, which would be the logical places for the outlaws to try and get out of the mountains on their way to Mexico. There is an old trail that leads from the Klondyke and Hot Springs country into the San Pedro river and another one that comes into the river near the old Redus place about forty miles below Benson. Sheriff Earhart of Santa Cruz county has posses out watching the country in the vicinity of Elgin and Cannile and the border in the vicinity of Santa Cruz is being patrolled by a detachment of the Tenth Cavalry.

Lived in Don Luis

John and Tom Powers are said to be brothers of "Maricopa Slim" Powers who was killed a few years ago. The boys lived at Don Luis a few years ago and Tom was arrested for causing trouble at a dance there and was fined before Judge Smith in the Lowell court. If they are the brothers of Slim Powers they have a sister living in this district.

Bisbee Daily Review, Feb. 14, 1918, courtesy of Arizona State Library, Archives and Public Records, obtained from http://adnp.azlibrary.gov/, p. 1 and 5.

MURDERERS DRIVEN INTO COCHISE STRONGHOLD BY OFFICERS; HILLS GUARDED

Hundreds of Deputies Surround Noted Retreat in Dragoon Mountains to Prevent Escape of Fugitives

With hundreds of armed deputies from Bisbee, Tombstone, Douglas, Gleeson, Pearce, Cochise, Willcox, Dragoon and other points in this county, aided by Deputy Sheriff Rye Miles and his posse and possibly others, Tom and John Powers and Tom Sisson are facing almost certain capture today. The murderers of the three Graham county officers were located last evening in Cochise Stronghold, in the Dragoon mountains and this morning a complete cordon of officers will surround the natural hiding place and barrier.

First reports reaching Bisbee last evening were to the effect that the three fugitives had been seen in the neighborhood of West Well, about seven miles east of Pearce. This information, however, proved false. The murderers had been located while going into Cochise Stronghold, however, and little chance is given them for escape.

Hot Trail Found

Sheriff Miles of Pima county took up the trail of the killers, sometime yesterday. According to a Tucson dispatch the officer found their trail at 3 o'clock. If, however, the three men were in the

Reddington (lower San Pedro) country yesterday the distance to be covered in getting into the Stronghold was too great in but three or four hours. The sheriff's office received word last evening that the men had stolen two horses and a mule from a rancher in the lower San Pedro region, supplanting their jaded animals, ridden since the morning of the murder in Rattlesnake canyon.

Leaving the Reddington country the three struck in a southeasterly direction crossing the Southern Pacific in the neighborhood of Dragoon. From that point theiy [sic] are supposed to have gone over the rim of Cochise Stronghold. Miles and his posse was [sic] but a short distance behind the outlaws as night closed in. His horses were so jaded that no further progress could be made.

Many Posses Formed

At least three separate posses were organized in the Warren district early last evening and immediately dispatched to the region of Gleeson to aid in the hunt for the man killers. The Dixie canyon country and all tributary avenues of escape are closely guarded.

This morning will see all of the posses organized under one head: probably under the direction of Sheriff Harry C. Wheeler or his chief deputy, guy Welch. At daylight the men will be split into small groups and placed at every point where there is a possibility of the Powers boys and Sisson making their escape.

Cochise Stronghold

Cochise Stronghold is a natural hiding place. It has two entrances, chief of which is located about eight miles west of Pearce. The Stronghold is a slice cut out of solid rock and there are few paths and trails by which either man or beast can get either in or out. Its walls are precipituous [sic] in the extreme and will make a natural hiding place for the outlaws. There is ample water in the deep canyon but few places where food can be secured.

The spot secured its name from the Apache chief by the same name, Cochise. It was in this canyon that Cochise, in July 1871, retreated with his band of renegade Apache Indians, after stealing a herd of cattle from a rancher in the neighborhood of Fort Bowie. In an attempt to enter the Stronghold after Cochise and his warriors Captain Jerry Russell and his troop of the Third cavalry was ambushed. So far as is known this is the first time since the Cochise episode that the defile has been utilized on a large scale, as a barrier and hiding place by outlaws.

BLOODHOUNDS ON TRAIL
(By Review Leased Wire)

TUCSON, Feb. 13 – The posse of Sheriff Miles of Pima county has finally struck the trail of John and Tom Powers and Thomas Sissons [sic], slayers of Sheriff McBride of Graham county and his deputies, Kempton and Wootan. The mule and one of the horses taken by the slayers from their victims were found on the Cross X ranch in the San Pedro valley this morning at 11:30 o'clock, they having been abandoned after being ridden to total exhaustion. With the remaining horse, which apparently they are using as a pack animal, the three slayers are doubling back to the scene of the crime in Graham

(Continued on Page Five)

MURDERERS ARE SURROUNDED IN COCHISE COUNTY

county, and Sheriff Miles left Benson at 3 o'clock this afternoon with bloodhounds which will take up the trail of the slayers where it was found on the Cross X ranch. Word of the finding of the trail has been sent to other posses and it is believed that the fugitives will soon be overtaken.

The place where the horse and mule were found is two miles from Deep Wells, twenty miles east of San Pedro and twenty-five miles from the scene of the crime.

Chief Deputy United States Marshal Willetts announced today that he had asked the department of justice to offer a reward for the capture of the men, to be added to $4000 reward already offered. Willetts, who is directing the search for the United States marshal's office doubts that the slayers know they are being hotly pursued, as they no doubt think they killed all the officers in the posse that went for them.

The possibility that the pursuit of the Powers-Sissons [sic] trio may lead to a general round-up of draft evaders is being taken into consideration by the possemen. The presence of many draft evaders, of all nationalities, in the southwestern corner of New Mexico and the adjoining section of Arizona is known to officers. Some officers were inclined to suspect that they may be trying to effect a junction with the draft evader colony in the forestry wilds, which border Mexico. In the event the pursuit should lead to a general round-up of draft evaders officers who know the country say that it would require soldiers with a mountain field piece to dislodge them.

Wylie Morgan, an uncle of the Powers boys, in Tucson today, said that the Powers boys were under the domination of Thomas Sissons [sic], who he said was a radical pro-German and caused the Powers boys to evade the draft. Morgan says he warned McBride that the boys would kill him if he sought to arrest them and the Powers boys sent him a warning that they would kill him if he did not stop talking.

TROOPS PATROL BORDER
(By Review Leased Wire)

DOUGLAS. Feb. 13. -- Colonel George H. Morgan, commander of the Arizona military district, tonight dispatched two troops of cavalry to patrol the international boundary east of Douglas to prevent Tom and John Powers and Tom Sisson, Graham county slayers of Sheriff R. F. McBride and two deputies last Sunday morning from escaping into Mexico. These troops have orders to leave orders [sic] to leave the border patrol if it is thought that by so doing they an [sic] aid in the capture of the men. Colonel Morgan said tonight that the international line would be carefully guarded to keep the fugitives from crossing.

Deputy United States Marshal J. F. McDonald tonight formed a posse of local officers and citizens to take up the trail of the slayers in West Wells, forty miles north of here, where it was learned early last night that the trio had procured fresh horses and doubled back. The possemen left here at 11:30 in automobiles and expect to be where the outlaws are reported to have been seen within two hours.

Ranchers in the section through which the fugitives are expected to pass have been warned and are organizing to assist in apprehending the men.

Local Man Tells Notable Facts of Powers Family

Charlie Jones, of this city, was up at the Powers' claims at Abandoned mine, a gold property, in Rattlesnake canyon, two years ago looking at the mine and knows the father and son [sic], who are being sought by officers for the killing of three deputies. Jones had planned to return there with a party of Los Angeles engineers next week but has cancelled the trip owing to the trouble.

The country around Rattlesnake canyon, Redfield canyon and Redfield pass is very rough, according to Jones, and in fact at the pass, a narrow defile in the mountains, one man could stand off a regiment. The country is heavily timbered and only accessible by pack horses.

According to Jones the Powers boys as well as their father Tom are excellent shots and he tells of the marksmanship of one of the boys who was at the claims when he was there. The boy would go out and bring down ducks on the wing with a rifle with greater ease than the average man would do so with a shotgun.

Family of Adventurers.

The father has been a frontiersman all his life as were his father and grandfather before him, both of whom died with their boots on. His mother and wife lived in Rattlesnake canyon when the family first moved over with their cattle from the New Mexico line. The log cabin which the father and sons erected caved in and killed Powers' [sic] wife while his mother was killed when a young horse ran away throwing her from a buggy.

When the Powers family first moved to Rattlesnake canyon the father made a wagon by cutting down a large tree and hollowing it out for the bed of the wagon while the wheels were round blocks from a tree.

The Powers family formerly had a cattle ranch near Klondike [sic] but sold this out and moved what cattle they kept up to Rattlesnake canyon. This canyon received its name due to a den of snakes making it their home. These were so deadly and caused such heavy losses among the Powers' cattle that the father and two sons finally "gassed" them.

The Abandoned mine was originally located by Bullard and Tucker. The latter was killed at the mine by a forest ranger and it was his interest which the elder Powers has handled.

No Relations Here.

Tom Powers and his sons are not related to Bill "White Oaks" Powers, formerly of Bisbee, and his brother "Maricopa Slim" Powers, who was killed by circus thugs four years ago at Maricopa in the performance of his duty as an officer, according to H.E. Grover, deputy sheriff, former Texas ranger and old timer in this section.

Grover knew "White Oaks" and "Maricopa Slim" well and speaks highly of both. Bill Powers served in the army during the Spanish-American war and later was in business in Porto [sic] Rico. From there he went to the Panama Canal zone and two years ago was in Phoenix, planning to go to Alaska to work on the Alaskan railroad.

Tom Powers and his family hail from Goose Creek, according to Grover, and John was foreman of the L.C. cow outfit years ago near Silver City, N.M.

Bisbee Daily Review, Feb. 16, 1918, courtesy of Arizona State Library, Archives and Public Records, obtained from http://adnp.azlibrary.gov/, p. 1 and 2.

MURDERERS DOUBLE BACK ABANDONING ALL MOUNTS
Posse Forces Graham County Murderers to Take to the Mountains On Foot. Late Details Are Lacking.

Sheriff Harry C. Wheeler, who, with Sheriff Rye Miles of Pima County, is directing the chase of the slayers of the three Graham County officers, telephoned to his office at Tombstone early this morning that the three murderers had been located in the immediate region of the old Vernie Young ranch, about twelve miles from Light, and in the foothills of the Chiracahuas.

Posses were leaving Bisbee early this morning for more volunteers to aid in guarding the southern side of the mountains to prevent the fugitives from making their escape into Mexico. The cattlemen of the Swisshelm and Chiricahua mountains have rounded up their horses and will supply "chuck" wagons to provision the various parties of officers through the hills.

American soldiers, customs guards and Mexican soldiers and guards have been appraised [sic] of the situation and their cooperation solicited. This morning bloodhounds from the Pima county sheriff's office, trained in the work of pursuing human beings, will arrive in Douglas on the Golden States Limited and immediately rushed to the neighborhood of Light.

Where the outlaws are now reported to be is some few miles distant from the Rock Creek country where they abandoned their horses shortly before dark and started afoot to make their escape.

Tom and John Powers and Tom Sisson, murderers of Sheriff McBride and Deputies Wootan and Kempton of Graham county last Sunday morning, are fleeing from several hundred deputy sheriffs on foot, according to information received last evening at the sheriff's office in Tombstone by Under Sheriff Guy Welch. The three men, apparently pressed close by a part of the posse, gave up their jaded horses at Rock Creek at dark. The horses, saddled, were found by the deputies.

Rock Creek, where the latest evidence of the killers was found, is located in the western edge of the Chiricahua national forest reserve. It is about fifteen miles from Moore ranch in Rucker canyon where the outlaws were reported yesterday afternoon. Rock Creek is northwest of Rucker and it would appear that the fugitives are doubling back on their own trail.

Inquiry failed to determine, last evening, whether Sheriff Rye Miles, who with Sheriff Harry C. Wheeler, of Cochise, is directing the manhunt, had his bloodhounds with him. It is known, however, that William Hudson, a rancher living about four miles from the Riggs ranch in the Dos Cabezas region, has some dogs which may be used for the purpose of tracking the murderers, now that they have abandoned their mounts.

Undoubtedly this morning will see a closing in of the posses which are scouring the mountains for the much-wanted men. The country in which they are hiding is particularly rough and in some cases very precipitous. The region is very sparsely settled and forest rangers are located at various points through the reserve.

POSSES INCREASE.
(By Review Leased Wire)

Five hundred civilians and soldiers tonight were closing in on the Swisshelm mountains, twenty-five miles north of Douglas, in the hopes of apprehending Tom and John Powers [sic] and Tom Sisson, alleged slayers of Sheriff R. F. McBride and Deputies Kempton and Wootan of Graham county last Sunday. The fugitives were last heard from at the Frank Moore ranch where they changed horses this morning.

Three posses left here late this afternoon to reinforce those already in the field, one striking directly at the southern outlet of the Swisshelms, and the two others heading respectively for the Slaughter ranch and Guadalupe canyon, both near the international boundary.

Sheriffs [sic] Harry C. Wheeler of Cochise county and Sheriff Rye Miles of Pima county are directing operations from the field, with Sheriff Henry Hall of Pinal county rushing to assist them. Former Sheriff Jeff

(Continued on Page Two)

Adams of Maricopa county left here late today to help direct the civilian patrol along the border. Deputy Sheriff Putnam of Deming, N.M., was directing the co-operation of New Mexico posses along the Arizona-New Mexico line to cut off escape of the trio into the Mogollan mountains.

Fifteen hundred dollars additional reward has been offered by cattlemen of Graham and Cochise counties, making a purse of $5500 now hanging over the heads of the pursued men.

The patrol of United States troops north of the international line and Mexican soldiers south of the line was maintained today with some American cavalrymen going into the hills to join in the chase.

(By Review Leased Wire)

DOUGLAS, Feb. 15.—Posses led by Sheriffs Harry C. Wheeler of Cochise county and Rye Miles of Pima county late today found the horses and saddles used by Tom and John Powers and Tom Sisson, alleged slayers of Sheriff R.F. McBride and Deputies Wootan and Kempton of Graham county last Sunday, in Chiricahua mountains, according to word received here tonight. It was reported that the fugitives had taken to the mountains afoot.

Kempton brings Details of Crime

That five instead of three murders may be charged against the Powers boys, who are now being sought by hundreds of men in the Chiricahuas, is the statement of J.A. Kempton, night chief of police in Bisbee, and a brother of Deputy Mark Kempton who was killed in the tragedy in Rattlesnake canyon last Sunday morning. Kempton returned yesterday from Safford, Graham county, where he was in atendance [sic] at his brother's funeral.

Attention was first called to the Powers' family when the two boys, about two weeks before the murder of the officers, came into Klondike [sic] with a report that their sister had committed suicide. They stated she had been dead twenty-eight hours. A coroner and a physician went to the Powers house, in Rattlesnake canyon, and examined the corpse. It was determined, by the state of preservation of the body, that the girl must have been dead several days at least. Signs of strangulation were present and it is the opinion of the Graham county officers that the brothers murdered the girl.

One motive is assigned for the possible killing of the sister by the Power boys. The girl is said to have been meeting a young man, a neighbor who did not suit the fancy of the two brothers. It is said that the Powers boys warned the suitor to get out of the country or they would kill him. It is supposed that he was killed at the same time the sister was strangled. The man has not been seen or heard from for several weeks.

According to Kempton the Powers boys are crack shots and enjoyed a none too favorable reputation in the Rattlesnake canyon country of Graham county. Tom Powers, declares Kempton, shoots wild pigeons with a rifle. It is not [sic] said that Powers, with a revolver, at a distance of twelve to fifteen steps could mark a cross or a circle with bullet holes.

Mohave County Miner, Feb. 16, 1918, courtesy of Arizona State Library, Archives and Public Records, obtained from http://adnp.azlibrary.gov/, p. 1.

SLACKERS KILL OFFICERS AND ARE LATER SLAIN BY PURSUERS

R.F. McBride, Cain Wooton [sic] and M. B. Kempton were killed at the mining camp of the Powers fathers [sic] and brothers in the Galiuri [sic] mountains of Graham county, Arizona, last Sunday, when officers tried to arrest the boys as slackers. McBride was sheriff and the other two men were deputies. The officers, in company of Deputy U.S. Marshal Haynes, went to the camp and as they arrived at the cabin the father of the Powers boys came out with a gun and ordered them away. A fight resulted and the old man was shot through the shoulder. The other men then commenced shooting and the three officers were killed. Tom Sisson, a paroled convict, was also in the fight.

Two hundred cowboys and officers are close on the trail of the men and it is believed that they are surrounded, in the old Cochise stronghold, but are sure to be smoked out. If captured they will be given short shrift, as the murdered men were among the most popular in southern Arizona. The dead officers leave large families.

Judge George H. Crosby, who is holding court in Kingman, was a warm friend of the dead officers and their untimely death was a great shock to him. He prosecuted Sisson, when he was district attorney of Graham county, on a charge of horse stealing, and secured a conviction.

As the Miner is going to press a report comes from Bisbee that the outlaws were all killed in a fight with the cowboys near their old home in the Galiuri [sic] mountains, but there has been nothing confirmatory of that report.

Bisbee Daily Review, Feb. 19, 1918, courtesy of Arizona State Library, Archives and Public Records, obtained from http://adnp.azlibrary.gov/, p. 1 and 2.

Posses in Man Hunt Battle Blizzard to Apprehend Fugitives

(By Review Leased Wire)

Bowie, Feb. 18. – In a blinding snow and sleet storm which is one of the worst in the history of southeastern Arizona, the posses pursuing Tom and John Powers and Tom Sisson tonight continued on the trail of the three men wanted for the murder of Sheriff McBride and Deputies Kempton and Wootan regardless of weather conditions.

A fresh pack of bloodhounds from Globe was dispatched to the sheriff's posse at midnight last night. A long distance telephone message received here tonight stated that these bloodhounds, followed by Sheriff Slaughter of Greenlee county and his posse, had struck a fresh trail in the snow at the head of Turkey and rock creeks, on the west slope of Summit mountain. The message added that the outlaws were apparently only a few hours ahead of this posse and were heading northeast toward the head of Cave creek.

Indians Picked Trailers.

Men familiar with the Summit mountain country tonight predicted that, if the outlaws remain on the Summit it will be easy for the Apache Indian trailers from the San Carlos reservation to pick up their train [sic] in the morning by the tracks in the fresh snow. These Indian trailers were selected from the entire San Carlos reservation for their ability as trailers and are the best in the state.

It was also predicted here tonight that the outlaws would be overtaken and either captured or killed tomorrow as the snow is expected to make their escape almost impossible.

A carload of fresh horses arrived here at noon today and were rushed to the front to take the places of the fatigued animals which the posses have been riding. A number of men from Globe left with these horses to relieve ehsausted [sic] possemen who have been in the saddle night and day.

INDIANS TAKE TRAIL.
(By Review Leased Wire)

TUCSON, Feb. 18.—Three Apache Indians have left Willcox, Ariz., to trail Thomas Powers, John Powers and Thomas Sisson, wanted for the killing of three Graham county officers February 10, according to a report to Sheriff Rye Miles from Willcox today.

The fugitives are reported to have been trailed to Cottonwood canyon, in the western edge of the Chiricahua mountains, 40 miles north of Douglas. They have discarded their cowboy boots and are wearing hobnail shoes, according to the report.

U.S. MARSHAL JOINS CHASE.
(By Review Leased Wire)

DOUGLAS, Feb. 18.—United States Marshal Joseph P. Dillon left here late today for ottonwood [sic] canyon, 40 miles north, to help Sheriff Harry C. Wheeler direct posses searching the Chiricahua mountains for the three outlaws, Tom and John Powers and Tom Sisson, hunted for the murder of Sheriff R.F. McBride and Deputies Kempton and Wootan of Graham county more than a week ago. Late today word reached here that the trio had abandoned their rendexvous [sic] in Cave creek, crossed back to the west side of the mountains and were headed south into Cottonwood canyon. One thousand men continue to search for the outlaws. Eight troops of United States cavalry from Douglas are engaged in the man-hunt, having been sent out to capture the two Powers boys as draft evaders. A cold rain started falling here at 7 o'clock tonight, and it is expected to hamper the trailers.

GraPhic [sic] Story of Tragedy.

The following story of the killing of Sheriff McBride and deputies is taken from the last issue of the Graham Guardian and gives a graphic account of the murder of the officers. The accompanying pictures show John G. Powers on horseback. Tom Powers is the central figure in the group with the girl, Ola Powers,

(Continued on Page Two)

his sister, who was mysteriously killed being strangled to death, and his brother John. The other picture is that of Thomas J. Sisson, taken at the time he was an inmate of the state penitentiary. It is said that no members of the Powers family can read or write. The pictures indicate that all three men are far below the average in reasoning power. It was partly investigated the death of Olla Powers that the officers made the trip that cost their lives [sic].

(Report from Graham Guardian, Feb. 15, 1918, follows at this point in text - included in original manuscript.)

MAN HUNTING LOSES GLAMOR WITH REALITY.
By Review Correspondent.

Man hunting isn't half as much fun as many of the younger fellows in the hills seeking the Powers brothers and Tom Sisson imagined it would be and numbers of these no doubt wish now that they had remained home where three square meals daily and an honest to goodness bed at night are assured.

Those who are enjoying the man hunt most are the Arizonans who are fond of liquor and who prefer it oftener and at a cheaper cost than when secured from bootleggers.

Rodeo is the mecca of most of the posses and numbers of these are either making that town their headquarters or else find it necessary to go there often for supplies and information In fact, it is safe to say that Rodeo is the most popular town of its size in New Mexico at present.

Contrary to the general belief of those who have never visited the New Mexico town all of the buildings there are not saloons. There is a hotel and a railroad station there, also. The writer feels duty bound to set the public right in this respect.

One thing is certain and this is that Arizonans who depend on bootleg brought from Rodeo for their liquor supply need not worry that the town will be captured and the wet goods confiscated by the Powers boys and Sisson. Rodeo is amply provided with deputies to prevent such a tragedy.

Sunday Not Off Day.

Sunday is not an off day in Rodeo, judging from the frequent trips made by dusty and weary deputies backdoorward to the rear of the saloons. There medicine, which is highly recommended for sore throats, bad colds and snake bits [sic], was dispensed at a neat profit to the saloon men. At least it is believed that such is the case, since sore throats and colds disappeared as if by magic when the travelers returned to the main street, calmly wiping their mouths on their coat sleeves and grinning.

It is an ill wind that blows no one some good and it is believed that certain Rodeo merchants hope the Powers boys elude the posses for weeks.

What is brought home strongest to one after a trip to Silver Creek, Apache, Rodeo, Hilltop mine, Paradise, Cave Creek and the immediate neighborhood of the Chiricuahua [sic] mountains, is that the country in which the three Graham county murderers are biding is an immense territory in which with luck the outlaws could keep away from pursuers possibly for weeks or months. One has to see the country to realize what an immense territory it covers.

Hundreds Patrol Country.

Tired and weary, unshaven and hungry, gaunt eyes from loss of sleep, but armed to the guards with enough heavy artillery to capture and police Mexico, hundreds of men from Bisbee, Douglas, Tombstone, New Mexico and from Graham, Pinal and Pima county, are doing their best to patrol the country and capture the murderers and slackers.

A corps of barbers could do a land office business up in the Cave Creek vicinity for dark, stubby beards as well as lighter hued ones, ranging down to those of the near-peroxide type are disported by all of the deputies, excepting the very youngest who have not yet reached that estate of manhood where they find use for a razor.

For the most part residents throughout the country being patrolled and in the vicinity are not in much fear of the outlaws. One deputy residing at the Hilltop mine mentioned that the Powers brothers, or at least two men that he believed to have been members of the gang, had been seen less than a mile from there Friday night. Yet he was not worried. It might be possible, however, that the men seen were members of one of the posses.

Cave Creek Best Guarded.

Cave Creek, because of its nearness to Rodeo, was the strongest guarded point Sunday. Nearly 100 men were there. Humorous stories are told by the deputies of the length of time which it takes to get news from the New Mexico town. Couriers fail to return and sometimes it is necessary to send a dozen to town before the first one who went in can be rounded up and sent back with the latest word of the outlaws. One man was more than six hours covering the short distance and returned in a very happy frame of mind.

One noticeable thing is that the men in the posses as a rule know less about what is going on and where Sheriffs Wheeler and Miles are each day with the dogs. Reports they get, usually from Rodeo, but these are often conflicting. The telephone lines in places on the mountain tops have been cut or else the wires put out of commission by the snow for some of these have not been working for several days.

Man hunting has its pleasures as well as sorrows, but the writer advises any and all amateur man hunters to go fully equipped with warm blankets and if traveling by auto to be sure that the lining of all tires are in place as a record of 12 punctures in one tire in a day is possibly something to brag about, but changing tires is a real man's sized job. If you don't believe this consult Eugene V. Tracy, Arthur J. Tracy, Fred A. McKinney, Earl C. Murray or Chas. Mahan.

The Coconino Sun, March 8, 1918, courtesy of Arizona State Library, Archives and Public Records, obtained from http://adnp.azlibrary.gov/, p. 3.

MURDERER SISSON WAS SERGEANT IN U.S. CAVALRY

Tom Sisson, who with John and Tom Powers murdered three Gila county officers on the upper Aravaipa creek on Sunday morning, February 10th, was an old cavalryman. Some twenty or twenty-five years ago he was Sergeant Sisson of the 1st U.S. cavalry, then stationed at old Fort Grant, on Indian duty. It was the duty of the cavalry in those days to ferret out the hiding places of the Apaches and in hunting for these elusive Indians Sisson and his comrades became familiar with every rock and crevice of the mountain ranges of eastern Arizona, and it was to these old haunts that he led the Powers boys after the brutal murder of the Gila county peace officers, and it is due to his knowledge of the country that they were able to evade the hundreds of man hunters on their trail these three weeks past.

The Coconino Sun, March 15, 1918, courtesy of Arizona State Library, Archives and Public Records, obtained from http://adnp.azlibrary.gov/, p. 4.

"ONLY SOME OF HIS BOYS"

Tom Sisson, the man paroled by Governor Hunt, who with John and Tom Powers killed Sheriff McBride and his two deputies, Kempton and Wooten [sic] last February in Graham county, were finally arrested by U. S. troops while attempting to cross the border into Mexico, last Friday. The Powers brought their dead sister into Bowie for burial under suspicious circumstances and after burial her body was taken up and it was found that her neck had been broken. Sisson, the ex-convict had been living with the Powers' family. The two Powers boys were also wanted for being slackers and when the three officers went to their cabin to make the arrest the outlaws opened fire without warning, killing the three officers. Coldblooded murder in this state only earns the murderer the title of "one of my boys." Some day the people of Arizona will rise up and declare an "open season" on murderers, likewise the criminal element that is congregating here from all parts of the country.

The St. Johns Herald, March 21, 1918, courtesy of Arizona State Library, Archives and Public Records, obtained from http://adnp.azlibrary.gov/, p. 1.

IN SAD SITUATION.

When at Nogales recently Judge A. G. McAllister informed a friend who repeated the sad story to The Oasis, that the families of the three Graham county officers, killed by John and Tom Powers and Tom Sisson, are in straightened circumstances, and that moreover they are very large and the small children are numerous.

Judge McAllister stated that Sheriff R. G. [sic] McBride left a widow and seven children, with another expected shortly; Under-sheriff Kempton left a widow and seven children; while Deputy Sheriff Kane Wooten [sic] left a widow with four children and another expected.

The count is eighteen helpless children made fatherless by the murderers.

Neither McBride or Wooton [sic] left any means or property, but Kempton's widow has about 40 acres of land.

All three families are in need of assistance, and it is said that an effort will be made to have Governor Hunt include in his call for a special session of the legislature a provision to pass a relief act. --Oasis, Nogales.

Bisbee Daily Review, June 16, 1918, courtesy of Arizona State Library, Archives and Public Records, obtained from http://adnp.azlibrary.gov/, p. 9

MINE PROPERTIES OF POWERS BOYS HISTORIC CLAIMS
TUCSON. June 15. Negotiations have been on for several weeks for the purchase of the gold property in the Rattle Snake Canyon, scene of the tragedy where the Powers boys and Tom Sissons [sic] shot and killed the Sheriff of Graham county and his officers in resisting arrest for evading the draft, after the father of the Powers boys had been killed.

The Powers have a well developed tunnel and a mill on the property and at the time of the shooting, were about to realize from the milling of the ore they had developed. The property is now in the hands of Charles Powers.

264

Rattlesnake Canyon was first located as a gold prospect by Black Jack Gardener some years ago. He had a partner at the time. The partner sold his interest for $1000 to Francis Hartman and Col. Randolph, it is understood. After a company was formed and possibly $50,000 was spent on the property, it was abandoned. It is said the property finally came into the hands of the caretaker who sold it to the Powers who completed the work and opened up the gold ledges in a crosscut tunnel. The story of the discovery of the prospect as told by Gardener is a romance of the early days in the hills.

"I had been in Tucson," said Gardener, telling the story, "and I nearly went broke, so I thought I would hit out for the high hills and see if I couldn't pick up something in the hills where there had never been anybody.

"So I started out with my burro, a side of bacon, a bag of flour, a rifle and a prospecting outfit. I prospected all the east of Tucson until I came to the San Pedro river. One night I camped all alone on the bank of the river, when along came another fellow with a burro. He asked me how the water was and might he camp here, and I told him he sure could, for a [sic] always like to have a partner to chin to. He said he was from Oklahoma. Wasn't any prospector at all; just out to see the country. Didn't have anything but some beans. I told him he could be a partner of mine if he wanted to. He said he did not have anything and I told him I had about as much so that was fair enough. And so he chucked in.

"After a couple of days prospecting I wanted some fresh meat and we came to a steer and I shot it, believing I'd make good paying for it after a while. So that night we had fresh meat and we camped on the top of the ridge just above Rattlesnake Canyon. The next day we caught sight of some cowboys and we knew they found where that steer had been killed and we sneaked down into the Canyon, not waiting to argue with cowboys about that steer. Well, we waited there until the cowboys went by on the trail along the canyon and then we made camp there for two days and I went out to examine the dyke that runs across the canyon between the two ridges there. I saw one gold stringer after another on the face of that dyke and so I told my partner that we had better stay right there. And we did. I went up on the dyke and began to make the seams of gold ready for saye. You know I just went along them chipping off the rock around them so that they would show up and a man could see them. I worked two days. The second day I heard somebody pecking away at the rock with a hammer and I looked up and seen my partner with a little Durham sack, cracking off them seams I had dressed. Taking away the gold I had exposed. I roared at him and bawled him out so he wouldn't speak to me for a couple of days and when he did he said he was willing to sell out his share. So I said, 'Will you take a thousand dollars?' and he said he would, so I said, 'Come on back to Tucson.' So we came back to Tucson with specimens and I went to Francis Hartman and Col. Randolph and got him his thousand dollars.

"After that they organized a company or somebody did and they worked there but they couldn't make it pay and they wanted to hydraulic all the ground sloping down to the river for the gold that had eroded off the dyke. But they never did, although you could get color anywhere. So that was the end of Rattlesnake Canyon until the Powers family took it up."

The Coconino Sun, August 30, 1918, courtesy of Arizona State Library, Archives and Public Records, obtained from http://adnp.azlibrary.gov/

(Under "Range and Market News," p. 6)

Another chapter was written in the Powers-Sisson tragedy recently in Graham county, when the widows of the slain Graham county officers secured judgments against the Powers boys for the death of their husbands, and the famous mine in the Rattlesnake canyon was attached to secure the judgment.

The three widows were suing for damages as follows: Mrs. McBride, $50,000; Mrs. Kempton, $20,000; and Mrs. Wootan, $50,000. When suit was started, in order to attach the property, it was necessary to file a bond in an amount of double the amount sued for. Mrs. Kempton was the only one of the widows financially able to make the bond, and, not being able to make a bond of $100,000, she voluntarily reduced her claim to $20,000 and made bond for $40,000.

Graham Guardian, November 1, 1918, courtesy of Arizona State Library, Archives and Public Records, obtained from http://adnp.azlibrary.gov/, p. 3.

NOTICE OF SHERIFFS SALE

In the Superior Court of the County of Graham, State of Arizona.

Clara McBride, plaintiff, vs. John T. [sic] Power, Tom Power, and the Estate of Jeff H. [sic] Power, deceased, defendants.

Under and by virtue of an execution and order of sale, issued out of the Superior Court of the County of Graham, State of Arizona, in that certain action wherein Clara McBride is plaintiff and John T. Power,

Tom Power, and the Estate of Jeff T. Power deceased are defendants, upon a judgment rendered in said action, on the 14th day of August A. D. 1918, in favor of the said plaintiff and against said defendants by the terms of which judgment it was adjudged that the plaintiff have and recover from the defendants, the sum of Thirty Thousand ($30,000.00)Dollars with interest thereon at the rate of six per cent per annum until paid, together with Ten ($10.00) Dollars, costs and disbursements, at the date of said judgment, and accruing costs.

I, the sheriff of Graham County, State of Arizona, have levied on the following mining claims, to-wit:

Abandon No. One, amended location notice of which is recorded in Book 18, Records of Mines of Graham County, Arizona at page 228.

Abandon No. Two, amended location notice of which is recorded in Book 18, Records of Mines of Graham County, Arizona at page 229.

Abandon No. Three, amended location notice of which is recorded in Book 18, Records of Mines of Graham County, Arizona at page 230.

Abandon No. Four, location notice of which is recorded in Book 16, Records of Mines of Graham County, at page 98.

Gold Leaf No. One, location notice of which is recorded in Records of Mines of Graham County, Arizona, in Book 23, at page 48.

Gold Leaf No. Two, location notice of which is recorded in Records of Mines of Graham County, Arizona, in Book 23 at page 49.

Lee No. One and Lee No. Two.

All of the above mining claims being in Rattle Snake Mining District, Graham County, State of Arizona.

Now, therefore, notice is hereby given that on the 15th day of November, A.D. 1918, at the hour of 2:00 o'clock p.m., at the front door of the Court House, in the Town of Safford, County of Graham, State of Arizona, I will sell at auction, to the highest bidder for cash, lawful money of the United States, all the right, title and interest of the said defendants in the above described property to satisfy the said execution and costs.

Given under my hand this 18th day of October, A. D. 1918.

B. F. Stewart, Sheriff of Graham County, State of Arizona.

By J. C. Layton, Deputy Sheriff

First publication, Oct. 25, 1918.

Last publication, Nov. 8, 1918.

Made in the USA
San Bernardino, CA
06 January 2015